Generative Phonology

Iggy Roca

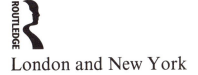

London and New York

First published 1994
by Routledge
11 New Fetter Lane, London EC4P 4EE

Simultaneously published in the USA and Canada
by Routledge
29 West 35th Street, New York, NY 10001

Set in 10/12 pt Times by Megaron, Cardiff
Printed and bound in Great Britain by T J Press (Padstow) Ltd,
Cornwall

British Library Cataloguing in Publication Data
A catalogue record for this book is available from the British
Library

Library of Congress Cataloging in Publication Data
applied for

ISBN 0-415-04140-6   0-415-04141-4 (pbk)

He who speaks does not know; he who knows does not speak

(Buddhist saying)

[*u* segment] → [− segment]

(Chomsky and Halle 1968: 404)

Contents

Series editor's preface

The Linguistic Theory Guides have been commissioned with a rather special readership in mind – the typical linguist, who knows a good deal about a small number of theories in his or her area of specialism, but is baffled by the problem of keeping up with other theories even in that area, to say nothing of other areas. There just aren't enough hours in the day to read more widely, and even if there were it wouldn't help much because so much of the literature is simply incomprehensible except to the initiated. The result is that most of us cultivate our own garden reasonably conscientiously, but have very little idea of what is happening in other people's gardens.

This theoretical narrowing is a practical problem if you are expected to teach on a broad front – say, to give a course of lectures on syntactic theory – when you only know one theory of syntax. Honesty demands that one should tell students about alternative approaches, but how can you when you have at best a hazy idea of what most theories have to say? Another practical problem is the danger of missing pearls of wisdom which might be vitally important in one's research, because they happen to have been formulated in terms of some unfamiliar theory. There can be very few linguists who have not rediscovered some wheel in their area of specialism, out of ignorance about work in other theories.

However, there is an even more serious problem at the research level, because one of the main goals of our joint research effort is to work towards the best possible theory (or set of theories), and this can only be done if we constantly compare and evaluate all the available theories. From this perspective, it is simply pointless to spend one's life developing one theory, or some part of it, if it is already outclassed by some other theory. It is true that evaluation of theories is quite a subjective matter, and is far too complex for any kind of absolute certainty to be arrived at. All we can do is to make a reasonably dispassionate, though subjective, assessment of the strengths and weaknesses of the alternatives, in the full expectation that our colleagues may disagree radically with our verdict. Total ignorance of the alternative theories is clearly not a good basis for evaluating them – though it is arguably better than the misinformation that can be used to bolster one's confidence in one's favourite theory.

It is with these problems in mind, then, that we have planned the Linguistic Theory Guides. Each book in the series will focus on one theory that is currently prominent in the literature (or in a few special cases, on a range of such theories). The list of titles is open-ended, and new titles will be added as new theories come into prominence. The aim will be both to inform and to evaluate – to provide enough information to enable the reader to appreciate whatever literature presupposes the theory concerned, and to highlight its strengths and weaknesses. The intention is emphatically not to sell the theory, though the valuation will naturally be sufficiently positive to explain why the theory is worth considering seriously. Several of the theories are already well provided with textbooks which say a great deal about their strengths and very little about their weaknesses. We assume that our typical reader finds such books irritating at best. What they want is clear exposition at the right level of sophistication (i.e. well above first-year undergraduate level), and wise evaluation, both internally and in relation to other theories.

It is not easy to write a book with these qualities, and we have selected our authors with great care. What we have looked for in each case is essentially someone who is a sympathetic outsider, rather than a devotee of the theory – someone who has experience of working within other theories, but who is well-disposed to the theory concerned, and reasonably well-informed about it. We hope that this recipe will produce books which will be acceptably non-partisan in tone, but we have also taken steps to make them factually reliable as descriptions of the theories concerned. Each book has benefited from detailed comment by at least one prominent devotee (a term which we do not apply disparagingly – without their devotees theories would not come into being, still less develop, and there would be no theoretical linguistics), as well as by an outside reader. Needless to say, the authors have been allowed to stick to their evaluations if the protests of their devotee readers have failed to change their minds.

It is our sincere hope that these books will make a significant contribution to the growth and development of our subject, as well as being helpful to those who read them.

Dick Hudson

Preface

When Dick Hudson first suggested writing a phonology book for 'syntacticians' (a shorthand for linguists not specialising in phonology), I optimistically anticipated a very straightforward operation, simply involving the compilation of a digest with the main strands of current phonological theory. However, as the project began to take shape, both in my own mind and on the sheet of paper before me, things started looking substantially different. In a nutshell, not only is 'current phonology' scattered around a range of rather heterogeneous sources, but the fit between many of the diverse proposals is not immediately obvious. Soon in the day it thus became clear that the collation of a ready-made 'summary' for syntacticians would be hopelessly premature, the prerequisite being a cohesive account of the body of phonological theory as it stands at present.

As in other areas of linguistics, generative phonologists are brought together by a shared set of problems and questions. Such a set constitutes the fabric on to which current phonology is (being) built, the thread that fastens the various trends and their proponents. One positive result of the present study has been the realisation that there is no disagreement of principle among those who, one way or another, call themselves 'generative phonologists'. Such unanimity does however break down as soon as answers to specific points are called for, and it is here that the task of assembling the conceptual and formal edifice of generative phonology faces the most arduous difficulties.

Fortunately, Chomsky and Halle's monumental *The Sound Pattern of English* (*SPE*) has provided an enduring foundation stone for the discipline, one which has signalled the point of departure for all research into generative phonology. Thus, to a larger or lesser degree, we are all still ploughing through the consequences of Chomsky and Halle's work, weaving and reweaving its multiple yarns, in the hope of achieving a better match with the variegated phonologies of the world's languages.

This ancestral source of current generative phonology is also reasonably well known to non-specialists whose linguistic education took place during the 1960s, 1970s, or even much of the 1980s, and therefore I have adopted the practice of referring to it more or less systematically at the beginning of each chapter. In this way, the non-phonologist will not feel thrown into the deep end from the word go, and will hopefully be motivated to go ahead with the reading.

My goal has been to provide a clear account of the various elements that make up present-day generative phonology, and of the relations between these elements. Note that by elements I mean both the several components of the model and the proposals (*prima facie* sometimes at loggerheads) put forward by practitioners. I have at all times tried to relate and unite, looking for woods beyond trees, and for similarities behind disparities of terminology and formal presentation. In doing so, I have taken to heart John Goldsmith's advice that 'the task of the linguist is not to *choose* among theories so much as it is to select and then integrate the best of all currently available frameworks into a new, more satisfactory model' (Goldsmith 1985: 254). If my interpretation of the state of the art is correct, there are surprisingly few differences between phonologists. In particular, I have not found any strong evidence for the existence of different 'schools', as has sometimes (perhaps somewhat lightheartedly) been claimed, albeit with less emphasis than in other fields of linguistics. On the other hand, the question remains open as to whether the principles of phonology are fundamentally distinct from those of syntax, or whether a formal unification of the two sister disciplines can be envisaged. The claim in Bromberger and Halle (1989) is that there are genuine discrepancies, as reflected for instance in the endurance of rule ordering, which 25 years of post-*SPE* research has been unable to eradicate.

As is inevitable in an enterprise of the present kind, coverage is anything but boundless. Clearly, at a general level, a line must soon be drawn in order to stunt encyclopaedic growth. In the present case, moreover, stringent and persistent length guidelines were imposed as a matter of editorial policy. These limitations notwithstanding, I am satisfied that both the main areas and the main approaches are dealt with at a reasonable level of depth, and in a manner sufficiently explicit to permit the outsider to follow the exposition without recourse to additional sources.

I now turn to the agreeable task of acknowledging help. The following phonologists have been involved in reading and commenting on various parts of the book at various stages of its evolution: Diana Archangeli, Monik Charette, François Dell, Colin Ewen, Carlos Gussenhoven,

Morris Halle, John Harris, Dick Hayward, Scott Myers, Marina Nespor. My colleague Peter Trudgill gave me a lay linguist's opinion and much encouragement at a time when I particularly needed it. Geert Booij kindly read the whole finished manuscript and unwittingly stepped into the shoes of the editor's 'prominent devotee', thus providing me with very useful feedback that I have endeavoured to incorporate in the text. The selection and accuracy of the Yoruba data, which figure rather prominently throughout the book, have greatly benefited from the advice of Akin Oyètádé.

For a special round of thanks I must single out Morris Halle and Dick Hudson. Throughout the two years of writing, Morris has always been there in the role of guardian angel, his invisible, but very real, presence having had the obvious salutary effects both on my own state of mind and heart and on the final product. Dick has, as the series editor, been a constant source of support, and an indefatigable reader and purger of rougher and more polished drafts. Needless to say, none of the cited bears responsibility for any errors or omissions, which accrue exclusively to the author. Finally, I am grateful to the Routledge staff (in particular Emma Cotter) for editorial advice, and to the Department of Language and Linguistics at Essex for material assistance and for sabbatical leaves which enabled me to get on with the writing.

Abbreviations

abl.	ablative
abs.	absolutive
acc.	accusative
ant	anterior
antipass.	antipassive
ATR	advanced tongue root
BAP	Basic Accentuation Principle
CG	Clitic Group
comm.	commutative
cons	consonantal
cont	continuant
cor	coronal
CU	Contrast-based Underspecification
dat.	dative
EC	Elsewhere Condition
ECP	Empty Category Principle
f.	feminine
F	foot
GC	Government and Charm
gen.	genitive
imp.	imperative
inst.	instrumental
IP	Intonational Phrase
lab	labial
LP	Lexical Phonology
m.	masculine
MCR	Margin Creation Rule
MOR	Maximal Onset Realisation Parameter
MOS	Minimal Onset Satisfaction Principle
n.	neuter

nas	nasal
nom.	nominative
OCP	Obligatory Contour Principle
OCR	Onset Creation Rule
pl.	plural
PP	P Phrase
pres.	present
PU	P Utterance
purp.	purposive
PW	P Word
RROC	Redundancy Rule Ordering Constraint
RU	Radical Underspecification
SCC	Strict Cycle Condition
sg.	singular
SLH	Strict Layer Hypothesis
son	sonorant
SSP	Sonority Sequencing Principle
syll	syllabic
UG	Universal Grammar

1 Phonological representations

1.1 THE ARRANGEMENT OF ELEMENTS IN *SPE*

We shall start our discussion with a brief summary of the basic formal fabric underpinning the *SPE* model of phonology (*SPE* = Chomsky and Halle 1968), with which we assume a certain familiarity.[1] This will give us a useful basis of comparison with subsequent developments, with which the body of this book is primarily concerned.

In *SPE* a phonological representation was made up of a linear array of feature matrices. Let us consider the simple word *pen*. Each of the three segments of this word was broken down into more elementary particles, called 'distinctive features', each essentially representing one aspect of its pronunciation. Formally, each *SPE* feature was assigned one of two values, positive or negative. Simplifying somewhat, the formal *SPE* representation of /p/ will therefore be as follows:

(1) *SPE* representation of /p/

$$
\begin{bmatrix}
-\text{syll} \\
+\text{cons} \\
-\text{son} \\
-\text{voice} \\
+\text{ant} \\
-\text{cor} \\
-\text{nas}
\end{bmatrix}
$$

The feature matrix in (1) is of course incomplete, but will suffice at this point in the exposition.

Given such decomposition of segments into features, the word *pen* will be formally represented as in (2):

(2)   Formal representation of *pen* in *SPE*

$$
\begin{bmatrix}
-\text{syll} \\
+\text{cons} \\
-\text{son} \\
-\text{voice} \\
+\text{ant} \\
-\text{cor} \\
-\text{nas}
\end{bmatrix}
\begin{bmatrix}
+\text{syll} \\
-\text{cons} \\
+\text{son} \\
+\text{voice} \\
-\text{high} \\
-\text{low} \\
-\text{back}
\end{bmatrix}
\begin{bmatrix}
-\text{syll} \\
+\text{cons} \\
+\text{son} \\
+\text{voice} \\
+\text{ant} \\
+\text{cor} \\
+\text{nas}
\end{bmatrix}
$$

As we shall see in Chapter 3, distinctive feature theory has evolved substantially since the time of *SPE*, but this is not important for our immediate purposes. Also negligible at the moment is the exact interpretation of each of the feature labels in terms of articulation, acoustics, etc., which we will introduce step by step as we go along (see Chapter 3 for a more thorough discussion). What is significant at the present point is the arrangement of the matrices into unilinear strings characteristic of *SPE*. In fact, from this perspective, the representation in (2) is equivalent to that in (3):

(3) /pen/

Both (2) and (3) are made up of a linear array of elements, strung together like beads in a string. There is an obvious formal claim implicit in this arrangement, namely, that phonological representations consist of sequences of elements (whether distinctive feature matrices, as in (2), or phonemes, as in (3)) drawn out of a basic vocabulary and capable of entering linear relations of precedence with each other. This is a particularly simple and commonsensical conception of phonological structure, one that also runs through IPA transcription and conventional orthographic writing, where phonetic symbols or letters follow each other in a linear fashion. This mode of representation could therefore easily be thought to be directly rooted in phonetic facts, and thus to constitute the null hypothesis for the representation of sound. As is well known, however, it is in fact not possible to draw up precise boundaries between sounds, for the simple reason that in real life both articulatory and acoustic events form a continuum.

For greater explicitness, we shall now review the relevant formal aspects of the model under scrutiny. Let us say that, for a hypothetical language *L*, the vocabulary of phonological elements consists of three members, as follows:

(4) Vocabulary of phonological elements for *L*
      {p, e, n}

Moreover, let us imagine that no restrictions are imposed in L on the precedence relations between these elements. The following sequences will thus be licensed:

(5) pen
    pne
    enp
    epn
    nep
    npe

All these strings will be possible phonological words in this language. The number of well-formed phonological objects could of course be easily increased by bringing optionality and recursion into the picture (*p, pe*, etc.; *penpen, penpne*, etc.), but such additional complexity is unnecessary for our present purposes. What is important to realise is that the language under consideration has an inventory of three phonological elements, as in (4), and a grammar which allows these elements to enter into unrestricted unilinear relations with each other. A graphic representation of this grammar is given in (6):

(6) $x_1, x_2, x_3, \ldots, x_n$

The *x*s in (6) stand for phonological elements, and the subscripted digits indicate sequential ordering. The precedence relationship (call it '$<$') has the properties of transitivity, antisymmetry and irreflexivity (see Sagey 1988a). Thus, in (6), $(x_1 < x_2)$ and $(x_2 < x_3)$ entails $x_1 < x_3$ (transitivity). Given $x_1 < x_2$, it follows that it is not the case that $x_2 < x_1$ (antisymmetry). Finally, it is also not the case that $x_j < x_j$, i.e. no element can precede itself (irreflexivity). This is the gist of the formal representational machinery made available by *SPE*.

As we shall now see, a revolution that started in the 1970s has profoundly transformed the formalisation of phonological structure in generative phonology. Specifically, the unilinear geometry which characterises *SPE* has now been abandoned in favour of multilinear representations.[2] In order to understand the meaning and implications of this far-reaching change, we shall first briefly examine its basic rationale.

1.2 COMPLEX SEGMENTS

1.2.1 Affricates

The analysis of affricates has long puzzled phonologists, because of the Janus-like nature of these sounds, which behave simultaneously as mono- and bisegmental. Thus, consider the affricate sound [tʃ], which occurs twice in the word *church*. The following question arises: does such a sound correspond to one or two phonological elements? Specifically, is there in English a phonological element /ʧ/, directly corresponding to the affricate, or should this sound be analysed as a sequence of the individual elements /t/ and /ʃ/, which are attested in *tut* and *shush*, respectively. As it happens, there is evidence supporting either stand.

On the one hand, English only allows one obstruent word-initially, with the notable exception of *s* + obstruent clusters.[3] Thus, alongside *tar* [tɑː] we have *star* [stɑː], but orthographic *tsar* is not pronounced *[tsɑː], at least by linguistically unsophisticated speakers, but rather [zɑː]. Note that, irrespective of their pronunciation, words like *tsar* and *tsetse* are felt as exotic, in clear contrast with such everyday non-oddities as *church*, *chat*, *much*, and so on, all containing [tʃ]. So, from the point of view of the phonotactic constraint prohibiting word-initial (in fact, syllable-initial) obstruent clusters we would wish to treat [tʃ] as a single element.

In *SPE* affricates are indeed treated as monosegmental, and differentiated from other plosives by a positive value for the feature [delayed release], which suggests an opening of the [t] closure in two stages, the first, partial one corresponding to the frication [ʃ]. This treatment is however at odds with the fact that single obstruent stops can usually be followed by liquids (*prawn*, *plot*, *treat*, *crown*, *clog*) but [tʃ] + liquid clusters are impossible (cf. hypothetical *chrat*). Such a distributional gap naturally points to a bisegmental status for [tʃ].

Further evidence for a bisegmental analysis comes from the behaviour of [tʃ] with regard to inflectional allomorphy. Thus, consider the conjugation of the verb *to match*: *matches*, *matched*. What is interesting is that in the third person the affricate patterns with other sibilant[4] fricatives in selecting the long allomorph [əz] [mætʃəz] (cf. *mashes* [mæʃəz], *passes* [pæsəz], etc.), while in the past the short form /d/ (→ [t]) is selected: [mætʃt]. In this, therefore, *matched* contrasts with other forms with a final coronal[5] non-continuant, which select the long variant [əd]: *patted* [pætəd], *prodded* [prɒdəd], etc. Now, if [tʃ] is analysed as a single segment, this behaviour becomes mysterious, since such a segment would clearly have to be defined as a non-continuant coronal (as indeed it was in *SPE*), and therefore we would expect it also to select the long past allomorph [əd].

1.2.2 Other complex segments

Before offering a solution to the puzzle posed by affricates in English and other languages, we shall point out the existence of additional types of complex segments in many of the world's languages: prenasalised stops [^{m}p], [^{n}d], [^{ŋ}g], etc.; rounded stops [p^{w}], [b^{w}], [k^{w}], [g^{w}], etc.; labiovelars [kp] and [gb]; palatalised consonants; aspirates; and so on. These sounds raise similar problems to those encountered with affricates, in particular whether they should be analysed as one or two segments.

A revealing language in this connection is Kinyarwanda, discussed in Walli-Sagey (1986). At first blush, this language allows consonant clusters of considerable complexity, as witness such words as *mɲaanhoreye* 'you (pl.) worked for me', *tkwaaŋga* 'we hate', and, more dramatically, *kariindgwi* 'seven'. This clashes with the evidence provided by the process of nativisation of (German) loan words, which ostensibly aims for a C(onsonant) + V(owel) distributional pattern: *Burgermeister* > *burugumesitiri*, *Republik* > *repuburika*, *Präsident* > *paatirisiya*, *Präfek* > *perefe*. Walli-Sagey's suggestion is that Kinyarwanda syllables, like those of other Bantu languages, indeed have the pattern CV, and therefore apparent surface clusters must be analysed as instances of complex segments, i.e. segments which count as one for the phonotactics of the language, while still being multiply articulated.

The formalisation of such ambiguous entities leads to a logical contradiction in *SPE* theory. Thus, remember that in this theory only one row of segments is countenanced. This inevitably leads to representing *kariindgwi* as indeed /kariindgwi/, but this is at odds with the noted monosegmental treatment of the string /ndgw/ by the phonotactics of the language. Similarly, of course, we would have to represent the English affricate [ʧ] as /tʃ/, and this again would be inconsistent with the part of the evidence that suggests monosegmentality. The alternative would be to try to accommodate the change of state within a single matrix, as represented in (7):

$$(7) \begin{bmatrix} -\text{syll} \\ +\text{cons} \\ +\text{ant} \\ +\text{cor} \\ -\text{nas} \\ -\text{cont}, +\text{cont} \end{bmatrix}$$

Such formalisation, however, directly contradicts the *SPE* principles of matrix formation. As mentioned above, in this model all segments are mappable onto matrices, a matrix being simply an unordered collection of valued features. Crucially, because the purpose of matrices is the (phonetically based) cross-classification of segments, only one value can be present for any one feature. In (7), however, the feature [cont] is assigned two values, − and +, which must moreover appear in the order given ([tʃ] is obviously distinct from [ʃt]).

1.3 MULTILINEAR REPRESENTATIONS

1.3.1 Parallel tiers

We seem to have reached an impasse with regard to the formalisation of multiply articulated but phonologically unitary segments. Such an impasse is however an artefact of the *SPE* unilinearity constraint on the geometry of representations, as we shall now show.

Starting off with affricates, suppose we capture the idea that these objects are effectively one consonant with two articulations by means of the structure represented in the following diagram:

(8)   C
        ╱ ╲
       t   ʃ

The interpretation of (8) is all but obvious, and must be contrasted with that of (9):

(9) C   C
    | |
    t   ʃ

(9) stands for a sequence of the consonants [t] and [ʃ]. On the other hand, (8) is intended to represent one consonant with two articulatory phases, the first equivalent to [t] and the second to [ʃ].

Before proceeding to sample a large body of empirical evidence in support of this novel mode of representation, we must ensure that it is not a simple notational variant of that in (7), where a single matrix encompasses the two opposite values of a feature. As was pointed out then, such formalisation is nonsensical in the context of the *SPE* model, where phonological representations consist exclusively of a unilinear array of matrices, and where, by definition, each matrix can therefore only contain one value for each feature. Embodied in (8) is a relaxation of the unilinearity constraint. In particular, we have taken the feature [−syllabic] (= 'C', informally) on to an autonomous representational tier (the precise status of the *SPE* feature [syllabic] will be discussed in Chapter 4). According to this alternative approach, phonological representations consist of a number of such autonomous tiers coordinated by means of association lines, as abstractly illustrated in (10):

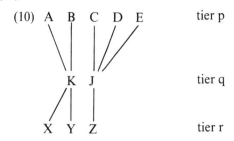

(10) A B C D E   tier p

        K J   tier q

        X Y Z   tier r

In (10), tier p includes five elements, tier q two elements, and tier r three. The association lines connect elements across tiers, as shown.

A number of questions arise in connection with such diagrams, among them the following: how many tiers are allowed? Which elements are assigned to which tier? How are the association lines drawn? We shall be providing answers to these and other questions in the remainder of the chapter. First, however, we shall make explicit some of the advantages inherent in the representation in (7).

Clearly, (7) appropriately encapsulates the ambiguous behaviour of affricates described above. Thus, their patterning with single obstruents as regards starting (or finishing) the syllable by themselves can be captured very naturally by stating this distribution at the level of the CV tier (the tier containing all and only the CV elements, which, as already mentioned, formalise the syllabic value of the corresponding segments), since in this tier affricates indeed correspond to a single unit. On the other hand, the presence of the two elements [t] and [ʃ] in the segmental tier accounts for the treatment of affricates as bisegmental with regard to such constraints as the prohibition to team up with liquids (see Clements and Keyser 1983 for a detailed exposition of English syllable phonotactics in this framework; syllables are discussed in Chapter 4 below). Finally, the precedence relationship [t] < [ʃ] also in the segmental tier explains why [ʃ], but not [t], influences the selection of suffixal allomorph.

At this point we shall introduce some basic principles and standard terminology. The model of phonology countenancing multilinear representations along the lines of (10) is known as 'autosegmental phonology'. While the intuition underpinning this model can be traced back to such authors as Bloch, Firth, Z. Harris, or Haugen (see e.g. Harris 1944, Bloch 1948, Haugen 1949, Firth 1957), the emergence of autosegmental phonology can be ascribed to John Goldsmith's (1976) thesis, which develops work carried out by William Leben and Edwin

Williams in the early 1970s. Central to this theory is the idea of relative autonomy of segments (or, more precisely, phonological elements) in any one tier with respect to elements in other tiers, whence the replacement of the label 'segment' with the blend neologism 'auto-segment', and the dubbing of the theory itself as 'autosegmental phonology'. As we have been seeing, autosegments are organised in tiers, each composed of elements obeying strict precedence relations. Obviously, the articulation of the autosegments from the different tiers must be coordinated, in a way similar to the lyrics and the melody of a song, and this is expressed by means of the association lines linking elements across tiers.

1.3.2 The timing tier

The representations in (8) and (9) above contain two tiers. In one of these tiers we have represented the phonemes [t] and [ʃ][6] (which in a more detailed formalisation would of course be broken down into their constituent features). The other tier lodges the feature [$\pm$ syllabic] ([$-$ syllabic] = 'C', in the two cases at hand). The autonomy thus granted to this feature corresponds well with the idea that, in some way, the alternation of vowelness and consonantness makes up the basic skeleton of speech (see e.g. Öhman 1967): what we are now seeing is that the phonological evidence parallels this phonetic observation. As will become clear as we go along, the tier in question performs a central role in the organisation of phonological structure, hence the labels 'core' and 'skeleton' which are often assigned to it. Besides bearing at this point the burden of establishing the syllabic status of phonemes (a different approach to this matter will be discussed in Chapter 4), the skeleton serves the purpose of determining the length of the elements associated to it, and is therefore also known as the 'timing tier' (a fourth label, 'CV tier' is self-explanatory). Thus, the existence of the skeleton or timing tier allows us to dispense with the *SPE*-inspired feature [$\pm$ long], whose obvious syntagmatic content is at odds with the paradigmatic nature of the main stock of distinctive features. Vowel length and consonant gemination will accordingly be represented as in (11) and (12), respectively (NB '[ ]' is intended here to represent a variable corresponding to a distinctive feature bundle):

(11) Vowel length

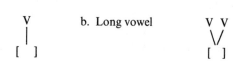

(12) Consonant gemination

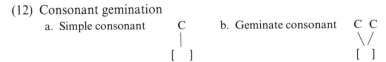

a. Simple consonant   C   b. Geminate consonant   C C

(11) and (12) thus add to (8) to complete the range of association possibilities: a one-to-one correspondence between skeletal and segmental elements, or a mismatch in either direction, which makes the segmental element either long (if there is one such element associated with several skeletal slots, as in (11b) and (12b)), or extra short, i.e. one of several fractions of a timing unit (whenever several segmental matrices share the association with only one skeletal position, as in (8)).

The mode of representation we are proposing is indeed supported by phonetic facts. An interesting case is Polish, where the configurations in (8) and (9) above are in actual contrast, as illustrated in (13a) and (13b), respectively:

(13)   a. [t͡ʃ]   b. [tʃ]

Czech	'Czech'	trzech	'three-gen. m.'
czy	'whether'	trzy	'three'
czysta	'clean-f.'	trzysta	'three hundred'
oczyma	'eyes-instr.'	otrzyma	'will obtain-3 sg.'
paczy	'warps-3 sg.'	patrzy	'looks at-3 sg.'

Obviously, the contrast may not be attributed to the internal composition of the sounds, which are [t] and [ʃ] in both cases. A study by Brooks (1965) shows that in [t] + [ʃ] clusters the frication is consistently longer than in their [t͡ʃ] affricate counterparts. This is as predicted by our formalism, which assigns a larger number of timing units to the cluster than to the complex segment.

The phonological evidence for autosegmental phonology is overwhelming, and there is at present no challenge to the idea that phonological representations must be autosegmentalised.[7] Problem areas are located in the technical details of the theory, as we will have occasion to see. First, however, we shall review some of the phenomena which provide strong support for autosegmentalism.

1.4 EVIDENCE FOR AUTOSEGMENTAL PHONOLOGY

1.4.1 Length phenomena

We saw above that, contrary to appearances, Kinyarwanda syllables are extremely simple: they consist of a consonant and a vowel, arranged in this order. Consider now the following underlying representations, made up of a prefix and a stem:

(14) /imi-nsi/   'days'
      /ba-nde/   'who?'
      /ku-ngana/   'to be equal'

Given the CV pattern of syllables in Kinyarwanda, we would expect the following surface realisations, with /n/ as a simple prenasalisation of the following consonant:

(15) [imi^{n}si]
      [ba^{n}de]
      [ku^{ŋ}gana]

The correct forms are however those given in (16):

(16) [imii^{n}si]
      [baa^{n}de]
      [kuu^{ŋ}gana]

In all cases we observe a lengthening of the vowel preceding the prenasalised consonant. This phenomenon would remain essentially unexplained in a model which resorted to brute force to express the change ('N' = [+nasal]):

(17) $V \rightarrow [+\text{long}]/\_\_^N C$

By contrast, the autosegmental formalism allows a principled account of this distribution. All we have to assume is that in underlying representations the assignment of CV slots is one-to-one, the unmarked option. Such associations will be altered in the course of the derivation, to make them compatible with the syllabic strictures of the language. In the case at hand, the nasal will switch its skeletal affiliation on to the slot of the obstruent, as in (18) (NB conventionally, a dotted line stands for the command 'associate', and the crossing out of a continuous line for the command 'sever the association', or 'di(sa)ssociate'):

(18)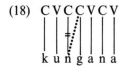

The effect of the change in (18) is double. First, it creates the prenasalised complex segment [^{ŋ}g], thus implementing the desired CV syllabification. Second, it sets free the skeletal slot previously associated to /n/. What will now happen to this slot? Although all Kinyarwanda syllables must be open (i.e. *CVC), there is no constraint on the length of the vowel. This allows the association of the vowel segment /u/ to the freed C slot, as follows:

(19) C V C C V C V

k u n g a n a

The appearance of a phonetically long vowel [uː] is thus an automatic consequence of the formation of the complex segment [ᵑg], a type of phenomenon usually known as 'compensatory lengthening'.

An interesting aspect of the derivation in (19) is the association of the vowel /u/ to a C timing slot, in addition to the V slot to which it is originally linked. The association of a vowel to a C slot will undoubtedly be the motive of some puzzlement. This matter will be addressed directly in Chapter 4, but a brief comment is necessary at this point. Simply, although the origin of the C/V labelling of slots can be seen in the *SPE* feature [±syllabic], as mentioned above, the two representations are in fact not isomorphic, the CV slots having achieved a certain degree of formal independence, particularly as a result of the work of Clements and Keyser (1983). This independence allows such slots to be associated with the 'wrong' type of segment, although the usual situation indeed is for vowels to link to Vs, and for consonants to Cs.

Psychological evidence for phonological structure is often forthcoming from the area of 'language games' or 'ludlings', i.e. systematic distortions of standard forms for purposes of play or privacy. Clements (1986a) reports on one such game in Luganda, known as 'Ludikya', which sheds additional light on the CV tier. Ludikya words are the syllabic mirror image of Luganda words, as illustrated in (20):

(20) kimuli   →   limuki   'flower'
     mukono   →   nokomu   'arm'
     mubinikilo   →   lokinibimu 'funnel'

As in Kinyarwanda, Luganda vowels can be long, as well as short:

(21) baana   'children'
     bageenda   'they are going'
     kutegeeza 'to inform'

Observe now the Ludikya counterparts of these words:

(22) naaba
ndageeba
zageteeku

Crucially, there is no transposition of length, which instead remains in the same position as in the source. This would be a strange phenomenon in a unilinear framework making use of the feature [±long], since this feature would be part of the same matrix as the other features which indeed get transposed. In the multilinear formalisation of autosegmental phonology, however, all we have to assume is that the syllabic transposition only affects the phonemic material (also commonly referred to as the 'melody'), leaving the CV tier intact, as we now illustrate for 'children':

(23)

1.4.2 Reduplication

Further evidence for autosegmentalism and for the CV tier comes from the phenomenon of reduplication. This is a common word-formation strategy, whereby a word has a part of itself (or, in some cases, its entire melody) affixed to create another related word.

Marantz (1982) analyses reduplication as involving the affixation of a certain string of CV elements (specific to the language or to the affixation process in question). In particular, he reduces the process to the affixation of a skeletal template, i.e. a template made up of a sequence of Cs and Vs, assuming that such a template will have access to the melodic tier. Thus, consider the following cases, where the reduplicated material in the right column has been italicised for ease of identification:

(24) a. Quileute
ci·phókwat′	'Negro'	*ci*ci·phókwat′	'Negroes'
qa·x	'bone'	*qa*qa·x	'bones'

b. Tagalog
lākad	'walk'	pag-*la*lākad	'walking'
kandīlah	candle'	pag-*ka*kandīlah	'candle vendor'

c. Agta
takki	'leg'	*tak*takki	'legs'
na-wakay	'lost'	na-*wak*wakay	'many things lost'

d. Chukchee

jilʔe-	'gopher'	jilʔe-*jil*	abs. sg.
nute-	'earth'	nute-*nut*	abs. sg.

In (24 a–c) the material has been prefixed, while in (24d) it appears as a suffix. On the other hand, the reduplicative template is CV in (24a) and (24b), and CVC in (24c) and (24d). This suggests the following procedure to derive *taktakki* 'legs':

(25) Reduplicative prefixation

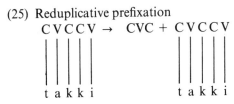

At this point the skeletal prefix CVC must be given some segmental content. One possibility would be simply to link its elements to the available stem melody *takki*, as follows:

(26)

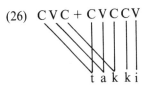

The resulting string is *taktakki*, as sought. This achievement notwithstanding, it is the common view that the procedure embodied in (26) is too powerful, since it also allows the derivation of many undesirable outputs, as exemplified in (27) for *kandīlah*:

(27)

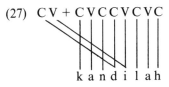

The output **(pag)dikandīlah* is at odds with the correct *(pag)-kakandīlah*. Moreover, such a type of process, where the association between skeletal and melodic elements takes place with obvious disregard of the precedence rights of autosegments (the string *kan* precedes *dī* in the word in question), is universally unattested, and should consequently be ruled out by the theory. In order to achieve this result, the following constraint on association has been proposed:

(28) No crossing constraint
Association lines may not cross.

This universal principle is one of the pillars sustaining the edifice of autosegmental phonology.

We must at this point find an alternative to the procedure in (26). A simple solution propounded by Marantz (1982) is to make the whole stem melody available to the skeletal affix by a copy convention, as illustrated in (29):

(29) C V C   + C V C C V
         | | | | | Stem Melody Copy
      t a k k i   t a k k i

The remaining two steps in the derivation of *taktakki* are as in (30):

(30) C V C   + C V C C V
      ⋮ ⋮ ⋮ ⋮ | | | | | Association
      t a k k i   t a k k i

      C V C   + C V C C V
      | | | | | | | | Clean-up
      t a k   t a k k i

The one-to-one association of the skeletal material CVC with the leftmost segmental string *tak* follows from the other core principle of autosegmental phonology, the 'Association Convention':

(31) Association Convention
     Associate free elements one-to-one from left to right.

The procedure discussed, which can of course be extended to the other cases of reduplication under scrutiny, effectively reduces reduplication to ordinary affixation, the only difference being that reduplication involves a CV template with no lexical melody. While this discussion is far from exhausting the interesting area of reduplication, to which we will be returning below, it has provided us with further illustration of the role of the skeleton in phonological structure.

1.4.3 Harmony

Many languages exhibit constraints on the class of vowels (or, rarely, consonants) which can occur in a given domain, typically the word. This phenomenon is commonly given the name 'harmony'. Thus, for instance, in Turkish all vowels usually agree in backness across the word, as illustrated in (32) for monosyllabic roots:[8]

(32)		nom. sg.	gen. sg.	nom. pl.	gen. pl.
'rope'		ip	ip-in	ip-ler	ip-ler-in
'hand'		el	el-in	el-ler	el-ler-in
'girl'		kiz	kiz-in	kiz-lar	kiz-lar-in
'stalk'		sap	sap-in	sap-lar	sap-lar-in

This paradigm shows that, while the root vowel remains constant, suffixal vowels undergo minimal changes to adapt to the backness value of the root: the genitive oscillates between *-in* and *-ɨn*, and the plural between *-ler* and *-lar*.

A particularly simple way of construing such alternations rests on the assumption that there is no lexical value for [back] in suffixes. Instead, the value carried by this feature in the root spreads to the suffixal vowels. This is illustrated in (33) for the genitive plurals *iplerin* and *kizlarɨn*:

(33) a. [− back]   b. [+ back]

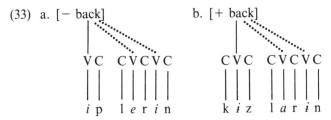

In (33) the feature [back] has been autosegmentalised, i.e. taken out of the common melodic matrix and assigned its own tier (the vowel symbols in the melodic tier have accordingly been italicised to informally signal their incompleteness, i.e. the fact that the matrices they stand for lack the feature [back]). The skeleton or CV tier occupies a central position, mediating between the two autosegmentalised subsets of features, as corresponds to its core structural role hinted at above. We are assuming, somewhat gratuitously, that the feature [back] comes associated to the root vowel from the lexicon: alternatively this association could take place in the course of the derivation by the Association Convention (31). This convention does not however provide for the spreading of this (valued) feature to the suffixal vowels, since it specifically requires the associating elements to be free, and [± back] is already attached to the stem vowel. Data such as these led Goldsmith (1976) to propose a Well-formedness Condition on auto-segmental representations, which we now formulate slightly adapted for our present purposes (a fuller version appears in (54) below):

(34) Well-formedness Condition (preliminary)
   At any stage in the derivation, all autosegmental elements must be associated.[9]

Given a dynamic interpretation of this condition, additional spreading will take place until all the vowels in the domain bear a value for [back], as shown in (33). At this point, therefore, association takes place in two stages, first one-to-one association of free elements according to (31), and then remedial spreading to make the representations comply with (34). As will be seen below, the appropriateness of such remedial spreading has subsequently been strongly called into question.

Turkish backness harmony is not always as simple as in our example, but additional details are orthogonal to our present interests. One aspect of the derivation in (33) must however be clarified. This concerns the fact that the spread of the feature [back] only selects vowels as targets. One simple way of achieving this result, which we will provisionally adopt at this point, is to assume that vowel harmony does not operate on the complete CV tier, but, rather, on the V 'projection' of the CV tier,[10] as illustrated in (35) for *iplerin*:

(35)

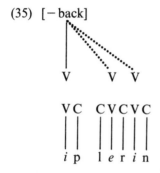

Clearly, Cs are not available at the projected level, and consequently only Vs will be possible targets of the spread. The mechanism of projection, attributed to J.R. Vergnaud (see e.g. Vergnaud 1977), is however too powerful, since it allows any element to be thus singled out arbitrarily (for instance, we could have limited projection to the segment *l*). Not surprisingly, therefore, more principled alternatives have been sought, and we will be returning to this matter at several points throughout the book, in connection with the various representational mechanisms to be proposed.

1.5 TONAL PHONOLOGY

We have by now achieved a reasonable degree of familiarity with the basic mechanics of autosegmentalism, and presented some evidence to justify the approach. Building on these foundations, we shall next explore the area which played the pioneering role in the emergence and development of autosegmental phonology: tonal phonology. In so doing, we shall extend the data accountable for by this model of phonological structure, and will introduce important refinements in the formal machinery made available so far, the details of which will become more explicit as we go along.

1.5.1 What is tone?

Given the importance of tone and the relative unfamiliarity of the phenomenon to the speaker of 'Standard Average European', we shall first dispense a few words of encouragement and clarification.

No human language is spoken in a monotone, in the manner of robots in science fiction motion pictures. Equivalently, all human languages are effectively sung. Now, when we think of a song in everyday life, we think of the coupling of some lyrics with a musical melody. In language, the lyrics are the words as they would sound if pronounced in a monotone, and the musical melody is the 'humming' which normally accompanies vocal delivery. In languages like English such humming is technically known as 'intonation'. We all know, for instance, that we can pronounce the word *yes* as a statement (-*Are you coming? -Yes*), as a question (-*You are coming, yes?*), as an invitation to further speech (-*You are coming. - Ye_ees*), and so on. What changes here is not the pronunciation of the three individual sounds making up (in some way still to be fully elucidated) the word *yes*, (i.e. [j], [e] and [s], in IPA transcription), but rather something apparently less tangible. Objectively speaking, however, this first impression of vagueness is simply mistaken. In fact, what differs is the humming which colours the delivery, and this humming can be most readily understood and measured, since it simply consists of (different rates of) vocal fold vibration.[11]

In English, differences in the pattern of humming do not affect word identity. In other languages, however, they do. When humming contributes to the shape of individual words, rather than just utterances, it is not referred to as 'intonation', but as 'tone'. One language which is commonly known to have tones is Chinese. Thus, in Chinese, words can be, and often are, kept apart by their tonal melodies alone. Specifically, Mandarin Chinese has four surface tonal melodies, as follows:

(36) level pitch
      pitch rise
      pitch fall
      pitch dip (i.e. fall followed by rise)

The functional importance of tone in Mandarin is brought out by such minimal contrasts as in (37):

(37)		Level	Rising	Falling	Dipping
bao	'wrap'		'hail'	'report'	'treasure'
huo	'hoeing'		'mix with water'	'perhaps'	'fire'
ling	'carry'		'actor'	'another'	'mountain range'
mo	'feel'		'plan'	'end'	'smear'
pin	'put together'		'poor'	'engage'	'product'
rang	'shout'		'avert'	'give way'	'earth'
shu	'write'		'sorghum'	'technique'	'category'
xi	'sunset'		'exercise'	'play'	'wash'

As can be seen, differences in tone signal lexical differences.

While most European languages lack tone (perhaps all, depending on the analytical perspective one adopts), many of the other world's languages have it. Many of these languages only have one tonal contrast. In order to describe such a contrast it therefore suffices to refer to one (relative) point in the pitch range, such that the tone corresponding to a pitch higher than that point is referred to as the 'high' tone, and, correspondingly, the tone with a lower pitch is known as the 'low' tone. In terms of binary features it is of course straightforward to translate these labels into [+high tone]/[−high tone], or [−low tone]/[+low tone]. Indeed, the standard formalisation of the contrast is by means of one such binary feature, [±upper], which splits the tonal register into an upper and a lower region, in the obvious way (see Yip 1980, Pulleyblank 1986, Snider 1990). For simplicity, however, we shall continue using the informal terms 'high' and 'low', abbreviated to 'H' and 'L', respectively. Other languages include a third, in-between tone, which we shall name 'M(id)'. One and perhaps even two more tones are possible, but rare.[12] For our purposes, it is sufficient to know that in some languages some vowels are pronounced as H and some as L (and perhaps some as M). Note that this classification is in fact considerably simpler (conceptually, auditorily and instrumentally) than the one which divides vowels into front, central and back, to give but one example. Moreover, such simple elements as H, M and L can end up making up truly intricate patterns, hence their heuristic usefulness to the student of phonology.

1.5.2 Phonological properties of tone

1.5.2.1 Unboundedness

We shall now sample some of the evidence for the autosegmentalisation of tone. The first argument concerns the possible distribution of one tone throughout a word domain, similarly to the distribution of [back] in Turkish vowels. Thus, consider the following tonal contours of verbal stems in the Southern Manyika dialect of Shona, discussed in Myers (1987) (such stems can for instance be prefixed with *ku-* to form infinitives; ' + ' = morpheme boundary):

(38) + téng + á   'buy'
      + téng + és + á   'sell'
      + téng + és + ér + á   'sell to'
      + téng + és + ér + án + á 'sell to each other'

What is of interest is the fact that all the suffixes (maximally causative + applicative + reciprocal + final vowel) carry a high tone (conventionally, an acute accent represents a high tone, and a grave accent a low tone). This could of course be taken to indicate that these suffixes are so marked in the lexicon. Consider, however, the data in (39):

(39) + èrèng + à   'read'
      + èrèng + ès + à   'make read'
      + èrèng + èr + à   'read to'
      + fùng + ìdz + ìr + àn + à 'suspect each other'

Here the same suffixes show up with a low tone. The key to the alternation is to be seen in the tonal specification of the verbal root, which we will assume is H for *teng*, and L for *ereng* and *fung*. As anticipated above, what now follows is reminiscent of Turkish vowel harmony, with an autosegmentalised feature spreading freely over the whole domain. We illustrate with *téngéséráná*:

(40)

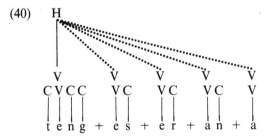

As before, we are assuming that the feature comes preattached to one segmental element in the lexicon, spreading from there to the rest of the domain. Before eventually putting this assumption to the test, we point out that, also as in the case of Turkish vowel harmony, the spreading operation takes place, not on the full line of CV elements, but rather on its V projection, as corresponds to the fact that universally only syllabic segments (vowels in particular) usually carry tone.[13] We accordingly talk about Vs as being 'tone-bearing units'. The notion of 'bearing unit' with regard to a particular autosegmental feature is of course central to the procedure, since we obviously want this feature to attach only to such units. The fact that autosegmental features can spread along on to any number of bearing units constitutes very strong evidence for the autosegmental approach.

The representation in (40) contains a lone H tone in the tonal tier, but this tone is realised over no less than five syllables. Given this configuration, we would expect that any process affecting this tone would be reflected in the tonal implementation of the five syllables. As we shall now see, this expectation indeed corresponds to fact.

Let us consider a dissimilation process quite common in Bantu languages and generally known as 'Meeussen's Law'. Thus, in another dialect of Shona, Zezuru, the word for 'axe' in isolation is *démó*, with two Hs. However, after concatenation to the prefix copula *í-*, also with an H, *demo* surfaces with two Ls: *ídèmò* 'it is an axe'. A similar effect takes place in longer strings of Hs, as shown in (41) for inflected forms of the by now familiar verb stem *téngésá* 'sell' (for general discussion see Myers 1987: 194ff.):

(41)   + chá + tèngèsà   'will sell'
       + ká + tèngèsà   'sold (before today)'
       + ngá + tèngèsè   'could sell'
       + á + tèngèsà   'sold (today)'

A ready account of such data can be given if the structure in (42) is assumed for *téngésá* (NB in the third form in (41), *ngátèngèsè*, the final vowel exhibits the allomorph *-e*):

(42)

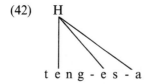

In particular, along the lines of our preceding discussion, the root *teng* carries a lexical H, which subsequently spreads on to the lexically toneless suffixes *-es* and *-a*. Meeussen's Law can now be formalised as a highly natural rule of tone dissimilation:

(43) H → ∅ /H___

The derivation of *-chá-tèngèsà* is illustrated in (44):

(44)

Putting aside for the moment the question of the source of the surface Ls on *tengesa* in this construction (see 1.6.2.1 below), we have now accounted for the simultaneous disappearance of H from the last three syllables of this word.

1.5.2.2 Persistence

We have mentioned the fact that tone-bearing units must be syllabic. The question therefore arises of what the fate of a tone will be when the vowel carrying it gets deleted (also when the vowel is desyllabified, i.e. when it becomes a glide). If tone were a feature of the phonemic melody, on a par with, say, [nasal] or [round], the tone ought to disappear with the vowel upon deletion. If, on the other hand, tone is autosegmental, we expect it to remain unaffected by such processes, as is actually the case.

In Margi the verb *tlà* 'to cut' undergoes vowel elision when suffixed by *-wá* to signify 'to cut in two' (Williams 1976). Such a loss of a tone-bearing unit would inevitably result in the obliteration of the tone if the tone was indeed embedded in the segment. Given the autosegmental formalisation, however, the natural outcome is for the tone to stay, as indeed it does. We know this to be so because the derivative 'to cut into two' is not pronounced **tlwá*, but rather *tlwǎ*, with a rising tone on its only tone bearer, *a*. If we analyse such a rising tone as a complex of L + H, as we will see we have plenty of motive to do, a highly natural derivation follows:

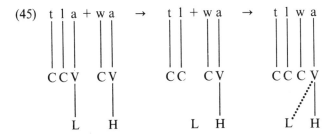

(45)

The L has been made to 'float' (a technical expression applied to unassociated autosegments) by the deletion of *a*. By the Well-formedness Condition (34), such a floating tone must attach to the nearest element capable of bearing it, as indeed it does. Note that this attachment takes place irrespective of the fact that the element in question is already linked to one tone. Such accumulation of tones on one vowel is sometimes referred to as 'dumping', to keep it distinct from the multiple linking of one tone to many vowels, which is simply known as 'spreading'.

1.5.2.3 Contour tones

The representation of surface contour tones as structurally composite lends additional support to the autosegmental analysis of tone. Note first that the evidence for such representation is quite compelling. Thus, consider such alternations as *vĕl* 'to jump' vs *vèlání* 'to make jump' in Margi. Assuming that the suffix *-ani* is not marked for tone in the lexicon, as was also the case with the Shona suffixes considered above, and that the tonal sequence LH is part of the lexical representation of the stem, the following derivations result (in the interest of graphic simplicity, the CV tier has been omitted):

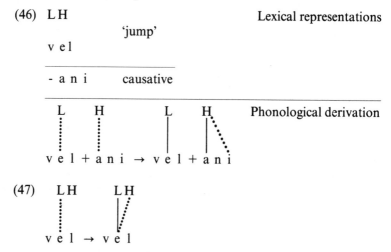

Notice that, departing from the practice so far, the underlying representations in (46) and (47) contain no association lines between the tones and the melody line. As must be clear by now, this formalisation is made possible by the Association Convention (31). Besides its obvious simplicity, we will see in 1.5.2.4 that such lexical independence of tones is in fact often forced on us by the facts.

What is of relevance to the matter at hand is the fact that alternations of the type being considered would be bizarre in the extreme if, e.g. the rising tone in *vĕl* was given independent formalisation, say, as R, since now there would be no apparent reason for the alternation R ∼ L, nor for the fact that the occurrence of the simple tone L in the stem is a function of the realisation of an H in the suffix.

A similar, possibly even stronger, argument for the composite analysis of contour tones comes from the phenomenon of tone assimilation, which is extremely common in tone languages. Simply, the sequence low + high tends to become low + rising, and the sequence high + low tends to become high + falling. These two mirror-image changes are readily formalisable autosegmentally by means of a rule spreading the first tone rightwards, as follows ('C^n' = any number of consonants):

(48)   a. Rise formation   b. Fall formation

The naturalness of the process is obvious, and can intuitively be related to the strength of the tendency for left-to-right tonal association, encapsulated in the Association Convention (31). One language which disfavours the abrupt transition from H to L or L to H is Yoruba. Thus, when the Yoruba copula *ó*, with an H, combines with the adjective *dùn* 'sweet', with L, the result is not **ó dùn*, but rather *ó dǔn* 'it is sweet' (cf. *kò dùn* 'it is not sweet'). Likewise for the H in *dún* 'to sound', which becomes rising in *kò dǔn* 'it does not sound' (cf. *ó dún* 'it sounds'). Clearly, these facts are derived straightforwardly if two rules with the effect of (48) are postulated for Yoruba.

The representation of contour tones as sequences of level tones inevitably leads to an autosegmental formalism. Thus, were we to preserve *SPE*'s unilinearity, we would run into the same problem as we did above for affricates, namely, the contradictory specification of a feature within a matrix. In particular, because a vowel clearly cannot be simultaneously high and low in tone, i.e. [+ upper] and [− upper], the representation in (49) is ruled out:

(49)

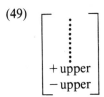

As we have seen, a rising tone requires a sequential representation [− upper, + upper], but this is difficult to accommodate within the *SPE* single matrix approach:

(50)

$$\left[\begin{array}{c} \vdots \\ - \text{upper}, \, + \text{upper} \end{array}\right]$$

As in the case of affricates, the problem with (50) is that *SPE* only allows for one feature value per matrix, because, as pointed out above, the function of the *SPE* features is to cross-classify the segment. The prediction made by the *SPE* formalism therefore is that contour tones ought to be confined to geminate vowels, since only such vowels can be analysed as containing two segments, each of which could then be assigned one of the tones. As we are seeing, however, this prediction is blatantly contradicted by the facts, and we must consequently conclude that the *SPE* formal machinery indeed needs reforming in the direction of autosegmentalism.

1.5.2.4 Autonomy

If tones are autonomous from vowels, nothing ought to rule out tones without vowels in the lexicon, and the evidence indeed supports this prediction.

Consider for instance the case of the Shona verbal stem *pá*, where *-a* must be analysed as a 'final vowel' morpheme, thus leaving *p* as the sole representative of the root. Should tones be an integral part of vowels, an obvious problem would arise, since the 'final vowel' is lexically toneless in Shona (see the data in (38) and (39) above), and the root is vowelless. The consequence of this analysis would obviously be that the surface H tone of *pá* would lack a source altogether, a paradoxical result. By contrast, if we allow for tones to be assigned to whole morphemes, rather than to individual vowels, as we are suggesting, the desired form will be readily derivable, as follows:

(51)   H   Lexical representations
              'give'
        p
        _____
        -a   Final Vowel
        _____
           H   Phonological derivation
           ⋮
           ⋮
           p a

Clearly, H has no other place to dock on than the Final Vowel − *a*.

Further evidence for the autonomy of tones is provided by the phenomenon of 'tonal melodies'. In particular, in many languages the number and identity of lexical tones is independent of that of phonemes. An oft-quoted example is Mende, where, in Leben's (1978) analysis, the

tone pattern of (most) monomorphemic words is drawn out of the pool
H, L, HL, LH, and LHL. As illustrated in (52), the number of syllables in
the word (more specifically, the number of tone-bearing units) bears no
relation to the selection of tone pattern:

(52) H   kɔ́   'war'   pélɛ́   'house'   háwámá   'waistline'

     L   kpà   'debt'   bɛ̀lɛ̀   'trousers'   kpàkàlì   'tripod chair'

     HL   mbû   'owl'   ngílà   'dog'   félàmà   'junction'

     LH   mbǎ   'rice'   fàndé   'cotton'   ndàvúlá   'sling'

     LHL   mbǎ̀   'companion'   nyàhâ   'woman'   nìkílì   'groundnut'

The last line is particularly telling, with a rise-fall on the monosyllable
mbǎ̀, a fall on the last syllable of the disyllable *nyàhâ*, and three simple
tones across the trisyllable *nìkílì*. Data such as these provide striking
support for the Association Convention (31) and the Well-formedness
Condition (34). Note in particular that dumping takes place, as
predicted by the Well-formedness Condition (34), and that it takes place
in the rightmost position, as follows from the conditions imposed on
association by the convention in (31), specifically one-to-one pairing of
free elements and left-to-right directionality. For greater clarity, we
illustrate these points with the derivation of *nyàhâ*:

(53)   L H L   Lexical representation

           'jump'

   n y a h a

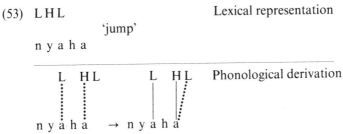

      L   HL   L   HL   Phonological derivation

   n y a h a   → n y a h a

The first step in the derivation takes place strictly in accordance with the
Association Convention (31), after which the Well-formedness Condition (34) comes into play to effect dumping of the floating L.

In the two cases considered so far we have found that the number of
tones in a morpheme need not match the number of tone-bearing units,
and we have interpreted this as additional evidence for the autosegmentalisation of tone. An even stronger case can be made from the
fact that it is possible, indeed quite common, for tones to be provided
independently of phonemes altogether. We have already encountered
morphemes without tones (cf. e.g. the Margi suffix *-ani*, discussed
above), and the question naturally arises as to whether the opposite
situation also obtains, namely, whether there are morphemes which do
not have segmental melodies but do have tone. The answer is an
unreserved yes, and we will come across two such morphemes for Tiv

(an L- prefix for the general past and an -H suffix for the recent past) in the course of our discussion below.

1.6 PRINCIPLES OF ASSOCIATION

1.6.1 Early autosegmental phonology

The model of association presented up to this point rests on the Well-formedness Condition (34), which we now formulate in Goldsmith's (1976) version:

(54) Well-formedness Condition

At any stage in the derivation, all vowels are associated with at least one tone, and tones are associated with at least one vowel.

(Goldsmith 1976:27)

Clearly, (54) acts as a filter on representations, such that it allows the structures in (55) to go through, but not their counterparts in (56) ('V' = tone-bearing unit; 'T' = tone):

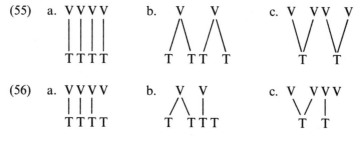

(56a) and (56c) illustrate underspreading (one of the Vs remains unassociated), while in (56b) there has been no dumping of the unmatched floating tone.

Because of its filter-like nature, the Well-formedness Condition is obviously insufficient to generate all and only the grammatical outputs. Thus, while, as noted, all the representations in (55) are compatible with the Well-formedness Condition, those in (55b) and (55c) manifestly violate the Association Convention (31), since they include multiple associations outside the rightmost edge. Notice also that the Well-formedness Condition has nothing to say about the No Crossing Constraint. In particular, the structure in (57) would comply with the former, but not with the latter:

(57) V   V   V   V
        ╳   ╳
      T   T   T   T

Clearly, thus, the Well-formedness Condition reduces to a statement of an ideal of association exhaustiveness, without specifying how this ideal must be reached. The machinery we have effectively been using to accomplish this aim is now summarised in (58):

(58) Principles of early autosegmental phonology
  i   associate free tones and tone-bearing units
      a one-to-one
      b from left to right
  ii each tone must be associated with at least one tone-bearing unit; tones remaining unassociated after (i) associate to the last tone-bearing unit
  iii each tone-bearing unit must be associated with at least one tone; tone-bearing units remaining unassociated after (i) associate to the last tone
  iv association lines may not cross

(58i) corresponds to Association Convention (31) above, and (58iv) to the No Crossing Constraint in (28). (58ii) and (58iii) simply spell out the Well-formedness Condition (54).

Ongoing research suggests that drastic reductions in the list in (58) may be necessary. Specifically, an examination of the recent literature leaves (58ia) as the only principle that can be accepted without any qualifications as an absolute universal ((58iv) is also commonly accepted). As we shall now see, the other clauses have been reinterpreted as preferred settings of a given parameter or seen their status demoted to that of simple language-particular rules.

1.6.2 Incomplete association

The Well-formedness Condition (54) requires all tones to be associated at all stages in the derivation. Equivalently, it prohibits floating tones at all levels but the lexical. Strong evidence against this constraint has however been emerging over the past decade, especially in the work of D. Pulleyblank (1983, 1986).

1.6.2.1 Against automatic spreading

We presented above the case of the Shona verbal stem *-téngéséránà* 'sell to each other', and suggested that the uniform H tone was the result of spreading, since there is evidence that all the suffixes are in fact lexically toneless (cf. *-fùngìdzìrànà* 'suspect each other'). The question we must now address is whether such spreading is brought about automatically, as the result of a universal convention, or whether it requires a language-specific rule. For ease of exposition, we have been following the former tack, which corresponds to the early belief in the context of autosegmental phonology. Contradictory data are however not in short supply.

In some languages tonal association takes place in one fell swoop after morphemes have been strung together to form words. In other languages, however, tonal association takes place in step with the morphological structure of the word. This mode of rule application is also available to other (non-tonal) processes, and is known as the 'cycle'. For each phonological process we must therefore specify whether its mode of application is cyclic or non-cyclic (see Chapter 5 for specific discussion).

In our present context, the availability of the cycle entails that automatic spreading cannot be universal. Thus, consider the behaviour of the Tiv Recent Past tonal suffix -H (an instance of a purely tonal morpheme). Because there is evidence that tonal association in Tiv is cyclic, we can test the correctness of the two competing hypotheses, multiple spreading vs strictly one-to-one association, as illustrated in (59) and (60), respectively (see Pulleyblank 1986: 78 for discussion):

(59)　L　　　　　　　　　　　　　　　Lexical representations

　　　　　　　　　　　'refuse'

　　vende

――――――――――――――――――

　　-H　　　　　　　　Recent Past

――――――――――――――――――――――――――――――――

　　　　　　　　　　　　　　　Phonological derivation

(60) L   Lexical representations
                          'refuse'
      vende

-H   Recent Past

                                    Phonological derivation

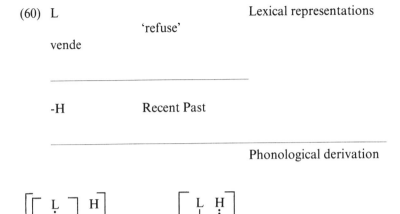

The respective outputs are *vèndě and vèndé. The ungrammaticality of the former is obviously due to the fact that the L has overspread in the inner cycle, a result which is avoided if association is exclusively one to one, as shown. Note that the argument against multiple spreading is independent of the implementation of dumping, since the output *vèndè, with no dumping of the H but with multiple spreading of L in the inner cycle, would be equally unacceptable.

The existence of cyclic tonal association makes the case against automatic spreading extremely compelling. Now, if we limit association by universal convention to one-to-one linking, we must clearly find an alternative way of accounting for the data presented above as suggestive of multiple spreading. The obvious such alternative is a language-specific spreading rule. One important difference besides cost between multiple spreading by universal convention and multiple spreading by rule is that in the former case there will be no directionality restrictions, whereas in the latter a specific directionality will be built into the rule. Consider in this light the following data from Margi (Pulleyblank 1986: 89ff.):

(61) tsárí   'to knock at'
     nàrì   'to tell a person'

The suffix -*ri* is toneless, and therefore takes its surface tone from the root, which we must consequently assume carries H for *tsa* and L for *nǝ*.

Such data of course constitute the stock-in-trade of automatic spreading.

Now, if spreading were induced by the Well-formedness Condition, we would expect at least some prefixes to exhibit similar tonal alternations. This expectation is however not fulfilled. A plausible account of this asymmetry relies on the postulation of a special rule of tone spreading for Margi, as follows (NB ringing indicates floating status):

(62)

(62) predicts that tones will spread rightwards on to vacant V slots, but not leftwards. This prediction matches the noted different tonal behaviour of prefixes and suffixes.

Another area which clearly shows the impossibility of automatic spreading is tonal default. Thus, it has been widely noticed that the distribution of tones in any one language is usually not symmetric, but rather one of the tones appears to be favoured (typically, L in two-tone systems, and M otherwise, as mentioned in note 12 above). The general issue of default and underspecification will be examined in depth in Chapter 2. Suffice it to say here that a language like Tiv, with H and L, must be assumed to have a rule supplying L to otherwise toneless syllables, which we will formulate, somewhat informally, as in (63):

(63) Tiv tone default

Consider now the following paradigms of general past tensed verbs (see Pulleyblank 1986: 82):

(64) a. !úngwà   'heard'   b. vèndè   'refused'
          !yévèsè   'fled'   ngòhòrò   'accepted'

Putting aside the interpretation of '!' for the time being (see 1.6.2.2 below), we observe a difference between the two columns, in that the forms in (64a) contain an H, but not so those in (64b). The tonal pattern of the forms in (64b) could at this point be interpreted as the result of the spread of a lexical L, but clearly a similar analysis with H is not available for the forms in (64a), because this tone only occupies the first syllable. Several alternatives readily come to mind (we could, for example, postulate an HL melody for the (64a) forms), but a deeper probe into the facts of the language will prove them futile. Thus, consider the forms in (65), which correspond to the recent past:

(65) a. óngó   'heard'   b. vèndé   'refused'
          yévésè   'fled'   ngòhórò   'accepted'

Besides some changes in the vocalism and the absence of '!' in the (65a) forms, we notice that the second syllable is now invariably H in both columns. This identifies the recent past marker with a floating H (thus providing a further instantiation of a vowelless tonal morpheme), as follows:

(66) a.   b.

The first tone, which we represent already associated, is the lexical tone of the verb, while the second corresponds to the recent past morpheme. Obviously, this tone does not undergo iterative spreading (cf. *yévésé, *ngòhóró), but rather its association takes place strictly in accordance with the Association Convention (31), which only sanctions one-to-one linking:

(67) a.   b.

The last syllables *se* and *ro* will eventually be assigned a default L by rule (63):

(68) a.   b.

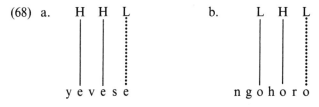

The desired surface forms *yévésè* and *ngòhórò* now result.

1.6.2.2 Against dumping

Having opened a first breach in the buttress of the Well-formedness Condition, we now proceed to show that universal dumping is also untenable.

Let us examine the tonal realisation of the copula *mba* in Tiv (Pulleyblank 1986: 34; NB in line with note 13 above, some consonants also carry tone in this language):

(69) ùnyìnyà mbâ   'there are horses'
      kásév mbâ   'there are women'

These data obviously appear to support dumping, since *mbâ* bears a composite HL tone. Consider, however, the forms in (70):

(70) mbá !vàǹ   'they are coming'
      kásév mbá !gá   'there are not any women'

Here, the same word is realised as *mbá*, with only an H tone. This notwithstanding, there is evidence that *mba* indeed carries two lexical tones, H and L, in this order, since the H of the words following *mba* in (70) is downstepped, as signalled graphically by the exclamation mark.[14] Clearly, the downstep is not inherent to *van* or *ga* (cf. e.g. *á kahà gá* 'he did not hoe', *á kèrà hìdè gá* 'he failed to return'), but rather has been induced by *mba*, as will obviously happen if this word indeed brings along an L:

(71)
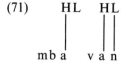

What is relevant to our present discussion is the fact that such an L remains floating. This would clearly not be the case if dumping was triggered by a universal convention. On the other hand, if we confine dumping to language-specific stipulation, we account for all the facts of Tiv by the postulation of the following rule:

(72)

The condition in (72) that the V be prepausal (' ‖ ') explains the preservation of the floating status of L in (70)–(71).

The analysis of Tiv dumping just presented is confirmed by the initial downstep on the general past form of the high-toned verbal stem *yevese* 'flee', which was already introduced above:

(73) H   Lexical representations
                          'flee'

      yevese

      ─────────────────────────────────

      L-   General Past

      ─────────────────────────────────

                                      Phonological derivation

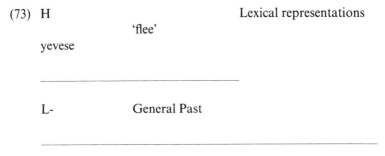

If dumping was universal, the floating L would associate to the first *e* in the second cycle. The result would be a rising tone on this vowel and no downstep (*yě . . .). Instead, *ye* surfaces with a downstepped H: *!yévèsè* (the additional Ls are supplied by default).

As in the case of multiple spreading, there is abundant cross-linguistic evidence that dumping does not take place universally. Consequently, Goldsmith's original Well-formedness Condition (54) must be tuned down to the more modest Association Convention (31), which simply pairs up free elements from left to right.

1.6.3 Directionality

In this section we review some evidence that casts doubt on the universality of rightward directionality. Such evidence will be drawn from the tone tier and the CV tier.

1.6.3.1 Right-to-left association

All the data reviewed so far are consistent with left-to-right association, as embodied in principle (58ib) above. In particular, we have seen multiple spreading or dumping (whether implemented by universal convention or by rule) to take place on the right edge of the domain. The distribution of tones in Hausa contradicts this prediction, however (data from Newman 1986):

(74) a. búhúnnàa   'sacks'
         shúugábáncìi   'leadership'

     b. hànkàakíi   'crows'
         bàbbàbbàkú   'be well roasted'

     c. yàaràntákàa   'childishness'
         cìnìkáyyà   'mutual trade'

Three different complex patterns are demonstrated in (74): HL (74a), LH (74b), and LHL (74c). In all three cases the direction of association is obviously right-to-left, since left-to-right association would generate such incorrect contours as *búhùnnàa, *hànkáakíi, or *yàrántàkàa.

Another area from which support for right-to-left association can be drawn is reduplication, which was introduced above. At the time we used reduplication to back up the more general left-to- right direction of association, but, as early as Marantz (1982), it was suggested that such direction of association is only unmarked for prefixes, suffixes usually associating right-to-left, as illustrated by the following form from Dakota:

(75) C V C C V   +   C C V C
      | | | | | ⋮ ⋮ ⋮ ⋮
      h ạ s k a   h ạ s k a

The skeletal suffix *CCVC* is a marker of verbal plurality. The re-duplicated form *hạskaska* 'be tall-pl.' shows that association must be right-to-left, subject to the language-particular proviso that vowels only associate with V slots, and consonants with C slots, as shown.

Marked directionality in reduplication can be exemplified with Chukchee, where suffixes associate left-to-right (see (24d) above), and with Madurese, which has prefixes associating right-to-left (e.g. *búwáq-án* 'fruit' → *wáq-búwáq-án* 'fruits', not *búw-búwáq-án*).

1.6.3.2 Edge-in association

The existence of right-to-left, in addition to left-to-right, association can be formalised by means of a directionality parameter, which we will see in subsequent chapters also plays a role in other areas of phonology (see in particular Chapters 4 and 5). Crucially, in both cases parsing takes place from one end of the domain to the other. In what follows we shall present some evidence suggesting that an additional parsing mode may be necessary: parsing from both ends inwards.

A few words are first necessary about what has come to be called 'root-and-pattern' or 'non-concatenative' morphology, since it is primarily in this area that edge-in association has been called in. Non-concatenative morphology has also played a prominent role in the development of autosegmental phonology, and has therefore an interest of its own for us here.

Put at its simplest, instead of or in addition to affixal morphology, some languages (especially Semitic languages) license a morphological process by which two lexical morphemes interleave their elements. Typically, one of these morphemes consists exclusively of vowels, and the other of consonants. For instance, in Arabic there is a lexical root /ktb/, with the general idea of 'write'. This broad semantic meaning gets narrowed down in specific forms to signify 'correspond', 'subscribe', 'make write', and so on. The way this is done is by means of skeletal templates, also provided by the lexicon, each of which carries a specific nuance of meaning. For instance, the template CVVCVC modifies the basic meaning of /ktb/ into the reciprocal 'correspond' (each such templatic-expressed meaning modification is given the name *wazn* in Arabic, although in generative phonology they are more commonly known under the Hebrew label *binyan*, plural *binyanim*; the set of binyanim can be reasonably interpreted as a conjugational paradigm). Let us now examine how this template will come together with the root /ktb/:

(76)

Simply, each root consonant associates to one skeletal slot, as predicted by the Association Convention. Consider, however, the causative binyan, with the template CVCCVC. Here there is one excess C position, and the question arises as to how association will take place. Left-to-right directionality predicts *katbab. The correct form, *kattab*, can however be obtained straightforwardly if association proceeds from each edge inwards:

(77)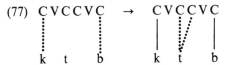

In the first step, the two peripheral root consonants associate to the template edges, after which the remaining consonant fills in the two medial slots.

In the derivations given so far the V slots have been left vacant. In the model of templatic morphophonology originally put forward by McCarthy (1979, 1981, 1986), the lexical vowels are assigned an independent tier, from which they associate to the template, as shown in (78):

(78)

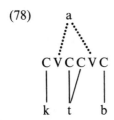

The assignment of vowels and consonants to different tiers can be justified on morpholexical grounds, since the Arabic vowel melody constitutes an independent morpheme, which expresses tense, aspect, voice, etc. It also follows from the requirement that association lines do not cross, as they would do if both vowels and consonants were located in the same tier:

(79) C V C C V C
      | ✕✕✕ \
      k t b   a

The evidence just presented for edge-in association is not isolated, and Yip (1988a) makes a plea for a wider application of the procedure, although a question remains as to whether melody-to-template association obeys the same principles as tonal association or other such autosegmental processes. As an additional argument from Arabic we can mention the vocalism of forms like *mutakaatib* 'writing to each other' (*muta-* derives from a skeletal concatenative prefix). If *uai* is factored out as the vocalic melody, left-to-right association predicts **mutakiitib*. On the other hand, edge-in association goes beyond generating the right output, since it allows the simplification of the lexical vocalic morpheme to *ui*, as we now show:

(80)

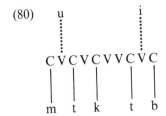

After association of the two vowel melodies to the edges, the remaining V slots can be filled in by simply supplying *a* by default (NB one-to-many association of the lexical vowels must thus be prevented in the present case), as corresponds to the general facts of (Classical) Arabic.

Further instantiations of edge-in association have been claimed to exist in such languages as Tigrinya (cf. the gemination of the medial *b* in the frequentative *säbabärä*, from the plain perfect *säbärä*), Tigre (*dǝmmäl* 'vengeance' vs the plural *dämämmǝl*), Cupeño (cf. the verb stem *cal* 'husk' with the habilitative form *caʔaʔal*, where *ʔ* is a default consonant), and others (see Yip 1988a: 573ff. for discussion). Overall, however, the evidence for such a mode of association is not compelling, and the proposal must therefore be approached with caution.

1.6.4 Line crossing

The outcome of the preceding discussion is that the obligatory asssociation machinery must be minimised. At this point, we have effectively reduced the list in (58) above to the Association Convention (31) and the No Crossing Constraint (28). We now turn to the examination of this constraint.[15]

In 1.4.2 above we discussed some facts of reduplication and interpreted them as evidence for the No Crossing Constraint. In particular, we suggested that derivations such as (26), repeated here as (81) for convenience, are undesirable:

(81) (= (26))

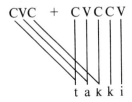

A different tack is explored in McCarthy and Prince (1986), who tentatively propose a relaxation of the No Crossing Constraint.

We will rehearse one of their arguments here. Winnebago has a process of vowel epenthesis, commonly known as 'Dorsey's Law', which destroys obstruent + liquid clusters by inserting a copy of the following vowel, as illustrated in (82) (cf. McCarthy and Prince 1986: 104):

(82) Winnebago's Dorsey's Law

krepna	→	kerepana
hoikwe	→	hoikewe
pras	→	paras
rupri	→	rupiri

At first sight, it may appear that the only possible formalisation of Dorsey's Law is as a copy rule along the lines of (83):

(83) Dorsey's Law as copy

$$\emptyset \rightarrow V_j \quad / \ C\underline{\hspace{1.5cm}}CV_j$$

$$[-\text{son}][+\text{son}]$$

The problem with such transformational formalism concerns its practically unlimited power (for instance, nothing would in principle prevent the same process from taking place between a string of *n* syllables). Consider, however, the following autosegmental account for *kerepana*:

(84)

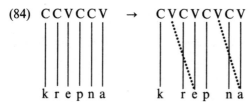

This autosegmental formalism brings out the naturalness of the process. In particular, although lines are crossed, they are crossed minimally. Thus, we would like to ban derivations such as the following:

(85)

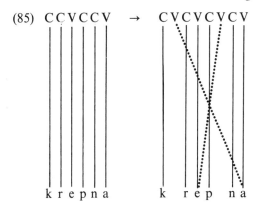

The output would be **karepena*. McCarthy and Prince propose to forestall such undesirable results, while preserving the naturalness of the autosegmental approach, by dropping the No Crossing Constraint (28) and postulating a new set of association principles, essentially as follows (see McCarthy and Prince 1986: 105):

(86) Skeleton Satisfaction Condition
All skeletal positions must be exhausted.

(87) Principle of Maximisation of Association
Associate as many different phonemic melody elements as possible.

(88) Principle of Crossing Avoidance
Do not cross association lines gratuitously.

These principles are assumed to apply in the order given, in the sense that Skeleton Satisfaction must be given absolute priority, and Maximisation of Association overrides Crossing Avoidance.

Thus, by Skeleton Satisfaction (86), the additional V slots introduced by a simplified Dorsey's rule ($\emptyset \rightarrow V /[-son]\_\_[+son]$) must be given melodic content. Only the derivation in (84) will however be consistent with the Crossing Avoidance principle in (88), since any other pattern of association (e.g. that in (85)) would cross more lines than strictly necessary for compliance with Skeleton Satisfaction (note that the direction of association must be stipulated on a language-specific basis: cf. *rupri → rupiri* vs **rupuri*).[16]

It is clear at this stage that the approach can profitably be extended to reduplication. In particular, the principles in (86), (87), and (88) will license the derivation of *taktakki* in (81) (= (26)), but not that of **(pag)dikandīlah* in (89):

(89) (= (27))

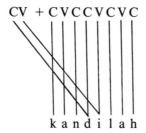

k a n d i l a h

Once more, the association lines linking the skeletal prefix in this derivation do not comply with the Principle of Crossing Avoidance (88), and therefore the derivation will be disallowed. The advantage of this procedure over the one adopted earlier concerns the fact that it dispenses with melody copy (and its attendant clean-up procedures), a clearly *ad hoc* device confined to reduplication.[17]

This gain notwithstanding, McCarthy and Prince explicitly present their proposal as tentative, as mentioned above, and the common consensus still supports the No Crossing Constraint in its original formulation (28). Indeed, Bagemihl (1989) makes a case for limiting legitimate violations of the constraint to the area of ludlings, 'backwards languages' in particular, which would thus depart from the norms of ordinary phonology. We illustrate in (90) with the derivation of *hatjob* from the Javanese *botjah* by means of maximum line crossing (*tj* = [ʧ]):

(90)

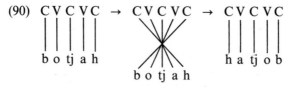

In the last step the melodies have undergone relinearisation precisely to correct line crossing, which Bagemihl contends is only tolerated in intermediate derivational stages.

1.7 CONCLUSION

We have gone some way in our exploration of phonological structure, and are now in a position to provide answers to the questions posed at the outset. Thus, there are as many tiers as autosegments, and any phonological element can in principle be autosegmentalised: individual phonemic features, as in harmony systems, tones, as evidenced by tone languages, and the syllabicity-related elements, which make up the skeleton. Given a number *n* of autosegmental tiers, the question arises as to how they relate to each other. This question has in fact two parts. First, have all tiers access to all other tiers? Second, given two mutually accessible tiers, how do their elements interact?

The basic answer to the first question is that the skeleton acts as a central autosegmental line to which all other tiers are connected (some refinements will be introduced in this idea as we go along). A useful analogy is provided by the hub and the spokes of a wheel, or, perhaps more accurately, by a book's spine and the pages which stem from it (this image is, I believe, originally due to Morris Halle; see Halle 1985). We illustrate graphically in (91):

(91)

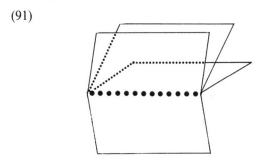

In (91) there is a central line of points, to be interpreted at this stage as a sequence of Cs and/or Vs. Out of this line comes a potentially infinite number of planes (strictly speaking, half planes), one for each class of autosegments. It is within each of these planes that the conventions mapping the autosegmental elements to the skeletal slots apply.

The association principles have been seen to be much impoverished in relation to their original formulation. At the present point, they would appear to reduce to a pairing algorithm (the Association Convention), possibly parametrised as to directionality, and to a prohibition of line crossing (conceivably weakened to a simple dislike for crossing, as embodied in the Principle of Crossing Avoidance). Armed with this essentially very simple machinery, we will continue our probe into the fabric of phonology throughout the ensuing chapters.

2 Lexical redundancies

2.1 THE ORGANISATION OF PHONOLOGY

It is the task of phonology to provide a formal representation of the phonic matter pertaining to the systems of natural languages. Typically, there are predictable, alongside unpredictable, aspects to such matter. Consider, for instance, the voice alternations induced by the suffix -*th* in English: *five* ~ *fifth*, *twelve* ~ *twelfth* (also *hundre*[t]*th*, *thousan*[t]*th*). Such contextual changes in the make-up of morphemes are of course formalised by means of phonological rules, which constitute the stock-in-trade of phonology.

There is, however, a second type of regularity, to be directly examined in this chapter. Thus, morpheme-internally in English, the common situation is also for adjacent obstruents to agree in voicing (see 2.3.2.1 below). Regularities of this kind are clearly not reducible to alternation, as they concern the distribution of features in the lexical representations themselves. Consequently, they cannot be accounted for by the mapping rule mechanism commonly held responsible for alternations.

2.1.1 The generation of lexical matrices

Lexical items are kept apart phonologically by means of contrasts in their distinctive feature matrices.[1] In particular, in the standard approach, Universal Grammar (UG) makes available a set of bivalent distinctive features, $[\pm F_1], \ldots, [\pm F_n]$. Maximal utilisation of these elements yields a number 2^n of distinct segments, for a segment defined as an exhaustive combination of valued features[2] (in line with Archangeli and Pulleyblank forthcoming, each such valued feature will also be referred to here by the convenient expression 'F-element'), as partially represented in (1):

(1) S_i S_j S_k S_l S_m . . .

F_1 + + + + +
F_2 + + + + −
F_3 + + + − +
F_4 + + − + +
.
.
.
F_n + − + + +

The segments 'S_x' in (1) are all distinct,[3] as they differ in the specification of (at least) one feature.

Languages, of course, only utilise subsets of the total set of features made available by Universal Grammar. Submatrices of the matrix generated by all the features available in L will in turn define lexical items in L, as illustrated in (2):

(2) a. S_i S_j b. S_i S_k S_l c. S_k S_l S_m
      F_1 + + F_1 + + + F_1 + + +
      F_2 + + F_2 + + + F_2 + + −
      F_3 + + F_3 + + − F_3 + − +
      F_4 + + F_4 + − + F_4 − + +
      .   .   .
      .   .   .
      .   .   .
      F_n + − F_n + + + F_n + + +

In (2) three possible lexical items of L are represented, with the segmental composition $/S_i\,S_j/$, $/S_i\,S_k\,S_l/$, and $/S_k\,S_l\,S_m/$.

While the number of lexical items constructable by this procedure is potentially quite large (given the sizeable set of binary distinctive features, and thus of segments, made available by UG), it is of course still finite. In the composition of lexical items, languages therefore characteristically break away from this constraint by availing themselves of recursion, and such items as in (3) could accordingly be present in the lexicon of L, alongside those in (2):

(3) a. S_i S_j S_i S_j b. S_i S_j S_i S_j S_i

F_1	+	+	+	+		F_1	+	+	+	+	+
F_2	+	+	+	+		F_2	+	+	+	+	+
F_3	+	+	+	+		F_3	+	+	+	+	+
F_4	+	+	+	+		F_4	+	+	+	+	+
.						.					
.						.					
.						.					
F_n	+	−	+	−		F_n	+	−	+	−	+

As usual, the linear order of segments within each item indicates relations of precedence. As discussed in Chapter 1 and reiterated in note 3 above, this order is an integral part of phonological representations, and a sequence such as $S_j \, S_i \, S_j \, S_i$ will therefore define a lexical item distinct from $S_i \, S_j \, S_i \, S_j$ in (3a).

2.1.2 Levels of representation

We have been referring to representations such as those in (1), (2) and (3) as 'matrices'. By a 'matrix' we therefore understand an array made up of rows and columns, the former defined by the set of feature labels, and the latter by successive permutations of the values assigned to such features, each distinct set of values defining a different segment. As we are seeing, lexical matrices fulfil a classificatory function, in that they serve the purpose of identifying (and thus differentiating) all and only the items capable of phonic individuation in a given language. The optimalisation of this function can (and typically does) entail significant representational differences with respect to the phonetic materialisation of such items. For instance, while the presence of aspiration in English is phonetically relevant, its distributional predictability obviously makes it redundant from the point of view of lexical classification.

As is well known, this dilemma is formally resolved in generative phonology by the postulation of two autonomous levels of representation; namely the lexical level, at which only lexical contrasts are expressed, and the phonetic level, at which all the information pertinent to phonetic realisation must be provided. The mapping between these two levels is carried out by a set of (phonological) rules, which can (and often do) yield intermediate representational levels.

The phonetic level constitutes the final state in a (full) phonological derivation. Its justification is ultimately phonetic, in that it must match some phonetic reality, such as the (idealised) set of instructions which must be issued to the articulators in order for phonetic implementation to take place. In turn, the representations at the lexical level, which constitutes the initial derivational state, are assumed to be maximally simple, subject to compatibility with their classificatory function and with the general condition of naturalness on phonological representations (see note 1 above).

2.2 COMBINATORY RESTRICTIONS

In real life the size of the matrix illustrated in (1) is curtailed in two ways. First, the phonetic substance of features imposes obvious universal combinatory restrictions, both segment-internally and across segments. Second, the remaining subset is typically underexploited in individual languages.

2.2.1 Markedness in *SPE*

The observation that phonetic substance has an influence on the combinatory possibilities of features intra- and intersegmentally forms the basis of 'Markedness Theory', given particular impetus by the work of Roman Jakobson. A specific formalisation of the markedness hypothesis is provided in *SPE*, and it will be useful to turn to it briefly as a preliminary to our discussion.

2.2.1.1 Absolute prohibitions

Certain combinations of valued features are banned universally. In *SPE*, the strongest such prohibition concerns the cooccurrence in the same matrix of the two opposing values of any one feature, as already embodied in the general formal apparatus of this model of phonology.[4] Other restrictions need however to be specifically stated, and this is done in *SPE* by means of a set of 'marking conventions'.

Among the universal prohibitions assumed in *SPE* are the following two:

(4) a. * $\begin{bmatrix} + \text{high} \\ + \text{low} \end{bmatrix}$

   b. * $\begin{bmatrix} - \text{coronal} \\ + \text{lateral} \end{bmatrix}$

The first of these prohibitions is usually interpreted as an instance of logical incompatibility, since, the argument goes, it is impossible for the tongue to be simultaneously raised and lowered from its neutral position.[5] The prohibition expressed in (4b) would by contrast be grounded on empirical fact, rather than on logic. In particular, it rules out the combination of the valued features [−coronal] and [+lateral], which clearly does not violate any of the principles of logic.[6]

The direct ban on the stated configurations embodied in the formalism in (4) corresponds to the idea of 'filter', or 'negative condition'. In *SPE* such prohibitions are however represented implicationally, along the lines of (5) and (6):

(5)   a.   [+low]   → [−high]
       b.   [+high] → [−low]

(6)   [−coronal]   → [−lateral]

If-then conditions of this kind are in fact logically equivalent to negative conditions, since $\sim(A \& B) = (A \rightarrow \sim B) \& (B \rightarrow \sim A)$. At this point, therefore, no obvious specific advantage accrues to either of the two formalisms, a matter we will return to in 2.6.2 below.

2.2.1.2 Universal tendencies

As is well known, in addition to absolute prohibitions on feature coocurrence, there exist universal trends by which certain combinations are favoured over others. Thus, sonorants tend to be voiced, back non-low vowels tend to be round, and their front counterparts non-round, low vowels tend to be non-round, irrespective of backness, and so on.

Combinatory preferences of this kind are also formalised in *SPE* as marking conventions, as illustrated in (7):

(7)   a.   [*u* voice]   → [+voice] / $\left[\begin{array}{c} \underline{\quad\quad} \\ +son \end{array} \right]$

       b.   [*u* round]   → [αround] / $\left[\begin{array}{c} \underline{\quad\quad} \\ \alpha back \\ -low \end{array} \right]$

       c.   [*u* back]   → [+back] / $\left[\begin{array}{c} \underline{\quad\quad} \\ +low \end{array} \right]$

Note that features are now specified as *u* in the input, and as + or − in the output (NB 'α' stands for either + or −). The symbol *u* designates the 'unmarked' value, which is assumed to be cost-free.

All in all, there are 39 separate marking conventions in *SPE*, many with internal branches and sub-branches. Between them, they purport to capture (albeit in a provisional way) what is expected in languages, both in terms of segment inventories (i.e. the restrictions obtaining on paradigmatic combinations of feature values) and of segment patterns (i.e. restrictions on syntagmatic cooccurrences). The programme of thus cataloguing and formalising markedness was continued in Kean (1975), after which it effectively came to an end.

2.2.2 Language-particular constraints

In addition to universally bound restrictions on certain cooccurrences of F-elements, languages exhibit parochial constraints. Thus, consider the vowel systems of English and Turkish. We know from Chapter 1 that Turkish allows all value combinations for the features [back] and [round], and therefore such vowels as /y/ ([−back, +round]) or /ɨ/ ([+back, −round]) are possible in this language. By contrast, in English the features [back] and [round] must agree in value in non-low vowels.

From the point of view of markedness, English therefore receives a higher evaluation than Turkish, since English, but not Turkish, complies with the marking convention (7b) above. In the markedness model of *SPE*, however, such conventions are purely evaluative, and thus have no power to ban marked combinations (such as [αround, −αback, −low]) from lexical representations. Clearly, thus, in order to exclude front rounded segments from the English lexicon we will need to interpret the statement in (7b) as a specific constraint on this language, rather than as a simple universal measure of cost, as explicitly expressed in (8):

(8) $[\alpha \text{back}] \rightarrow [\alpha \text{round}] / \begin{bmatrix} \underline{\qquad} \\ -\text{low} \end{bmatrix}$

Such language-specific constraints allow us to give formal characterisation to the fact that the set of unattested lexical forms of any one language includes possible, as well as impossible, items. An oft-cited example is the triplet *brick*, *blick*, *bnick* for English. The first of these words is of course part of the English lexical stock. The second is not, but could freely enter the language as she is today. The third item, *bnick*, however, is not a possible word of present-day English, since it violates a constraint of this language to the effect that initial stops can only be followed by oral sonorants:

(9) $[+\text{cons}] \rightarrow \begin{bmatrix} -\text{nas} \\ +\text{son} \end{bmatrix} / \#[-\text{cont}]\underline{\qquad}$

Crucially, the inclusion of this simple statement in the grammar allows us to substantially simplify the lexicon, in the obvious way.

Suppose now that we wished to rule out the occurrence of *blick*. The implementation of this ban would require the following constraint:

(10) $[+\text{son}] \rightarrow [-\text{lateral}] \,/\#b\underline{\quad}\text{ɪk}\#$

The payoff of (10) is confined to the one item in question, thus failing to offset the high cost of the constraint, as reflected in its formal complexity (thinly disguised by the informal segmental representation of the environment). This shows that the generalisation in (10) is spurious, in contrast to its counterpart in (9).

2.3 LEXICAL UNDERSPECIFICATION OF FEATURES

The term 'underspecification' will occupy a central position in the exposition in the remainder of the chapter, and is intended to describe a situation where some feature parameter has not been assigned a lexical value. Equivalently, underspecified features can be construed as simply being absent from the representation, as we will see.

2.3.1 Redundancies as blanks

Kiparsky (1982a,b) proposes to encode distributionally redundant values as lexical blanks. This is a natural, intuitively appealing, and simple formalisation of lexical redundancy, already adopted in early generative phonology (see e.g. Halle 1959, 1964; Chomsky 1964; and Chomsky and Halle 1965). Such an approach had however been abandoned following the demonstration by Lightner (1963) and Stanley (1967) that specious contrasts can arise through the application of phonological rules to matrices containing blanks.[7]

Crucially, however, such an objectionable practice presupposes the lexical availability of both the positive and the negative specifications of the feature in question, alongside its blank representation. The undesirable outcome can consequently be forestalled by the simple strategy of only accepting one of the two explicit values as lexical. In particular, Kiparsky proposes that for each distinctive feature there be a rule with the format of (11):

(11) $[\quad] \rightarrow [\alpha F] \,/\, X$

The provision by rule (11) of the appropriate value α to F in context X makes it possible to omit this value from lexical representations in this specific environment. By contrast, the complement value $[-\alpha F]$, also in environment X, must obviously be entered in the lexicon. The restriction that only one value per feature can be supplied by rule entails that only binary oppositions can ever be established: $[\emptyset F] (= [\quad])$ vs $[-\alpha F]$ in the lexicon, and $[\alpha F]$ vs $[-\alpha F]$ after the application of (11). Consequently, an approach of this kind satisfactorily answers the Lightner/Stanley objection to lexical blanks.

Kiparsky's proposal accommodates both universal and language-particular rules on the format of (11). The universal rules parallel the *SPE* marking conventions, with blanks formally substituting for *u*s in the input. These rules therefore provide the universally preferred value of each feature in each particular context. As we have seen, specific languages are also subject to specific constraints, hence the need for additional, language-particular redundancy rules.

Thus, within Kiparsky's system, lexical entries look very much like their *SPE* counterparts, with unmarked values now simply left empty, and marked values specified as $+$ or $-$, as appropriate. The empty values will at some point be filled in by rules with the format of (11). In addition to this feature-filling mode of application, however, such rules will be allowed to apply in a feature-changing mode, as we shall see directly.

2.3.2 Modes of rule application

We will now illustrate the procedure by considering the distribution of the value for [voice] in English, as discussed in Kiparsky (1982a,b).

2.3.2.1 Structure-building mode: the Elsewhere Condition

First, the following two markedness rules are assumed to be part of the stock of universal grammar:

(12) a. $[\quad] \rightarrow [+\text{voice}]$

b. $[\quad] \rightarrow [-\text{voice}] \quad / \quad \begin{bmatrix} \underline{\qquad} \\ -\text{son} \end{bmatrix}$

Rule (12b) predicts that obstruents will be voiceless, all other segments being supplied the value $[+\text{voice}]$ by (12a). Importantly, the context-free formulation of (12a) that we are adopting entails a disjunctive, bleeding ordering (12b) < (12a), as we shall now show.

Such application restrictions are in fact very natural. Clearly, both rules cannot be allowed to apply to the same input, since their outputs are contradictory. At first blush, it might be thought that (12a) ought to be given precedence, as it is context-free, and thus has maximal general scope. A moment's thought will however reveal that this approach cannot yield the desired results. Specifically, were a more general rule, R_g, to apply disjunctively before a more particular rule R_p, with the same input in a more restricted environment, R_p would never have a chance to apply, since it would systematically be bled by R_g. Therefore, R_p would be lost from the grammar. Consequently, in order for R_p, the more specific rule, to be preserved, it must precede R_g, the general case (appositely referred to as the 'elsewhere case'). In the event of application of R_p, R_g will be suspended by convention, since, if it wasn't, its application could undo the effects of R_p.

The principle which thus regulates the order of application of overlapping rules is known as the 'Elsewhere Condition' (EC), and is assumed to be part of Universal Grammar (it is in fact doubtful that the EC even needs to be stated as a principle of grammar, given the facts just considered):

(13) Elsewhere Condition
Given two rules R_p and R_g, such that (i) they have contradictory outputs, and (ii) the input of R_p overlaps with, but is more specific than, the input of R_g (more formally, the structural description of R_p properly includes the structural description of R_g), then only R_p applies to any input which meets the structural description of both R_p and R_g.

Thus, for instance, the three segments of the form *pan* will be left lexically unspecified for [voice], the application of the two rules in (12) taking place as follows:

(14)   p a n
    [voice]   lexical
    ─────────────────────────→
    [voice] −   by (12b)
    ─────────────────────────→
    [voice]   + +   by (12a)

In (14) the two rules in question have applied in a structure-building mode, their action being limited to the provision of some structure which is missing from the input. Such a structure-building mode of rule application, therefore, crucially presupposes the presence of blanks.

Let us now consider the form *ban*, where the voiced obstruent *b* manifestly contradicts the predictions of (12b). All that is needed in order to account for such exceptional behaviour, however, is to include the exceptional value in the lexical representation of this item. The legitimacy of this move is of course underwritten by the fact that the proposed lexical specification is complementary to the one supplied by the redundancy rule (12b). For clarity, the derivations of *pan* and *ban* are now compared. Note, crucially, that the mode of application of rule (12b) is still structure-building, and therefore the lexical value [+ voice] remains unaffected:

(15)   p a n   b a n
    [voice]   +   lexical
    ――――――――――――――――――――――――――――――――――→
    [voice] −   by (12b)
    ――――――――――――――――――――――――――――――――――→
    [voice]   + +   + +   by (12a)

According to Kiparsky, the two rules in (12) do not exhaust the description of the distribution of [voice] in English. In particular, a further regularity concerns the usual voice uniformity of obstruent clusters in this language, as we now capture in (16) (like the other rules mentioned in this chapter, this rule is of course formalisable auto-segmentally; we follow here the formulation found in the original sources):

(16) $[-\text{sonorant}] \rightarrow [\alpha\text{voice}] / \underline{\quad} \begin{bmatrix} -\text{son} \\ \alpha\text{voice} \end{bmatrix}$

Kiparsky construes the assimilation rule in (16) as language-particular (it is, however, far from unusual cross-linguistically), in contrast with its predecessors in (12), which are assumed to be universal. Like these, rule (16) will supply the appropriate value to the feature [voice] in the given environment (and, because of its greater specificity, it will be given disjunctive priority over (12b) by the Elsewhere Condition (13)), as we now illustrate with the *b* of *abdomen*:

(17)   a b domen
    [voice]   +   lexical
    ――――――――――――――――――――――――――――――――――→
    [voice]   +   by (16)

The [+ voice] lexical specification of *d* provides the context which triggers the action of (16), in the manner seen.

There are some exceptions to the voicing agreement of clusters.[8] Consider for instance a word like *absent*, where we consider *b* not to take on the [− voice] value of the following *s* (at least phonologically). As will be clear from the previous discussion, this result can be achieved by simply including [+ voice] in the lexical representation of the *b*, in a manner paralleling our treatment of the *d* of *abdomen*. On the other hand, *s* will have [− voice] supplied by the markedness rule (12b), and consequently such value can be left lexically blank:

(18)   a b sent
        [voice]   +   lexical
        ─────────────────────────────────────→
        [voice]   −   by (12b)

This completes the survey of the structure-building mode of application of the rules at hand, which, as shown, plays an important role in accounting for the lexical distribution of voice in English.

2.3.2.2 Structure-changing mode: Strict Cyclicity

Consider next the [+ voice] : [− voice] alternation in such pairs as *fi*[v]*e* : *fi*[f]*th*, *lo*[z]*e* : *lo*[s]*t*, etc., already referred to at the outset, a clear case of regressive voice assimilation. These data suggest that the rule in (16) is also applicable heteromorphemically, i.e. outside strict lexical representations.

Let us examine the change /v/→/f/ in *fifth*. The *v* in *five* must be lexically marked as [+ voice], in line with our discussion above. The environment of voice assimilation (16) is simply not met by this form in isolation. Upon addition of the nominalising suffix -*th*, however, an input is created for (16), which will accordingly apply:

(19)   fi v θ
        [voice]   + −   input representations
        ─────────────────────────────────────→
        [voice]   −   derivational cycle
                   fifth

The second step in derivation (19) illustrates the structure-changing mode of application of the rule under scrutiny, which of course also applies in a structure-building mode to underspecified lexical representations, as we saw above.

A crucial question at this point concerns the selection of mode of operation. Thus, for instance, in derivation (15) above it is not clear what prevents (12b) from also applying in a structure-changing mode to the lexical representation of *ban* and thus devoicing the initial obstruent, since, as formulated, the Elsewhere Condition only regulates the interaction of rules, not the interaction of rules and lexical representations.[9]

The answer to this question is given by another important principle, one whose effects are indeed apparent throughout phonology. Remember that we mentioned in Chapter 1 that some phonological rules apply cyclically. Now, an interesting cluster of properties has been found to converge on cyclic rules. One such property, known as the 'Strict Cycle Condition'(SCC), prevents cyclic rules from effecting changes in inputs which have not been created in the cycle in question (the identification of the set of rules where this prohibition is operative with the set of rules which apply cyclically is due to Mascaró 1976). We formulate this condition as in (20):

(20) Strict Cycle Condition
Structure-changing cyclic rules are only applicable to inputs created in the same cycle[10]

On an interpretation of (12b) as a cyclic rule,[11] it will follow from the SCC (20) that (12b) will be unable to effect changes in an input taken over directly from the lexicon, as is the case with *b* in (15), since this input cannot by definition have been created in the cycle in question. Consequently, the lexical specification [+ voice] will be preserved.

The effects of the SCC can be further observed in *five*, where (12b) cannot change the lexical F-element [+ voice] of the *v*. On the other hand, the application of (16) to /fiv + θ/ in (19) is not held back by the SCC, since this condition specifically does not block application to created inputs, as the one in question manifestly is, having arisen out of morphological concatenation. The upshot of this discussion therefore is that the effect of rules on any given representation falls out of the characterisation of the rule in question as cyclic or non-cyclic in conjunction with the checking effects of the SCC, a universal principle of grammar (cyclicity will be further discussed in Chapter 5).

2.4 LEXICAL CONTRAST AND UNDERSPECIFICATION

2.4.1 The transparency test

Implicit in any theory countenancing lexical blanks is a set of predictions with regard to the behaviour of lexically unspecified *vis-à-vis* lexically specified features. These predictions follow from the fact that feature values which are not included in the representation are concomitantly not available as triggers or blockers of phonological rules. Such predictions, in turn, constitute an empirical test on the adequacy of the theory.

One particularly rich body of evidence concerns the phenomenon of 'transparency', a term that refers to the invisibility of some feature or set of features to some phonological process. Thus, imagine a situation where a sequence ABC becomes ABA. Clearly, the assimilation of C to A has taken place irrespective of the presence of B. Assuming a strict locality constraint on the operation of phonological rules (as follows from the No Crossing constraint formulated in Chapter 1 in connection with the scope allowed to autosegmental processes), this behaviour becomes inexplicable unless we assume that, somehow, B does not 'count', i.e. is structurally invisible. This invisibility would follow automatically from leaving B out of the representation.

A theory of lexical redundancy to be referred to as 'Contrast-based Underspecification' (CU) contends that only lexically non-contrastive features can be left blank in lexical representation (see e.g. Steriade 1987 and Clements 1988).[12] Embodied in CU is therefore the expectation that transparent behaviour will be associated with lexical non-contrastiveness, and opaque behaviour with lexical contrastiveness. In other words, lexically contrastive values will act as triggers or blockers of rules, but lexically non-contrastive values will not until filled in by a redundancy rule. To this extent, therefore, underspecification will dispense with the need for projection (see Chapter 1) for the formal description of transparency effects.

2.4.2 Latin lateral dissimilation

As an illustration, we shall examine the process of lateral dissimilation in Latin. The facts are as follows. Latin has an adjectival suffix *-alis* (inherited as *-al* in English), which we exemplify in (21) (the reasons for the subgrouping will become clear directly):

(21)	a.	nav-alis	'naval'	cf. nav-is	'ship'
		voc-alis	'vocal'	cf. voc-is	'voice' (gen.)
		caus-alis	'causal'	cf. caus-a	'cause'
	b.	flor-alis	'floral'	cf. flor-is	'flower' (gen.)
		sepulchr-alis	'funereal'	cf. sepulchr-um	'grave'
		litor-alis	'of the shore'	cf. litor-is	'shore' (gen.)

So far, there is nothing worthy of mention.

Consider now the following additional forms:

(22)	a.	sol-aris	'solar'	cf. sol	'sun'
		milit-aris	'military'	cf. milit-is	'soldier' (gen.)
		Lati-aris	'of Latium'	cf. Lati-um	'Latium'

b. reticul-aris 'of the net' cf. reticul-um 'network'
   regul-aris 'regular' cf. regul-a 'rule'
   articul-aris 'articular' cf. articul-us 'joint'

Here the suffix is *-aris* (cf. the English cognates *-ar* and *-ary*), clearly an allomorph of *-alis*. Specifically, it involves delateralisation of /l/ into /r/. The question is why such a process takes place throughout (22), but not in (21).

Let us first examine (22a). Clearly, in these forms, but not in (21a), the root contains /l/. It is therefore quite reasonable to look at this segment as a possible source for the change from /l/ to /r/, and to interpret this change as dissimilation. Let us consequently formulate a rule of lateral dissimilation along the lines of (23):

(23) Latin Lateral Dissimilation
[+lateral] → ∅ /[+lateral]_____

The effect of this rule, reminiscent of Meeussen's Law discussed in Chapter 1, is simply the deletion of all but the first of a sequence of adjacent [+lateral] markings (cf. the Simultaneous Application Convention of *SPE*, by which a rule applies simultaneously in all the environments which meet its structural description at the point of application). Rules of this kind are in fact quite natural, and can be related to the pressure exerted by the so-called 'Obligatory Contour Principle' (OCP), which disfavours adjacent identically specified features (the OCP is an important principle of phonology, to be further referred to as we go along; see note 4 in Chapter 3 for some specific discussion). The derivation of *solaris* will consequently be as follows (in this and the following derivations, the autosegmentalisation of the feature [lateral] implies that all the symbols in the melody line must be interpreted as exclusive of this feature):

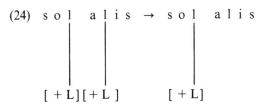

(24) s o l a l i s → s o l a l i s

    [+L][+L]   [+L]

Obviously, the resulting configuration must eventually be supplied with the missing values for [lateral]. In Latin, this feature is only distinctive, and thus lexically specified, for the class of liquids, the remaining segments being redundantly [−lateral], as expressed in the following rule:

(25) Latin Redundant Laterality
[   ] → [−lateral]

The *l* which becomes underspecified for [lateral] in (24) will therefore eventually be assigned [−lateral] by (25) (likewise for the segments lexically unspecified for this feature), and the desired *solaris* will ultimately emerge.

An obvious problem for the analysis of Latin lateral dissimilation just sketched is posed by the fact that the two relevant segments need not be skeletally adjacent, even if we were gratuitously to assume auto-segmental segregation of consonants *vis-à-vis* vowels, along the lines suggested for Arabic in Chapter 1. Thus, for instance, /t/ intervenes between the two liquids in both *militaris* and *Latiaris*. What we want to say is of course that such segments are transparent, but this status ought to be derived, rather than stipulative (note in particular that the projection solution tentatively adopted in Chapter 1 cannot be extended to the present situation on any principled basis).

In fact, the transparency of non-liquids follows directly from the preceding discussion, specifically from the lack of lexical specification for [lateral] in all segments but liquids. Thus, consider the lexical representation of *militaris*:

(26) m i l i t   a l i s

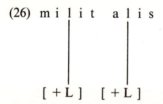

     [+ L]   [+ L]

In (26) the two [+ lateral] specifications are adjacent in their tier, and therefore the environment of Lateral Dissimilation (23) is met. The effect of the rule is shown in (27):

(27) m i l i t   a l i s

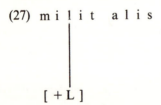

    [+ L]

The configuration in (27) will eventually be input to the redundancy rule in (25), which provides the value [− lateral] throughout, thus yielding the surface /r/ in *militaris*.

Consider now the forms in (21b), which also contain /l/ in the root, but where no dissimilation takes place. The lexical representation of *litoralis* is given in (28):

(28)

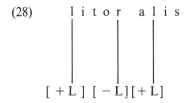

The two occurrences of [+ lateral] are not adjacent, because, as a liquid, /r/ is lexically marked as [− lateral]. The rule in (23) will therefore simply be inapplicable to this configuration. By contrast, although the forms in (22b) also contain /r/, such an /r/ is crucially not placed between the two /l/s, and consequently dissimilation will proceed as expected.

2.4.3 Algorithm

Having instantiated the correlation between lexical non-contrastiveness and transparent behaviour (and, correspondingly, between lexical contrastiveness and opaque behaviour), we will now make explicit the algorithm responsible for the formalisation of the appropriate lexical representations, essentially as summarised in Archangeli (1988: 192):

(29) Contrast-based Underspecification Algorithm
   a provide full specifications for all segments;
   b enumerate all pairs of segments;
   c single out segment pairs differing by a single feature specification (where necessary, eliminate features whose value is universally predictable);
   d designate such features as 'contrastive';
   e for each pair of segments, delete all non-contrastive feature specifications.

The workings of this algorithm can be illustrated with the simple vowel system /i, a, u/. The full specification of these segments for the four basic vowel features is given in (30):

(30)

	i	a	u
high	+	−	+
low	−	+	−
back	−	+	+
round	−	−	+

Proceeding to stage (29b), we enumerate all pairs of segments:

(31)

	i a	i u	a u
high	+ −	+ +	− +
low	− +	− −	+ −
back	− +	− +	+ +
round	− −	− +	− +

No two segments in these pairs differ by a single feature specification, a hint that at least one of the four features is non-contrastive throughout. Let us assume that one such redundant feature is [round], in line with the markedness rules formulated above (see (7)), which universally derive the value of this feature from the value for [back] (a reason for the non-contrastiveness of [round] will be given below, following Steriade's 1987 proposals). The ensuing simplification of the matrices under scrutiny is as in (32):

(32)

	i a	i u	a u
high	+ −	+ +	− +
low	− +	− −	+ −
back	− +	− +	+ +

In (32), [back] minimally keeps apart /i/ and /u/, and we thus designate such a feature as contrastive, following (29d). Turning now to /a/ – /u/, it differs in the values for [high] and [low], and we shall therefore (arbitrarily) dispose of [low] (cf. the marking conventions in (5) above). The resulting matrices are given in (33):

(33)

	i a	i u	a u
high	+ −	+ +	− +
back	− +	− +	+ +

The feature [high] now minimally separates /a/ and /u/, and must consequently also be declared contrastive. The chart in (34) thus summarises the lexical values present in this system:

(34)

	i a u
high	+ − +
back	− +

The values of the missing features ([+ back] for /a/, and either value of [low] and [round] throughout) will eventually be filled in by the corresponding redundancy rules to yield the surface forms.

2.4.4 Evaluation

Archangeli (1988) points out several problematic aspects of Contrast-based Underspecification. Four specific issues will be examined here.

2.4.4.1 The phonological primitive

The CU algorithm leads to an inventory of fully formed (albeit underspecified) lexical segments, as seen. Accordingly, the phonological primitive assumed by CU is the segment, rather than the simple F-element.

We are already familiar with the autosegmentalisation of special features, e.g. tones in tone languages, or some segmental features in harmony systems. Autosegmentalised features can by definition be granted lexical autonomy with respect to any one segment, for segment membership defined through skeletal association (see note 2 above). This situation is seemingly incompatible with the requirement of full lexical association implicit in the CU algorithm.

A possible retort by the proponent of CU would be that in such cases the pertinent features have become 'prosodic', i.e. autosegmentalised (more to the point in the present context, 'desegmentalised'), and therefore will no longer play a part in the definition of any one lexical segment. It is far from clear, however, how this conception of phonological structure can be made compatible with the more radical approaches to autosegmentalism, according to which all features can undergo autosegmentalisation. In fact, as we shall see in Chapter 3, current models of distinctive features award every feature an independent autosegmental plane, irrespective of overt behaviour.

Such theoretical developments aside, some clear cases of full lexical autosegmentalisation are attested, one of which will be discussed in 2.5.2.3.2 (the demonstration would be premature at this point). As expected, this creates an insurmountable problem for CU. Thus, consider again the matrix in (34), which contains the F-elements [+ high], [− high], [+ back], and [− back]. Were these elements to be detached from their postulated lexical associations, the segment /æ/ would also be derived, since [− high] could now freely associate with [− back]. Consequently, the more restricted inventory in (34) could not be generated.

2.4.4.2 Markedness and language specificity

The second problem concerns the fact that in CU naturalness is assigned quantitatively, rather than qualitatively. In particular, given the algorithm in (29), the markedness ranking of a system will be a function of the number of segments in the inventory, irrespective of the naturalness of the segments' identities or of their patterning.

Consider, for instance, the vowel systems of Swahili and Auca, to which the CU algorithm in (29) will assign the lexical specifications in (35) (Archangeli 1988):

(35) Contrast-based Underspecified vowel systems
a. Swahili   b. Auca

	i	e	a	o	u			i	e	o	ɑ	æ
high	+	−		−	+		high	+	−			
low			+		−		low			−	−	+	+
back		−	−	+	+		back		−	+	+	−	

The number of specified feature values is identical for both inventories, namely ten. This fact notwithstanding, the naturalness of the Swahili system in (35a) vastly exceeds that of its Auca counterpart. In particular, the Swahili vowels are those of the universally canonical vowel system, while the Auca system is unique in Maddieson's (1984) survey of 319 languages. We would obviously wish this disparity to have a formal reflection, but this desideratum is unachievable within the framework of CU.

Note that, ironically, considerations of universal markedness are claimed to be at the core of CU theory. Thus, Steriade (1987) speculates that some of the non-contrastive values are motivated by the need (or the convenience) to enhance perceptual saliency, in the sense of Stevens, Keyser and Kawasaki (1987), while other such values express the defective distribution of a 'content' feature within a class defined by means of 'stricture' features.[13]

According to Steriade, the adoption of such functional grounding for redundancy restricts the space of redundancy rules in interesting ways. For instance, it precludes the rule [+ round] → [+ high], postulated in Archangeli and Pulleyblank's (1986) analysis of the three-vowel system of Nyangumata, since both [round] and [high] are content features, and [high] does not enhance [round]. On the other hand, a rule like [αback] → [αround]/[$\overline{- \text{low}}$], which has played a role in some of the analyses above, will be permissible, the relationship between its input and its output being one of enhancement.

2.4.4.3 Structural vs functional asymmetry

The third, related problem for CU concerns the fact that, as will be seen in more detail in the next section, in most phonological systems one of the segments (typically within a major class, say, the class of vowels) behaves asymmetrically, in that it alone undergoes or fails to undergo certain changes, it alone constitutes the output of deletion or epenthesis processes, and so on. A theory of underspecification can be reasonably expected both to give structural reality to such an asymmetry and to identify the asymmetric segment correctly.

The lexical representations associated with CU indeed define one of the segments as asymmetric. For instance, in the matrices in (35) above, Swahili /a/ is minimally specified, with only one value (for [+low]), whereas in Auca /i/ is only marked as [+high]. Thus, the first of the two requirements is satisfactorily met by CU.

The structural asymmetries resulting from CU-framed analyses are however often at odds with the evidence. For instance, as we have just seen, /a/ comes out as the structurally asymmetric vowel of Swahili, but it is /i/ that exhibits functional asymmetry in this language (Archangeli 1988). More generally, the structural asymmetry of /a/ is inherent in the canonical five-vowel system, but, in many of the languages possessing such a system, one of the other vowels is functionally asymmetric: /i/ (Swahili, Japanese), /u/ (Telugu), /e/ (Spanish).

2.4.4.4 Descriptive shortfalls

In addition to the three problems mentioned, Archangeli (1988) points out that the CU algorithm in (29) simply fails to yield a contrastively specified matrix for the marked five-vowel system of Maranungku, /i, o, ə, æ, u/ . The specific problem concerns the distinction between /i/ and /æ/, as we shall now show.

The fully specified matrix of Maranungku vowels is given in (36):

(36) Maranungku fully specified vowel system

	i	ɑ	ə	æ	u
high	+	−	−	−	+
low	−	+	−	+	−
back	−	+	+	−	+

Operating on this matrix, the algorithm in (29) will yield the contrast-based underspecified matrix in (37) (NB both /i/ and /æ/ minimally contrast in backness with /u/ and /ɑ/, respectively):

(37) Maranungku Contrast-based Underspecified vowel system

	i	ɑ	ə	æ	u
high			−		+
low		+	−		
back	−	+		−	+

As anticipated, the segments /i/ and /æ/ fail to contrast structurally, although they function as distinct phonemes in the language in question. It is unclear how this difficulty can be circumvented without allowing more than one feature specification for every pair of segments. While this move would achieve the desired result, it cannot be accommodated within the CU algorithm as specified in (29) above.

2.5 RADICAL UNDERSPECIFICATION

The problems just considered are overcome in the theory originally proposed in Archangeli (1984), developing Kiparsky's ideas on underspecification discussed above. Because this theory takes lexical underspecification to the limit compatible with derivational binarism, it has come to be known as 'Radical Underspecification' (RU).

We have just seen that the Lightner/Stanley problem of specious ternarity is forestalled in Contrast-based Underspecification by the requirement that the feature responsible for each minimal contrast be given its full binary specification. In turn, in Kiparsky (1982a,b) only one of the two explicit values is lexically available for any one feature in addition to its blank representation. Clearly, thus, an overall ceiling of two lexical values per feature is necessary in order to cast away the spectrum of specious ternarity. On the other hand, nothing seems to prevent us from reducing the number of such values. Thus taking this possibility to its logical conclusion, Archangeli (1984) builds a theory of underspecification where one segment in each major class has all its features completely unspecified in the lexicon. The key to the approach is encapsulated in the 'Feature Minimisation Principle', which she states as follows:

(38) Feature Minimisation Principle
   A grammar is most highly valued when underlying representations include the minimal number of features necessary to make different the phonemes of the language.

(Archangeli 1984: 50)

2.5.1 Basic principles and algorithm

2.5.1.1 Segment functional asymmetries

The basic observation underpinning RU is that the behaviour of one of the segments (per major class) in each language is characteristically asymmetric. We shall exemplify with the Yoruba vowel /i/, as discussed in Pulleyblank (1988a).

The Yoruba vowel inventory comprises seven segments, as follows:

(39) Yoruba vowel system

  i u
  e o
  ɛ ɔ
   a

The asymmetry of the vowel /i/ concerns the following processes (as usual, ′ = H and ` = L; mid tones have simply been left unrepresented, as in the Yoruba orthography):

(40) Yoruba /i/ Asymmetry

 a. /i/ fails to trigger cross-word regressive vowel assimilation in possessive constructions:
   ará òkè → *aró òkè* 'northern Yoruba'
   vs *ará ìlú* 'townsman' ↛ **arí ìlú;*

 b. /i/ fails to trigger cross-word deletion of the preceding adjacent vowel, particularly frequent in verb + noun collocations; instead, it itself disappears:
   ra ɔ̀gɛ̀dɛ̂ → *r ɔ̀gɛ̀dɛ̀* 'buy bananas'
   vs *gba iṣé* → *gba ṣé* 'take a job';

 c. /i/ fails to trigger lateralisation of a preceding /n/ (NB vowel deletion (b) must be applied first):
   ní aṣɔ → *n áṣɔ* → *láṣɔ* 'have cloth'
   vs *ní iṣu* → *níṣu* 'have yam' ↛ **líṣu;*

 d. /i/ fails to trigger assimilation of the /o/ of the noun *oni* 'owner, maker, seller' to the first vowel of the noun to which it is prefixed (NB vowel deletion (b) and /n/ lateralisation (c) also take place):
   bàtà 'shoe' → *oníbàtà*
   epo 'palm-oil' → *oniepo* → *on épo* → *olépo* → *elépo*
   vs *igi* 'wood' → *oniigi* → *onigi* ↛ **inigi/*iligi;*

 e. /i/ alone changes to /u/ following *ki* prefixation and stem reduplication (cf. *dùrù* 'organ' → *dùrùkídùrù* 'any organ'):
   igbà 'time' → *ìgbàkíigbà* → *ìgbàkúgbà* 'any time, whenever';
   vs *ohun* 'thing' → *ohunkíohun* → *ohunkóhun* 'whatever' ↛ **ohunkúhun*

 f. /i/ alone can (variably) delete after a nasal consonant, which concomitantly becomes syllabic:
   oniṣɛ́ → *oṅ̩ṣɛ́* 'hard worker'
   vs *ɔ̀mùtí* 'a drunkard' ↛ **ɔ̀m̩̀tí;*

g. /i/ alone can (variably) delete in initial position (provided it carries a mid tone and the word has at least three syllables):
ibùsùn 'bed' → *bùsùn*
vs *ekùkù* 'edible worm which spins the silk when making its cocoon' ↛ **kùkù*.

The range of evidence for the special status of Yoruba /i/ is therefore very considerable. Crucially, none of the six remaining vowels can be thus singled out. Similar situations have been uncovered in many other languages.

2.5.1.2 Algorithm

Granting thus the possibility of functional asymmetry for one segment in any given language, we now proceed to the formulation of the algorithm responsible for the establishment of lexical representations under Radical Underspecification theory:

(41) Radical Underspecification Algorithm
   a. identify the functionally asymmetric segment;
   b. provide the fully specified matrix M of this segment;
   c. for each of the F-elements in M, write a rule supplying the F-element in question;
   d. ban from the lexicon all the F-elements thus provided by rule;
   e. set up lexical entries with the complementary F-elements.

The main learning load in RU thus concerns the identification of the functionally asymmetric segment, the rest of the system then following automatically from the universal principles in (41).

We shall exemplify the workings of this algorithm with the canonical five-vowel system of Swahili, already mentioned above, on the assumption that this language shares /i/ with Yoruba as the functionally asymmetric vowel. For ease of reference, the fully specified vowel matrix is first given in (42). It is important to bear in mind, however, that such fully specified matrix has no theoretical status in RU theory:

(42) Swahili fully specified vowel matrix

	i	e	a	o	u
high	+	−	−	−	+
low	−	−	+	−	−
back	−	−	+	+	+
round	−	−	−	+	+

Let us now start the application of the algorithm in (41). By steps (41a) and (41b), we obtain the matrix in (43):

(43) Swahili asymmetric vowel matrix

	/i/
high	+
low	−
back	−
round	−

Next, a set of 'Complement Rules' is created by clause (41c) to supply precisely the feature values specified in this matrix:

(44) Swahili Vowel Complement Rules
   a. [ ] → [+high]
   b. [ ] → [−low]
   c. [ ] → [−back]
   d. [ ] → [−round]

Finally, the F-elements provided by (44) are banned from lexical representations, which will instead be built on their complements. The underspecified matrix in (45) thus results:

(45) Swahili radically underspecified vowel matrix (Provisional)

	i	e	a	o	u
high	−	−		−	
low			+		
back			+	+	+
round				+	+

This matrix can be further simplified on the strength of the usual markedness rules, which are also an integral part of RU theory (and which Archangeli confusingly redubs 'Default' rules, with the initial capital in *default* as the only possible disambiguating mark between the technical and the lay uses of the word). Assuming thus that such markedness rules as in (5) and (8) above predict the incompatibility of [+high] and [+low], and the relationship between [back] and [round] in non-low vowels, we obtain the definitive radically underspecified matrix in (46):

(46) Radically Underspecified Swahili vowel matrix (Final)

	i	e	a	o	u
high	−		−		
low		+			
back			+	+	

The simplicity of this matrix compares favourably with that of its CU counterpart in (35a) (five and ten feature values, respectively). Moreover, as we shall see next, the approach provides satisfactory answers to the three general issues noted above as problematic for CU, namely the cross-linguistic differences in the identity of the asymmetric segment, the markedness differences between systems with an identical number of segments, and the need for full association in the lexicon.[14]

2.5.2 Overcoming the difficulties associated with CU

2.5.2.1 *Language-specificity of the asymmetries*

Clearly, RU has no difficulty in predicting the existence of segment functional asymmetry. In fact, as we saw in the previous subsection, such asymmetry constitutes the very keystone of the RU algorithm, the first step of which precisely consists in the identification of the functionally asymmetric segment (see (41a)). Functional asymmetry is then translated into structural asymmetry by clause (41d), by which all predictable F-elements are excluded from the lexicon.

Moreover, the RU machinery allows for the correct identification of the functionally asymmetric segment in each particular case. Specifically, the identity of such a segment is left open, as a matter of learnable empirical fact. This is in contrast with CU, where asymmetry is derived as a formal corollary of the system, a problematic approach, given that, as we have been seeing, structurally identical systems may contain different functionally asymmetric segments. RU and CU consequently approach the relationship between the overall system and the individual asymmetric segment from opposite ends. In CU the system comes first, the asymmetric segment being then identified on the basis of its position in the system. In RU, by contrast, the asymmetric segment is designated empirically, and the system then derived from the substance of the segment, with additional subsidiary rules where necessary, as will be seen below.

This contrast between the two theories brings to the fore a further, central problem for CU. This concerns the role played by minimal oppositions in the CU algorithm (see (29c) above). Simply, the only way to find out (for the linguist and the learner alike) minimal contrasts, as is necessary for the determination of lexical features in this system, is by previous acquaintanceship with the system, a learnability paradox.

2.5.2.2 *Markedness and RU*

Another of the problems enumerated above for CU concerns the evaluation of systems quantitatively but not qualitatively identical. These systems will inevitably differ in naturalness, contrary to the predictions implicit in the CU formalism, which will yield undifferentiated structures. By contrast, in RU all qualitative differences are brought out formally, as desired.

We shall illustrate with the vowel systems of Swahili and Auca, with which we are already reasonably familiar, both of which have five vowels, with /i/ lexically unspecified. The crucial point to bear in mind is that, as mentioned at the time, the Swahili system is canonical, while its Auca counterpart is highly unusual.

The Swahili radically underspecified lexical matrix and its corresponding Complement rules were given in (46) and (44), respectively. Their Auca counterparts are as in (47):

(47) a. Radically Underspecified Auca matrix

	i	e	o	ɑ	æ
High			−		
Low				+	+
Back			+	+	

b. Auca Complement Rules

i   [   ] → [+ high]
ii [   ] → [− low]
iii [   ] → [− back]
iv [   ] → [− round]

Both languages have identical Complement rules, as follows from the fact that they share /i/ as the underspecified vowel (see clause (c) in the RU algorithm (41) above). Consequently, it is far from obvious how the differences in the two underspecified matrices ((46) for Swahili and (47a) for Auca) can be generated.

The feature specifications of /ɑ/ and /æ/ in the Auca underspecified lexical matrix (47a) are particularly puzzling. First, these two segments ought to eventually become merged by the markedness rule in (7c) above, according to which low vowels are also back. Second, this same rule seems to make redundant the value [+ back] for /ɑ/. In addition, we would expect the Complement rule (47bi) to turn the segment labelled /o/ into /u/, also in contradiction with the attested facts of Auca.

The answer to all these questions is in fact straightforward, and rather commonsensical. Thus, if /i/ is the functionally asymmetric vowel in both Swahili and Auca, these two languages ought to have the same surface inventory of vowels, everything else being equal. Since they don't, everything else cannot be equal. Now, the set of Complement rules has to be identical, since Complement rules are automatically derived from the substance of the functionally asymmetric segment (see (41c)), which is /i/ in both cases. Therefore, the differences between the two languages must be located either in the markedness rules or in some other set of rules not yet discussed.

In fact, both kinds of difference are accommodated for in RU. First, there can be language-specific suspensions of markedness rules. Thus, in Auca, the markedness rule providing backness for low vowels, (7c), must obviously be blocked, for otherwise /æ/ could simply not be generated. Once we block this rule, it is clear that we must enter /ɑ/ as [+ back], since otherwise /æ/ would be generated by the Complement rule (iii) in (47b).

The solution to the /u/ puzzle requires additional machinery. Specifically, in order to prevent the generation of /u/ by the Complement rule in (47bi), we assume that the grammar of Auca includes a language-specific rule along the lines of (48):

$$(48) \quad [\;\;] \;\rightarrow\; [-\text{high}] \;/\; \left[\begin{array}{c} \underline{\qquad\qquad} \\[4pt] +\,\text{back} \end{array} \right]$$

By the Elsewhere Condition, rule (48) will precede (47bi), thus bleeding it, as desired. Rules such as (48) are dubbed 'Learnt' rules in RU. They contrast with 'Complement' rules and 'Default' rules (i.e. markedness rules) in that, as the name suggests, they must specifically be learnt. The two other types of rules are instead provided by Universal Grammar, markedness rules in the usual way, and Complement rules as automatically derived by the algorithm in (41) from the feature values of the functionally asymmetric segment.

At this point, the reader might wish to object to the complexity of the procedure responsible for the lexical specification of Auca vowels. The assessment is undoubtedly right, but an objection would be misplaced, since we precisely want a degree of formal complexity to correspond to the unnaturalness of the Auca system. This is achieved in a remarkably elegant manner in the context of RU, whereas in the CU framework the Swahili and Auca vowel systems score evenly, as we saw above.

2.5.2.3 *The lexical primacy of features*

We know from the previous section that the CU algorithm presupposes full lexical association of all F-elements, and we pointed this out as problematic at the time. This is in direct opposition with the emphasis laid in recent developments of RU (what is dubbed 'Combinatorial Specification' in Archangeli and Pulleyblank forthcoming) on the lexical autonomy of features. In what follows we shall first show the formal viability of this stance, and demonstrate then its empirical desirability.

2.5.2.3.1 Formal viability

Let us turn once more to Swahili and Auca. We have already noted that, because these languages share /i/ as the asymmetric vowel, they have an identical set of Complement rules and, correspondingly, of lexical F-elements, as listed in (49):

(49) Lexical F-elements in Swahili and Auca

[− high]
[+ low]
[+ back]

Let us now explore the possibility of granting these elements lexical autonomy. Specifically, we shall show that the set of contrastive segments of these languages can be generated by the free combination of such valued features, subject only to the constraints embodied in the corresponding redundancy rules.

Free combination of the F-elements in (49) will yield the following segmental matrices:

(50) Potential segmental matrices for Swahili and Auca

	1	2	3	4	5	6	7	8
high	−	−	−		−			
low	+	+		+		+		
back	+		+	+			+	

Given these representations, let us first consider how the Swahili system is selected. Quite simply, given the Complement and markedness rules considered, columns 1, 2, 4 and 6 will all lead to the segment /a/ (remember that [+ low] entails both [− high] and [+ back] by markedness rules); 3 will yield /o/, 5 /e/, and 7 /u/; finally, matrix 8 corresponds to the underspecified vowel /i/. The five vowels thus generated are precisely the five vowels of Swahili.

In the case of Auca, the Learnt rule (48) and the language-specific suspension of the markedness convention (7c) will interfere with this simple procedure, in the expected manner. In particular, columns 2 and 6 will now correspond to the vowel /æ/ (given the language-specific blocking of the markedness convention providing [+back] to low vowels), while 7 will merge with 3 and yield /o/, rather than /u/, in the context of the Auca Learnt rule (48), which bans high back vowels. Clearly, thus, there is no need to specify the permissible lexical combinations of F-elements, since such combinations are derivable from the redundancy rules operative in the language.

2.5.2.3.2 Empirical desirability

Having thus shown that the RU machinery enables us to have the F-elements floating in the lexicon, we shall now present evidence for the necessity of this mode of representation.

Our demonstration will follow Pulleyblank's (1988b) analysis of the distribution of vowels in Tiv. The surface vowel inventory of this language is given in (51):

(51) Tiv surface vowels

     i u
     e o
     a ɔ

Taking /e/ as the asymmetric vowel, for reasons which will become clear as we proceed, we obtain the following lexical matrix, with the concomitant Complement rules:

(52) a. Tiv radically underspecified lexical vowel matrix

	i	e	a	ɔ	o	u
high	+					+
low			+	+		
round				+	+	+

     b. Tiv Complement rules

        i [ ] → [−high]
        ii [ ] → [−low]
        iii [ ] → [−round]

The distribution of the non-low front vowels /i/ and /e/ is now sampled:

(53) a.   gér   'be in excess'
           èse   'sweep'
           bènde   'touch'
           yévese   'flee'

      b.   gbìl   'put a thing down'
           tíndi   'send'
           lìvir   'dislocate, sprain'
           nyíishi   'change one's mind'

      c.   pìne   'ask'
           híne   'hoot'
           kíne   'groan'

The words in (53a) and (53b) contain between one and three syllables, all with the same vowel, /e/ or /i/, while those in (53c) are disyllables with the pattern *i . . . e*. The mirror image sequence *e . . . i* is unattested.

The data in (53a) and (53b) directly fall out of lexical representations with floating F-elements. First, the forms with /e/ in (53a) will simply have no lexical vowel features, the Complement rules in (52b) effectively supplying /e/ throughout. For the forms with /i/ in (53b), we postulate a floating lexical feature [+ high], which will automatically associate to the leftmost vowel by the association convention examined in Chapter 1, on the plausible assumption that left association is the unmarked option for this parameter. After such association, rightward spreading will be triggered by the following rule:

(54) Tiv high-spread

This rule is of course reminiscent of the ones we used for tone and harmony in Chapter 1. As shown in (55), the desired result is indeed achieved:

(55) n y V̀ V s h V

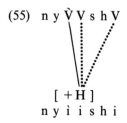

[+H]
n y ì i s h i

We shall put aside the forms in (53c) for the time being and proceed to the presentation and analysis of words with non-low rounded vowels, illustrated in (56):

(56) a. mòr   'puff out'
          kóso   'keep thing for a person'
          ǹghor   'receive'
          nyóoso   'be fully grown'

      b. búgh   'open'
          úndu   'leave person or thing behind'
          gúvul   'hem, make selvedge'
          gbúusu   'be abundant'

      c. únde   'mount'
          búme   'be foolish'
          hùre   'drive away'
          númbe   'play'

The patterns in (56) parallel those in (53), with roundness added. We can therefore account for these data by enriching the previous lexical forms with an also floating F-element [+round]. The failure of this element to spread in (56c) suggests that Tiv [+round] spread is 'parasitic' on [high] agreement (see 3.2.1.1 below for discussion of parasitic spreading), as represented in (57):

(57) Tiv rounding harmony

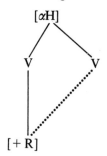

For clarity, the derivation of *gbúusu* is now provided:

(58)

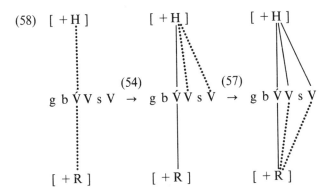

At this point, we must turn to the bisyllabic forms in (53c) and (56c), which appear as exceptions to [high] spreading. Pulleyblank accounts for this behaviour by means of 'extraprosodicity'. This device effects the invisibility of a peripheral element, i.e. an element placed at the edge of a domain, and will be seen to play an important role across the board in phonology. We thus simply assume that in the lexical representations of *pìne, únde*, etc. the final vowel slot is marked as extraprosodic. This mark will automatically make this element invisible to the rule of high spread, as desired (following current practice, extraprosodic material is enclosed in angled brackets):

(59)

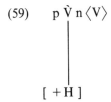

At some late point in the derivation the invisibility of *V* must obviously cease, since otherwise this lexical material would fail to receive a phonetic interpretation. We shall assume that at such a point the rule of high spread is no longer operative, the empty skeletal slot being therefore simply filled in by the Complement rules in (52b), which yield the surface vowel *e*.

Let us finally examine the distribution of [+low] segments:

(60) a. káse   'surround'
       vànde   'precede'

	dzàmber	'beseech'
	gbàngese	'be broad'
b.	nɔndo	'drip'
	dzɔmon	'twist'
	sɔsom	'approach'
	nyɔngoso	'run'

These forms reveal that there is no rule of [+low] spread in Tiv. In the absence of such a rule, the lexically floating feature [+low] will simply dock on the leftmost vowel, by the association convention, and the value [−low] will be filled in in the remaining positions by the appropriate Complement rule.

There are a few additional (and interesting) complexities in the distribution of Tiv vowels, but these do not affect the basic principles we have just examined. Central to the proposed procedure is the floating status of the lexical features responsible for vowels. Such formalisation is problematic for the theory of CU, which presupposes full lexical association of features, but can be readily accommodated within the RU framework, as we have seen.

2.5.3 Problems for Radical Underspecification

Some potential disadvantages of Radical Underspecification concern the transparency effect, the relationship between underspecified status and markedness, and the pattern of association of lexically floating features.

2.5.3.1 The transparency test revisited

The general success of Contrast-based Underspecification in predicting transparency effects, as discussed in 2.4 above, presents an obvious challenge to Radical Underspecification, given the different predictions made by the two theories in this connection. A small residue does however remain which is recalcitrant to analysis under Contrast-based Underspecification, and we shall deal with this first.

The problem is two-sided. On the one hand, non-contrastive features sometimes exhibit opaque behaviour. This is directly contrary to the predictions of CU that such features are lexically unspecified, and therefore should not be available as blockers. Thus, for instance, in Steriade's (1987) analysis of Hungarian vowel harmony, the vowel /aː/ prevents the spread of the harmonic feature [back], although it is unpaired for backness. Likewise, Barra Gaelic (plain) [n] and (palatal) [lʲ] behave opaquely with respect to an all-pervasive process of palatal assimilation, despite the fact that neither of these segments contrasts lexically for the palatalising feature [back] (Clements 1988). The standard answer to these facts is to declare the relationship between transparency and lexical non-contrastiveness asymmetrical, in the sense that, while transparent segments are indeed required to be non-contrastive (and they are invariably so in Hungarian and Barra Gaelic), non-contrastiveness need not result in transparent behaviour. Note however that this interpretation is contrary to expectation and thus cannot be accepted uncritically. As it stands, it simply amounts to a restatement of the facts, and sheds no theoretical light on the situation.

The second aspect of the transparency problem is even more serious, since it precisely concerns the transparency of contrastive features in a handful of cases: Japanese voicing, Finnish backness harmony, and Mongolian roundness harmony (Steriade 1987). We shall briefly review the Japanese case here.

Of relevance are two rules of Japanese, 'Rendaku' and 'Lyman's Law', formulated in (61) and (62), respectively (see Itô and Mester 1986 for more detailed discussion):

(61) Japanese Rendaku

$$[+\text{voice}]$$
$$\vdots$$
$$]_{X^0} [_{X^0} C$$

(62) Japanese Lyman's Law
$$[+\text{voice}] \rightarrow \emptyset \, / \, \underline{\hspace{1cm}} \, [+\text{voice}]$$

Rendaku voices the initial obstruent of the second member of a compound, and Lyman's Law is a straightforward voice dissimilation rule, along the lines of the Latin delateralisation rule discussed above. We illustrate the two processes in (63):

(63)	a.	iro	'colour'		
		kami	'paper'	irogami	'coloured paper'
		asa	'morning'		
		kiri	'mist'	asagiri	'morning mist'
		unari	'moan'		
		koe	'voice'	unarigoe	'groan'
	b.	kami	'God'		
		kaze	'wind'	kamikaze	'God-sent wind'
		mono	'thing(s)'		
		šizuka	'quiet'	monošizuka	'tranquil'

širo	'white'		
tabi	'tabi socks'	širotabi	'white tabi socks'

In (63a) the initial obstruent of the second component undergoes voicing by Rendaku, while in (63b) this result is cancelled out by Lyman's Law.

As expected, sonorants behave transparently:

(64) a. taikutsu   'boredom'
         haraši   'dispel'   taikutsubaraši 'time-killing'

      b. taikutsu   'boredom'
         šinogi   'endure'   taikutsušinogi 'time-killing'

In (64a) the voiced sonorant /r/ fails to trigger Lyman's Law on /h/, the output of Rendaku thus simply prevailing ([b] is an allophonic realisation of voiced /h/ in Japanese), while in (64b), the voiced sonorant in the middle syllable of the second word poses no obstacle to the triggering of Lyman's Law by the syllable-final /g/.

Consider now the compound form *onnakotoba* 'feminine speech' (*onna* 'woman'; *kotoba* 'word'). This form parallels *taikutsušinogi* in (64a) in having had Lyman's Law triggered by a non-adjacent voiced obstruent, namely /b/. Crucially, however, the intervening consonant is now an obstruent, /t/. Obstruents are contrastive for voice in Japanese, and therefore we would expect them to constitute barriers to Lyman's Law, as non-lateral liquids are to Latin delateralisation. The fact that this expectation is not fulfilled is obviously problematic for CU.

Notwithstanding the noted difficulties, the general success of CU in providing a formal account for transparency effects raises the question of how similar results would be achieved with the alternative RU machinery, given the fact that the two theories predict a different range of underspecified feature values (indeed, in the Japanese case just discussed, it is RU that yields the right result, on the reasonable assumption that [−voice] is the redundant value for Japanese obstruents). It thus seems inevitable to expect that some of the successful CU analyses simply cannot be replicated in an RU framework.

2.5.3.2 *Marked underspecified segments*

A second type of problem for RU concerns the relationship of this theory to markedness.

This relationship is in fact indirect. In particular, in RU, the role of the markedness conventions is limited to the provision of default values (hence Archangeli's label 'Default' rules) in the absence of language-specific information, whether in the form of Learnt rules, explicit suspension of markedness rules, or, more commonly, simple lexical value specification. All these devices cancel out the ordinary action of markedness rules.

The RU stand of incorporating language-specific underspecification statements alongside universal conventions has been shown above to be empirically supported. In particular, we have been seeing that a universal identification of the asymmetric vowel would be problematic, and we interpreted at the time the flexibility of RU in this respect as precisely one of the strengths of this theory. There is, however, a reverse side to the same coin. Thus, in the absence of specific universal constraints, the theory effectively allows for any segment to carry the privileged status. The prediction therefore is that there should be languages where, say, /y/ or /ɛ/ behave as default, but this prediction is not fulfilled, and it clearly runs counter to expectation.

The problem is even more serious for consonants, where the range of cross-language variability is much smaller than in vowels. In particular, it appears that the only consonants that can exhibit the characteristic effects of total underspecification are coronals (see Paradis and Prunet 1991). This fact clearly conflicts with the prediction implicit in RU that any consonant (including, e.g. a uvular trill!) could function as default.

2.6 BEYOND UNDERSPECIFICATION

The last of the three problems mentioned above for RU goes beyond the confines of this specific theory, since it affects the very claim that lexical regularities are best expressed by means of blanks, to be eventually filled in by redundancy rules. This claim is of course common to the three underspecification approaches we have been examining.

2.6.1 Yoruba [ATR] harmony

The process of [ATR] harmony in Yoruba shows that blank-filling redundancy rules have insufficient power to capture the totality of lexical redundancies. We first summarise the basic facts.

2.6.1.1 Basic facts

As displayed in (39) above, Yoruba has a seven-vowel system, with [ATR] contrastive for mid vowels (see note 10 in Chapter 3 for specific discussion of [ATR]). Both high vowels are [+ATR], and the low vowel [−ATR]. In mid vowels, the distribution of [ATR] in the word domain (and also within certain types of compounds) is subject to the following constraints:

(65) [ATR] Distributional constraints on Yoruba mid vowels

    a. mid vowels preceding /a/ uninterrupted by a high vowel are [−ATR]:

        ɛpà 'groundnut' (cf. *èpà)
        ɔjà 'market' (cf. *ojà)

        but:
        àjɛ̀ 'paddle', ate 'hat'
        aʂɔ 'cloth', àwo 'plate'

        èjìká 'shoulder'
        èrírà 'one that is rotten'

    b. mid vowels preceding a non-final high vowel uninterrupted by /a/ are [+ATR]:

        erùpɛ̀ 'earth' (cf. *ɛrùpɛ̀)
        èlùbɔ́ 'yam flower' (cf. *ɛ̀lùbɔ́)
        odídɛ 'Grey Parrot' (cf. *ɔdídɛ)
        òkùrɔ́ 'palm kernel' (cf. *ɔ̀kùrɔ́)

        but:

        ebi 'hunger', ɛ̀bi 'guilt'
        eku 'bush rat', ɛwù 'clothing'
        orí 'head', ɔ̀kín 'egret'
        ojú 'eye', ɔ̀run 'heaven'

        ilé 'house', ilɛ̀ 'land'
        ìgò 'bottle', itɔ́ 'saliva'

    c. otherwise the value of [ATR] is uniform for all mid vowels:

ebè 'heap for yams'	ɛsɛ̀ 'foot'
epo 'oil'	ɛkɔ 'pap'
olè 'thief'	ɔbɛ̀ 'soup'
owó 'money'	ɔkɔ́ 'vehicle'
ògèdè 'incantation'	ɔ̀gɛ̀dɛ̀ 'banana'
ehoro 'hare'	ɛkɔrɔ 'cunning way of doing'

        (cf. *ɛbè, *epɔ, *ɔlè, *owɔ́, etc.)

Archangeli and Pulleyblank's (1989) account runs as follows. First, they select [−ATR] as the lexical F-element for this feature. Importantly, they assume that such an F-element is lexically assigned to morphemes, rather than to specific lexical segments, thus being phonologically floating. This floating element will be anchored on to the rightmost vowel by a marked setting of the association convention, and will then spread leftwards from this position by a language specific rule. A context-sensitive Default rule will supply [−ATR] to all unmarked occurrences of the low vowel /a/, and a context-free Complement rule will supply [+ATR] generally.

For greater clarity, we catalogue this machinery in (66):

(66) a. lexical representation: morpheme-bounded floating [−ATR]

     b. [−ATR] processes:

        i. rightmost association:

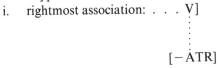

        ii. right-to-left spread:

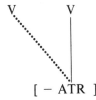

     c. redundancy rules:

        i. $[\ ] \rightarrow [-\text{ATR}]/ \left[\begin{array}{c} \underline{} \\ +\text{low} \end{array} \right]$

        ii. $[\ ] \rightarrow [+\text{ATR}]$

The results of this procedure are by and large as sought, as the reader will be able to verify without difficulty. In particular, most of the facts listed in (65) are accounted for either by rightmost association plus leftward spreading of [−ATR], or by simple default assignment of [+ATR] across the board. Three aspects are however in need of further attention. First, mid vowels uninterruptedly preceding low vowels are invariably [−ATR] (cf. (65a)), even in cases where this feature is not provided lexically as a floating element. Second, there are no [−ATR] high vowels, although nothing so far would prevent their creation via spreading of this F-element, in the obvious way. Third, [−ATR] mid vowels are disallowed before a non-final high vowel (cf. (65b) above), but, puzzlingly, not before final high vowels. We shall now deal with these three problems in turn.

2.6.1.2 The Redundancy Rule Ordering Constraint

The non-occurrence of [+ATR] mid vowels before /a/ and their free distribution after /a/ strongly points to harmony, precisely as follows from the machinery we have postulated. The problem is that the harmony rule (66bii) requires [−ATR] in the input, and it is not clear how this condition can be met in the case at hand, given the redundant nature of ATR-ness in low vowels, as captured by the Default rule (66ci).

What is in fact at issue is the interaction between redundancy rules, such as (66ci), and phonological processes, such as Right-to-Left Spread (66bii). The general assumption in RU is that redundancy rules apply as late as possible, a reasonable stand consistent with the behaviour of lexical blanks throughout the derivation. Clearly, however, in order for the distributional constraint under scrutiny to be derived from [−ATR] spreading, the F-element [−ATR] needs to be available to the spreading rule. This will be unproblematic in morphemes which include [−ATR] in their lexical representation. In the complementary set, however, [−ATR] will be absent from the lexicon, and will be supplied by the Default rule (66ci) where appropriate. Clearly, therefore, this rule must be allowed to precede the spreading rule (66bii), in order to make the F-element available to the latter.

Such ordering relationship is in fact not specific to Yoruba, but rather follows from the assumption in RU that feeding relationships thus involving redundancy rules are derived from a universal convention dubbed the 'Redundancy Rule Ordering Constraint'(RROC), which we shall formulate as follows (Archangeli 1984: 85):

(67) Redundancy Rule Ordering Constraint
       A redundancy rule (i.e. a structure-building rule) supplying the valued feature αF_i must apply prior to any rule making reference to αF_i in its structural description[15]

Because rule (66bii) mentions [−ATR] in the input, the RROC will enforce the prior application of the redundancy rule (66ci), which supplies this value. Note, importantly, that the RROC also acts as a further warranty against the Lightner/Stanley problem, since, given the RROC, any feature value relevant to a rule will be supplied across the board before the application of that rule, thus forestalling any possible misuse of blanks.

2.6.1.3 *Filters*

We now turn to the two remaining problems concerning the distribution of [−ATR].

Consider first the absence of [−ATR] high vowels. As the analysis stands, nothing will prevent the emergence of such segments:

(68) [+high]

$$[-\text{ATR}]$$

The configuration in (68) can be obtained either by [−ATR] association to the rightmost high vowel (by (66bi)), or by leftward spread (by (66bii)). In order to prevent this result either way, Archangeli and Pulleyblank (1989) enrich the machinery with the filter in (69):

(69) * $\begin{bmatrix} +\text{high} \\ -\text{ATR} \end{bmatrix}$

The addition of this filter to the grammar will obviously block the derivation in (68), as desired.

The filter in (69) also affords a very elegant solution to the third, remaining problem, which concerns the fact that [−ATR] mid vowels can occur before final high vowels, but not before non-final high vowels.

Thus, consider the fact that [−ATR] mid vowels are allowed before a word-final high vowel. The presence of [−ATR] in a mid vowel points to a lexical floating [−ATR], since otherwise [+ATR] would be provided by the Complement rule in (66cii). Such a lexical [−ATR] will try to associate to the rightmost vowel, by (66bi). Two possibilities exist: either this vowel is high or it is not. If the word-final vowel is [+high], filter (69) will prevent the association of [−ATR] to this vowel. Instead, [−ATR] will associate to the next rightmost vowel, thus generating such sequences as [...ɛ...i], [...ɔ...i]. If the word-final vowel is non-high, however, the floating [−ATR] will associate to this vowel, as illustrated in (70):

(70) ... [−H]   [+H]   [−H]

$$[-\text{ATR}]$$

The spread of [− ATR] to the penultimate high vowel is now blocked by filter (69). Consequently, the antepenultimate non-high vowel cannot receive a [− ATR] value by spreading either, given the requirement of adjacency on spreading, built into (66bii). Therefore, the noted gap in the distribution of mid vowels is accounted for.

2.6.2 Persistent rules

The postulation of filters alongside redundancy rules, characteristic of RU analyses, is shown by Mohanan (1991) to involve an element of formal redundancy. The demonstration is straightforward. Thus, given the fact that a given filter f forbids the cooccurrence of the F-elements $[\alpha F_i]$ and $[\beta F_j]$, such elements will never associate, either lexically or derivationally. Consequently, it will be idle to postulate a rule filling in precisely the value $[− \alpha F_i]$ in the presence of $[\beta F_j]$, since no other value of $[F_i]$ can associate to $[\beta F_j]$, given f. Notice that this demonstration further supports the claim of equivalence between negative and if-then constraints made in 2.1.1.1 above. We are now seeing this equivalence to concern structure-building rules in general, over and above their specific theoretical incarnation.

Addressing the particular case of Yoruba [ATR] harmony, Mohanan (1991) shows the viability of a more compact analysis than the one presented above, if the simple step is taken of interpreting all the (slightly reformulated) rules as feature-changing, as follows:

(71) a.   [+low] → [− ATR]
     b.   [+high] → [+ ATR]

     c.

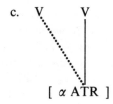

Notice that the source feature for the spreading is no longer specified as negative, either value of [ATR] being now allowed to spread. Assuming that final [+ high] vowels are extraprosodic, all the facts reviewed above fall into place. In particular, the [ATR] value of any one vowel will simply be determined by the value of this feature in the following adjacent vowel, with the proviso that all low vowels are [− ATR] (see (71a)), and all high vowels [+ ATR] (see (71b)). The formal advantages accruing to this approach are obvious, and need no further comment.[16]

Such a structure-changing mode of application of redundancy rules is essentially the language-specific counterpart of *SPE*'s universal 'linking' convention, by which marking conventions apply persistently to the output of language-particular rules. Some recent research in fact suggests that rules of this kind may not just be preferable to filters, or to structure-building rules supplemented with filters, but that they may indeed be empirically necessary.

Consider for instance the English vowel length alternation illustrated in (72):

(72) a. keep   b. kept
     leave   left
     deep   depth
     thief   theft

In (72), long /iː/ alternates with short /ɛ/. The trigger environment for shortening is obviously the consonantal cluster created by the addition of the suffixal consonant to the base (we are ignoring here the change in vowel quality, related of course to the Great Vowel Shift). We shall first attempt to formulate such a process by means of a filter, as follows:

(73) * V V C C]

(73) will indeed prevent the emergence of such forms as *keept*, *leaft*, etc. The problem is that it will simply block the outlawed configuration, either by stopping morphological concatenation (i.e. by ruling ill-formed such derivatives as *deep + th*), or by preventing the formation of the consonant cluster (thus predicting *deeth*, or perhaps *deep* in the sense of *depth*). Neither of these results is in accord with the facts. What we want instead is for vowel shortening to correct the effect of concatenation.

A straightforward way of achieving this aim involves the reformulation of (73) as a structure-changing rule, along the lines of (74):

(74) V V C C]

Suppose now that we allow rule (74) to be operative everywhere in the appropriate part of the grammar (namely the lexical representation and the first derivational stages in English). The obvious result is that we will at once prevent the outlawed configuration from entering the lexicon (it will simply be unlearnable, for want of evidence) and automatically correct any violations which may arise in the course of the morphological derivation. In other words, we will be accounting for the commonalities of distribution and alternation in one stroke, a highly desirable result.

Myers (1991) refers to rules of the type represented in (74) as 'persistent rules' (after Chafe 1968), and contends that such rules are likely to constitute the most appropriate formalisation for constraints affecting the internal structure of phonological elements both in lexical representation and throughout the derivation.

The diverse consequences emanating from the filter in (73) and from the persistent rule in (74), respectively, invite re-examination of our previous assertion of equivalence for negative and if-then conditions. The reason for the ambiguity of filter (73), as compared with its counterparts in (4) above, lies however in the fact that this filter, but not its congeners, contains a multiple conjunction of conditions (namely not V *and* V *and* C *and* C). Consequently, the injunction embodied in the filter can be resolved in a number of ways, as affecting any of these conjuncts. The equivalence between negative and if-then conditions is thus limited to two-term conjunctions involving an either–or choice, precisely the case of binary features. From this perspective, therefore, persistent rules indeed appear to pre-empt the need for filters, and hence to provide a more general formalisation for constraints.

2.7 CONCLUSION

In the present chapter we have investigated the formalisation of lexical redundancies. Different alternatives have been explored, namely lexical blanks, filters, and persistent rules. The misuse of blanks as a third feature value can be prevented by limiting to two the number of lexical contrasts for each feature, or by filling in all relevant values prior to the operation of a structure-changing rule (as per RROC (67)). Two sets of criteria for the determination of lexical blanks are in competition, as embodied in the theories of Contrast-based and Radical Underspecification. The use of lexical blanks has itself come under fire from the demonstration that the effect of filters encompasses that of blank-filling rules. Finally, the indeterminacy of output possibly associated with filters may yet tilt the balance in favour of structure-changing persistent rules.

Faced with such a range of choices, wisdom strongly recommends caution, while keenly awaiting the results of further research.

3 Basic Elements

3.1 THE *SPE* MODEL OF DISTINCTIVE FEATURES

In the previous two chapters we have accepted unquestioned the distinctive feature system of *SPE*. However, the autosegmentalisation of features proposed for, e.g. vowel harmony in Turkish or lateral dissimilation in Latin already hints at innovations in this area, to which we now turn. We will see that change has affected in varying degrees all aspects of the *SPE* system: number of features, identity of the features, relations between features, and feature valency.

As usual, a brief summary of the *SPE* approach will provide us with a convenient starting point. As has already been mentioned, *SPE* features had a classificatory as well as a phonetic function. In particular, they served the purpose of formally separating segments in the lexicon and throughout the derivation. Such a task can in principle be carried out by a system devoid of phonetic substance (see e.g. Fudge 1967). Indeed, abstract inventories are best suited to implement classification, their malleability allowing them to meet the precise requirements of any set of data. However, this formal virtue also constitutes the Achilles heel of this kind of system, since the sound patterns of human language are heavily constrained by the realities of articulation, acoustics and perception. Accordingly, Chomsky and Halle endow their features with specific phonetic content at all levels of representation. As well as simplifying the mapping, this permits us to capture the natural groupings of sounds with regard to both phonological processes and distributional regularities, as we have been observing throughout the preceding chapters.[1]

Included in the *SPE* system were the syntagmatically oriented features [unit] and [segment]. A positive marking for [unit] simply signalled the presence of phonological material, while plus and minus [segment] embodied the opposition segment vs boundary. The function of boundaries has since been rendered otiose by the direct interplay of

morphological structure with phonological representation, in turn
enriched with prosodic constituency (see Chapter 5 for discussion),
while the autosegmentalisation of features has resulted in the location of
segmental identity in the skeleton, as we have seen.

SPE segments were differentiated as to their content by means of the
remaining distinctive features. Such features numbered well over 20 if
prosodic features are included (*SPE*: 299–300), in sharp contrast with
Jakobson's inventory of only 12 (see e.g. Jakobson, Fant and Halle
1952). The reason for this divergence lies in the opposing conceptions
underlying the two systems. Specifically, Jakobson operated within a
structuralist framework rooted in the idea of phonemic contrast,
whereas Chomsky and Halle deliberately set out to describe 'the speech-
producing capabilities of the human vocal apparatus' (*SPE*: 297).
Following on from the conception of features as aspects of speech under
voluntary control, Chomsky and Halle admit the possibility of further
additions to their list, which must accordingly be considered open-
ended.

In *SPE*, segments were defined by means of unordered feature
matrices, as we illustrated for the word *pen* in Chapter 1 and repeat now
here for convenience:

(1) Distinctive feature representation of /pen/ in *SPE*

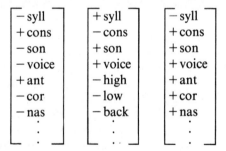

The order in which the features appear within each of the columns in (1)
is immaterial, and could freely be replaced by any of its permutations.
The only two relevant aspects of this representation are the completeness
of the inventory (subject to simplification in lexical representation, as
appropriate) and the positive or negative marking of each feature
(whether primary or derived from markedness considerations, as
discussed in Chapter 2).

Two consequences of this model need highlighting. First, the realisation of features is assumed to be segment-bounded. This limitation is of course directly at odds with the autosegmental approach, brought in precisely to overcome some of the difficulties inherent in this restriction. Second, all *SPE* features enjoy equal status. Specifically, no relations of subordination between features were accommodated for.

In addition, *SPE* features function binarily throughout the phonological representation ('each feature is a physical scale defined by two points, ... designated by antonymous adjectives: high-nonhigh ... '; *SPE*: 299). In particular, Chomsky and Halle liken phonological distinctive features in their classificatory function to such non-phonological lexical features as 'noun', 'animate' or 'transitive', and contend that 'the natural way of indicating whether or not an item belongs to a particular category is by means of binary features' (*SPE*: 297).[2] The obvious implication of this stand is that both polar values will play a role in the phonology. To the extent that this prediction is empirically substantiated, binarism will be validated. If, however, the prediction turns out to be factually void for one of the two values, a unary alternative, in which a given feature is simply present or absent from the representation, will be preferred.[3]

3.2 FEATURE DEPENDENCIES

We have just pointed out that, in *SPE*, features are viewed as mutually independent. In this section, however, we shall present evidence for dependency relations between features. This constitutes a first step towards the total hierarchisation of features, which will be seen below to have gained much favour in recent years.

3.2.1 Language-particular

3.2.1.1 Parasitic harmony

Consider the following data from the Yawelmani aorist (NB the underlying Yawelmani vowel system has four terms: /i, a, o, u/):

(2) a. lihim-hin   'ran'
         baṭin-hin   'fell down'
         hogin-hin   'floated'

     b. ʔugun-hun   'drank'
         ćumm-hun   'devoured'
         duulul-hun   'climbed'

The vowel of the aorist suffix -*hVn* is subject to progressive rounding harmony. Unsurprisingly, other suffixes are also affected by such harmony:

(3)   a.   xat-al   'might eat'
      b.   hoṭn-ol   'might take the scent'

Here, the vowel of the dubitative suffix -*Vl* rounds after the round vowel *o*.

Rounding does not however occur in all contexts:

(4)   a.   xayaa-hin   'placed'
           wan-hin   'gave'
           ʔohyoo-hin   'searched'
           ćow-hin   'touched'

      b.   diʔṣ-al   'might make'
           ṣuug-al   'might pull out'

Here we see the two suffixes show up in what appears to be their default, unrounded form, -*hin* and -*al*, respectively, irrespective of the specification for [round] in the preceding vowel.

The reason for the contrast between the two sets with regard to the application of rounding harmony must be sought in the respective value of the feature [high] in the trigger and the target vowels. Specifically, this value is uniform in (2) ([+ high]) and in (3) ([− high]), whereas in (4a) a [+ high] suffix (-*hin*) combines with a [− high] stem, and in (4b) a [− high] suffix (-*al*) is added to a [+ high] stem.

A direct formalisation of this situation, on the assumption of autosegmentalisation for [round] and [high], is as follows (see Cole 1987, and Cole and Trigo 1988):

(5) Yawelmani rounding harmony

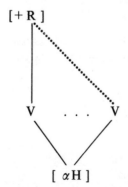

This type of formalisation, however, implicitly predicts the existence of rules of parasitic harmony along the lines of (6):

(6)

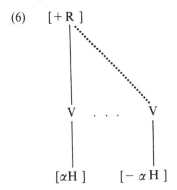

Rules parasitically depending on the disagreement of a feature value in the two protagonist vowels are unattested, and should therefore be barred on a principled basis.

3.2.1.2 Dependency analysis

The desired degree of constraining can be achieved by means of direct dependencies between the features. We shall base our exposition on Mester (1988), who makes interesting and decisive use of the Obligatory Contour Principle (OCP), already mentioned in the previous chapter[4] (antecedent analyses can be found in Archangeli 1984, 1985, where direct dependency is referred to as 'coplanar representation').

The approach is built on the premise that not all features need to connect directly to the skeleton, and can instead associate to some other feature. Suppose thus that we stipulate that, in Yawelmani, [±round] is a dependent of [±high], as represented in (7):

(7)

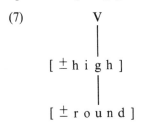

Consider now the derivation of *ʔugunhun*. First, the lexical representation of the stem for the relevant features will be as in (8):

(8)

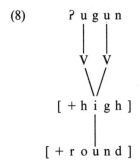

Note that a doubling of the valued feature [+high], as well as being unnecessary, will be banned by the OCP.

We next proceed to the formation of the aorist by concatenation of the suffix *-hVn*, the vowel of which we must assume is lexically specified as [+high] (the only alternants are *-hin* and *-hun*), but unspecified for roundness:

(9)

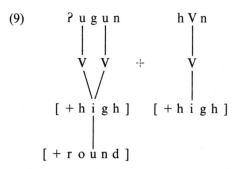

The representation in (9) contains a violation of the OCP. Mester's suggestion is that such a violation is automatically repaired through the fusion of the two adjacent identical [+high] F-elements (for discussion of repair mechanisms, see e.g. Paradis 1988–9):

(10)

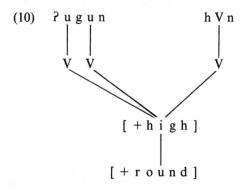

As can be seen, the desired rounding harmony has been obtained at no cost, without resort to stipulation.

It is clear that no harmony will take place where the values for [high] are not uniform. Thus, consider *ćowhin*, represented in (11):

(11)

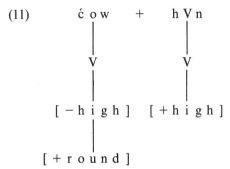

There is no OCP violation here, and therefore there will be no fusion. Instead, *-hVn* will have the value [− round] supplied by default, directly yielding the surface form.

It is important to note that, in Mester's proposal, directionality of dependency can be determined language-particularly. Thus, for instance, he postulates the opposite dependency between [high] and [back] in Ngbaka (where [high] dominates [back]) and in Ainu (where [back] dominates [high]), in order to account for OCP-related constraints in their lexical representations.

3.2.2 Universal

Some of the *SPE* features have since been found to have too broad scope, and have consequently been redefined. Such redefinitions typically involve universal dependencies. Moreover, facts of assimilation suggest that superordinate features are monovalent, thus causing a first dent in *SPE*'s contention of across-the-board binarism.

3.2.2.1 *[Coronal] dependencies*

The *SPE* inventory includes the features [coronal], [anterior] and [distributed], all related to place of articulation. The interaction between the first two features divides the buccal cavity into four regions, three of which correspond to the traditional groupings 'labial', 'dento-alveolar', and 'palato-alveolar', and the fourth one to the remnant.[5] The additional distinction between dentals and alveolars is implemented indirectly by means of [± distributed], a feature differentiating laminal from apical articulations.[6] Dentals will therefore be [+distributed], while alveolars will be [−distributed]. The same feature in principle captures the contrast between bilabials ([+distributed]) and labio-dentals ([−distributed]), velars ([+distributed]) and uvulars ([−distributed]), and so on. The non-coronal pairs are however all fricative, and also kept apart by the feature [strident], to be discussed below, the functional load of [distributed] being thus effectively limited to coronals. A similar restriction applies to [anterior], since anterior labials can be individuated simply by their labiality.

The facts of Sanskrit *n*-Retroflexion, examined in Steriade (1985) and Schein and Steriade (1986), confirm the dependency of [anterior] and [distributed] from [coronal]. In Sanskrit, the coronal nasal [n] is retroflected to [ṇ] after a retroflex continuant [ṣ] or [r]:

(12) pur-āṇa-   'fill' + middle participle
      cakṣ-āṇa-   'see' + middle participle
      kṣubh-āṇa-   'quake' + middle participle
      kṛp-a-māṇa-   'lament' + middle participle

As can be seen, the two segments need not be adjacent on the C projection.

The Sanskrit inventory of coronal consonants is as follows:

(13)   [anterior]   [distributed]
      t, s, n   +   +
      ṭ, ṣ, ṇ, r   −   −
      ʧ, ʃ, ɲ   −   +

Clearly, in order for [n] to become [ṇ] in, e.g. *purāṇa*, the value for *both* [anterior] *and* [distributed] must change from plus to minus. The motivation for such multiple assimilation is however obscure in the context of the *SPE* model of mutual feature independence.

Steriade's (1985) proposal involves the postulation of a (universal) dependency between the features in question, as follows:

(14)

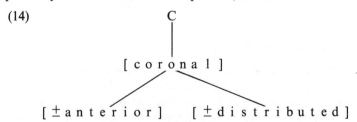

The essence of the proposal is therefore that the features [±anterior] and [±distributed] do not link directly to the skeleton, but rather through their dependency on [coronal].

All we now have to do in order to account for the Sanskrit facts is to postulate a structure-changing rule along the lines of (15):

(15)

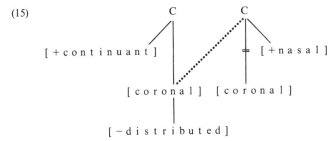

Implicit in this formulation is the prediction that the rule will be blocked by the presence of other coronals:

(16) kṣved-āna-   'hum' + middle participle
      kṛt-a-māna-   'cut' + middle participle

Here, the plain coronals [d] and [t] prevent the spreading of the [coronal] node to [n], precisely as falls out of (15).

By contrast, non-coronals fail to block coronal spread, as revealed by the appropriate data in (12) (e.g. *kṣubhāṇa*). If such segments were specified as [−coronal], however, blocking would be inevitable, since the F-element [−coronal] would stand in the way of [+coronal] spread (cf. the similar reasoning on the behaviour of Latin liquids in Chapter 2). One obvious solution (again, as in the case of Latin liquids) would be to have all Sanskrit non-coronals unspecified for [−coronal] at the time spreading takes place. The difficulty with this approach is that it contains the prediction that non-coronals could in principle also be lexically specified (given Steriade's own proposals for underspecification, discussed in Chapter 2), and thus act as blockers of coronal spread. This prediction remains however unfulfilled. The common response to such asymmetric behaviour has consequently been simply to assume mono-valency for [coronal], as we have already shown in (14) and (15).

An interesting consequence of the monovalency of [coronal] is the complete lack of specification of non-coronals for [±anterior] and [±distributed] at all levels of the derivation, phonetic form included. In particular, given the implicational relationship between these two features and the superordinate [coronal], the absence of the super-ordinate will automatically preclude the specification of the dependents.

Two other *SPE* features are relevant in the present context, namely [±strident] and [±lateral].

SPE identifies a positive marking for [lateral] with a lowering of the mid section of the tongue on the side(s), thus implicitly restricting the feature to coronal consonantal sounds. An apparent challenge to this restriction is posed by the velar laterals which have been reported in Papuan languages (see e.g. Ladefoged *et al.* 1979), where the main constriction is claimed to take place between the tongue body and the velum, with lateral airflow in the back molar area. However, in a detailed study of laterals, Levin (1988a) interprets these sounds as complex corono-dorsal segments. If so, their articulation will involve both the tongue blade and the tongue body, with the former formally manifested as [coronal], from which [+ lateral] can now hang as a dependent (the phonetic realisation of laterality on the velar is accounted for by the familiar lack of phonological timing restrictions between the component parts of complex segments).[7]

We must finally turn to [± strident]. This feature is characterised by the presence of a substantial degree of acoustic noise, and can therefore be used to differentiate a labiodental [f] ([+ strident]) from a bilabial [ɸ] ([− strident]), a uvular [χ] ([+ strident]) from a velar [x] ([− strident]), and so on, as noted above.

The construal of [± strident] as a dependent of [coronal] (see e.g. Shaw 1991, and Lahiri and Evers 1991) is more controversial than that of [lateral]. In particular, such a dependency would create an obvious problem for the parallel dependency proposed for [± distributed], which feature we have suggested can be dispensed with in non-coronals on the strength of [± strident]. Clearly, however, if [± strident] is also restricted to coronals, such distinctions will become inexpressible, at least within the standard feature frameworks.

The proposals we have examined result in a configuration of the [coronal] class along the lines of (17), where contentious assignments have been signalled by means of question marks:

(17)

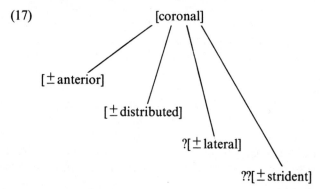

In (17), the mutual planar autonomy of the dependents is graphically indicated by their placement on different lines. Such planar autonomy is an important property of all features within the current autosegmental conception of phonology, and must therefore be borne in mind at all times.[8]

3.2.2.2 *Other dependency classes*

As expected, dependency relations are also found in other subsets of the feature inventory, and we shall now briefly review the most important ones.

3.2.2.2.1 [Labial]

Lip activity was formalised in *SPE* by means of the feature [round] ('rounded sounds are produced with a narrowing of the lip orifice' (*SPE*: 309)). Lip rounding must however be kept distinct from mere labialisation. Inevitably, therefore, an additional feature [labial] was brought in to capture general lip movement (see Hyman 1975 and the references therein), [round] now being specifically kept for rounding (see e.g. Halle and Clements 1983).

As discussed in Yip (1988b: 81ff.), labial consonants cannot cooccur in Cantonese morphemes (cf. *pim, *maːp). This restriction can readily be interpreted as an OCP effect on the feature composition of such morphemes. What is interesting for our present purposes is that, again morpheme internally, a round vowel cannot be followed by a labial consonant (*tup, *køm). The question which obviously arises is what a rounded vowel and a labial consonant have in common, so that the noted cooccurrence restriction can also be brought under the remit of the OCP. The answer is straightforward if there is a dependency between these two features, as is indeed proposed in Sagey (1986):

(18)   [l a b i a l]
                    |
                    |
        [± r o u n d]

Because [labial] is a superordinate of [± round], the presence of a round vowel will imply the presence of the feature [labial], hence the noted OCP violation.

As was the case with the [coronal] class, the superordinate feature [labial] is formalised as monovalent. Segments with no lip activity will therefore simply lack the specification [labial] (and, by implication, [± round]), and will thus be transparent to spreading.

3.2.2.2.2 [Dorsal] and [Radical]

The features [±high], [±low] and [±back] are presented in *SPE* under the heading 'features relating to the body of the tongue'. In her important 1986 study, Sagey proposes that such informal grouping be given formal status with the creation of a superordinate feature [dorsal], of which [±high], [±low] and [±back] will be dependents:

(19)

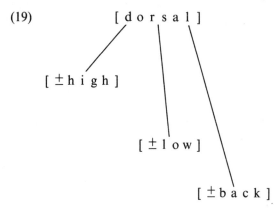

Besides considerations of symmetry,[9] Sagey (1986) mentions phonological evidence from Fante in support of this arrangement. Specifically, according to Welmers (1946), in this language the alveolar trill /r/ assimilates to a neighbouring vowel in all the dorsal features. Thus, /r/ becomes palatalised by /i/, /e/, and velarised by /u/, /o/, while the back of the tongue undergoes lowering when /r/ is in the vicinity of /a/. Clearly, these assimilatory changes receive a maximally simple description if the configuration in (19) is adopted, the process then being formally reduced to the spread of [dorsal] from the vowel to the consonant. Crucially, however, such spread does not include [±round], [±anterior], [±distributed], etc., all as predicted by the formalism being proposed.

The picture of the dependencies of place of articulation features is completed by the postulation of a superordinate feature [radical]. Note that the tongue root is an autonomous articulator, like the lips or the tongue body. Standard feature theory assumes that the tongue root either is advanced with respect to its neutral position or is not. The relevant feature effecting this division is [advanced tongue root], by which sounds are classified into [+ATR], with tongue root advancement, and [−ATR] without.[10] The feature [±ATR] is consequently treated as a dependent of [radical] by several (though by no means all) authors (e.g. Halle 1988, Sagey 1988b, Clements 1992):

(20)   [radical]

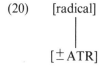

[±ATR]

3.2.3 Sum-up and some consequences

The two conceptions of feature dependencies we have been examining, universal (as in Sagey 1986) and language-specific (as in Mester 1988), are obviously at odds with each other. For instance, the postulated universal dependency of [±round] on [labial], and of [±high] on [dorsal], rules out Mester's (1988) dependency of [±round] on [±high] for Yawelmani. Which of the two opposing conceptions is correct is of course an empirical question, but so far the wind has blown (and continues blowing) in the direction of universal dependencies.

The superordinate features [labial], [coronal], [dorsal] and [radical] exhaust between them the possibilities for place of articulation. The proposed monovalency of such superordinates affords of course a maximally simple formalisation of the respective melodies, such that, e.g. a labial segment will simply be [labial], with no marking for the remainder of the place features, and so on. The planar independence of features makes however possible the accumulation of such super-ordinates in one and the same configuration. Specifically, as well as being marked for one of [labial], [coronal], [dorsal], or [radical], segments may carry multiple markings, say, [labial, coronal], or [labial, coronal, dorsal], etc. This result accords well with reality. In particular, Sagey (1988c) shows the existence of, among others, a labio-coronal [pt] in Margi, a labio-dorsal [kp] in Loko, a corono-dorsal [c] in Czech, and a labio-coronal-dorsal [tkw] in Kinyarwanda. The unitary behaviour of complex segments with respect to phonological processes, mentioned several times in the course of the exposition, thus falls out of the proposed representation, since, besides being attached to a unique skeletal slot, these superordinate features are not ordered with respect to each other.

3.3 THE HIERARCHY OF FEATURES

The reorganisation of features carried out in recent years does not end with the postulation of interfeature dependencies, and extends to the inclusion of all features in a constituent hierarchy.

3.3.1 Feature groupings

In a seminal paper, Clements (1985a) drew our attention to the functional unity of several sets of features with regard to rules (Clements acknowledges Mascaró 1983 and Mohanan 1983 as forerunners).

For instance, it is well known that in many languages nasals undergo total place of articulation assimilation to a following obstruent (see note 1 above). The representation of this process in *SPE* terms is as in (21):

(21) Nasal Assimilation

$$[+\text{nasal}] \rightarrow \begin{bmatrix} \alpha\text{coronal} \\ \beta\text{anterior} \\ \gamma\text{back} \\ \delta\text{distributed} \end{bmatrix} \bigg/ \underline{\quad} \begin{bmatrix} -\text{sonorant} \\ \alpha\text{coronal} \\ \beta\text{anterior} \\ \gamma\text{back} \\ \delta\text{distributed} \end{bmatrix}$$

This rule is obviously very cumbersome, in direct contrast with the cross-linguistic recurrence of the process. The formalism also incorrectly predicts the possibility of assimilation across features, as illustrated in (22):

(22) Pseudo-nasal Assimilation

$$[+\text{nasal}] \rightarrow \begin{bmatrix} \alpha\text{coronal} \\ \beta\text{anterior} \\ \gamma\text{back} \\ \delta\text{distributed} \end{bmatrix} \bigg/ \underline{\quad} \begin{bmatrix} -\text{sonorant} \\ \beta\text{coronal} \\ \gamma\text{anterior} \\ \delta\text{back} \\ \alpha\text{distributed} \end{bmatrix}$$

This result is prevented by our proposal in the previous section, but the simplicity problem remains, since even in the new framework the assimilation in (21) requires the spread of [labial], [coronal], or [dorsal] from the obstruent skeletal slot to its counterpart in the nasal. Implicit in this is the assessment of partial assimilation as less complex (and thus less marked) than total assimilation, again in conflict with the facts.

What we obviously want is a simple statement along the lines of (23) (see Harris 1969: 20):

(23) Assimilate place: $\begin{bmatrix} \underline{\quad} \\ +\text{nasal} \end{bmatrix}$ $[-\text{sonorant}]$

As it stands at the moment, however, the theory is unable to accommodate such a formalism.

3.3.2 Class nodes

The problems mentioned will disappear if all place of articulation features (at the moment [labial], [coronal], [dorsal] and [radical], each with its respective dependents) are gathered under a superordinate node, which we shall label {place}, and which we enclose in curly brackets as evocative of sets, for reasons that will become clearer as we proceed. In particular, the nasal assimilation rule can now be expressed with a minimum of fuss, as in (24) (the structure has been kept to a minimum for expository convenience):

(24)

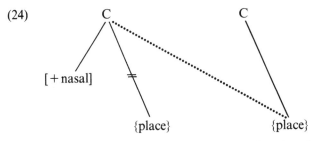

A number of such 'class nodes' will now be introduced and justified.

In Thai, larynx-related features act as a unit with regard to the neutralisation of several, glottally differentiated, stops. The data in (25) show the existence in this language of an opposition between voiced, voiceless unaspirated, and voiceless aspirated stops:

(25) Thai stop contrasts

a.	baa	'crazy'	b.	panya	'brains'	c.	pʰaa	'cloth'
	bil	'Bill'		pen	'alive'		pʰyaa	'title'
	bruu	'fast'		plaa	'fish'		pʰrɛɛ	'silk cloth'

These contrasts can be captured by means of the informal laryngeal features [± voice] and [± aspirated], as follows:[11]

(26) a. /b/ (voiced):

$$\begin{bmatrix} -\text{aspirated} \\ +\text{voice} \end{bmatrix}$$

b.   /p/ (voiceless unaspirated):

$$\begin{bmatrix} -\,\text{aspirated} \\ -\,\text{voice} \end{bmatrix}$$

c.   /pʰ/ (voiceless aspirated):

$$\begin{bmatrix} +\,\text{aspirated} \\ -\,\text{voice} \end{bmatrix}$$

Consider now the forms in (27):

(27)   Thai stop neutralisation

riip	'hurry'
sip	'ten'
rap	'take'

As illustrated in (27), all syllable-final stops in Thai are voiceless unaspirated (also phonetically unreleased). This category can plausibly be considered unmarked, and consequently the constraint can be interpreted as a prohibition against the lexical association of F-elements in that position, with the eventual provision of the structure in (26b) by default. As in the case of nasal assimilation, however, the fact that precisely these two features partake in such processes is not captured by the formalism. The problem obviously disappears if the two features are provided with a superordinate node {laryngeal}:

(28)   a. voiced   b. voiceless unaspirated   c. voiceless aspirated

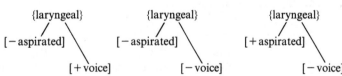

Given this configuration, the noted delinking and linking will take place between {laryngeal} and its superordinate node (a skeletal slot as things stand at the moment).

Groupings such as {laryngeal} or {place} are given a specific phonetic interpretation in Sagey (1986) ('involving the glottis as an active articulator', for {laryngeal}, and 'affecting formant structures in a manner resulting from changes in the shape of the resonator', for {place}). This author proposes the following overall hierarchy of distinctive features, or 'feature geometry' (in the interest of graphic simplicity, we omit the laryngeal and place dependents, which have already been discussed):

(29)

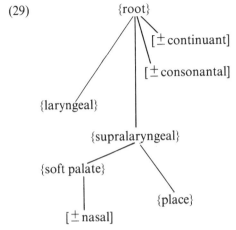

There are some novel nodes in this figure, and we shall now comment on them (the absent features [sonorant], [strident] and [lateral] are discussed by Sagey under the heading 'residue', on the grounds that their position in the hierarchy is unclear).

The {soft palate} node is self-explanatory, and is introduced by Sagey for reasons of symmetry with {place}, without apparent empirical justification. {Supralaryngeal} has the phonetic effect of 'distorting formant structures', while {root} 'simply corresponds to the phonological entity, the phoneme'.

Besides any possible phonetic reality, the postulation of such 'class nodes' has the expected phonological consequences. Note that implicit in this geometry is the prediction that assimilation (and, correspondingly, dissimilation and blocking) can operate at one of three levels: root level (total assimilation), terminal feature level (single feature assimilation), and class node level (partial assimilation). By contrast, assimilation of groups of features unaffiliated to the hierarchy is implicitly banned. These predictions indeed match the testimony provided by the world's languages.

Thus, spreading of the root node corresponds to such processes as gemination and copying, while delinking of this node formalises segment deletion with compensatory lengthening. Partial assimilations include those considered above (nasal place assimilation, vowel harmony, Sanskrit retroflection, etc.), as well as, e.g. regressive assimilation of voice and aspiration in Classical Greek. Moreover, as pointed out by Clements (1985a), rules of partial assimilation tend to show the same effects as rules of total assimilation with regard to opacity to epenthesis, a phenomenon that several authors (e.g. Steriade 1982, Hayes 1986, Schein and Steriade 1986) have related to the presence of multiple linkings in the corresponding structure,[12] such parallel behaviour obviously pointing to structural isomorphy. Finally, single-feature spreading is instantiated by place assimilation of coronal stops in English (Clements 1985a), voice assimilation in Russian (Hayes 1984a), etc.

Clements (1985a) and McCarthy (1988), among others, explicitly give priority to phonological over phonetic considerations in the construction of feature geometry. Clements (1989) reemphasises the autonomy of phonology from phonetics, which he compares to the autonomy of syntax from semantics, pragmatics, etc., one of the chief pillars of generative grammar. Such autonomy obviously implies that the evidence used to justify phonological constructs (be they the feature geometry or the features themselves) must be phonological.

Particularly thorough phonological testing of what can be regarded as 'core' feature geometry (i.e. the idealised common denominator of the various proposals, as sampled above) is carried out in McCarthy (1988). Three criteria are used to probe into the phonological robustness of the class nodes: assimilation (i.e. spreading), dissimilation (i.e. delinking), and dissimilatory blocking (i.e. effects related to the Obligatory Contour Principle).

The {soft palate} node cannot of course withstand such critical examination, since, as we said above, it was introduced by Sagey on exclusive considerations of configurational symmetry. Looking next at the {supralaryngeal} and {place} nodes, McCarthy contends that their functions are complementary, and thus that one of them is unnecessary. Consider for instance the phenomenon of debuccalisation, by which buccal (but, crucially, not laryngeal) articulation is lost.[13] Within feature geometry, this process has often been formally related to a delinking of the {supralaryngeal} node. As McCarthy points out, however, it can equally well be accounted for by delinking of the {place} node, indeed our practice above. Spreading of {supralaryngeal} is scantily represented in the literature, the few cases arguably being reanalysable as {place} spread. Finally, again according to McCarthy, OCP effects on {supralaryngeal} are unknown, whereas they are well attested for {place} (cf. for instance the so-called Prince-languages, after Prince 1984, where consonant clusters must agree in place of articulation).

The result of McCarthy's quest is the limitation of class nodes to {place} and {laryngeal}, the only ones for which he finds adequate support from phonological processes and constraints. Without denying the existence of the root, which is also well backed up by evidence, he contends that this position is not filled by a class node {root}, but rather by two formerly terminal features, namely [±sonorant] and [±consonantal]. The argument is straightforward, and follows the same lines as those concerning the dismissed class nodes. Simply, he does not find the two features in question engaging by themselves in processes of spreading or delinking, or exhibiting independent OCP effects. The consequence he draws is that such features are not formally autonomous from the rest, a situation he formalises by promoting them to the tree root itself. The resulting feature geometry is displayed in (30), which must be compared with the configuration in (29) above:

(30)

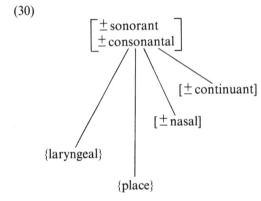

The conception of feature geometry embodied in this model is significantly at variance with that of its predecessors. In particular, the geometry in (29) exhibits a well-defined layered structure, with class nodes on top, monovalent superordinate features next, and binary dependent features ('terminal features') at the bottom of the tree. This symmetry is however lost in McCarthy's proposal in (30), where binary features act as superordinates, not just to other binary features (e.g. [±sonorant] to [±nasal]), but also to class nodes (e.g. [±sonorant] to {place}). The consequences of this shift are at present unclear, and we shall have nothing else to say on the matter here.

3.3.3 Autosegmentalism and class membership

3.3.3.1 Access to the skeleton

Consider the following paradigm from Icelandic:

(31) Icelandic declension

	f.sg.		n.sg.	
a.	rík	b.	ríkt	'rich'
	græn		grænt	'green'
	djúp		djúpt	'deep'

The forms in (31a) correspond to the feminine singular, and those in (31b) to the neuter singular, manifestly formed by *t* suffixation. In cases where the feminine singular base already ends in [t] we would consequently expect a sequence [tt] in the neuter, but we get [ht] instead:

(32) | | f.sg. | | n.sg. | |
|---|---|---|---|---|
| a. | feit | b. | fei[ht] | 'fat' |
| | sæt | | sæ[ht] | 'sweet' |
| | ljót | | ljó[ht] | 'ugly' |

The phenomenon by which the first of two adjacent identical voiceless plosives is changed into [h] (cf. also e.g. *ka*[hp]*i* 'hero', *þa*[hk]*a*, 'thank', etc.) is known as 'preaspiration'.

Facts such as these provide strong support for the autosegmentalisation of features. Specifically, on the assumption that Icelandic voiceless plosives are marked as aspirated ([+spread glottis] in the standard system of features), preaspiration can be approached as simply the loss of the supralaryngeal component in the first part of the geminate, a further instantiation of debuccalisation. Clements's (1985a) rule, inspired in Thráinsson (1978), is reproduced in (33):

(33) Icelandic Preaspiration (Clements 1985a)

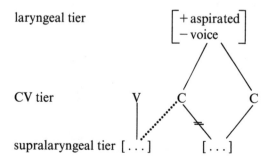

Hayes (1990) observes that in (33) both the laryngeal and the supralaryngeal elements are directly attached to the CV tier, with no participation of the root tier (or, effectively, of the laryngeal or supralaryngeal tiers, which are not part of the autosegmental configuration, as can be readily seen). This is at odds with Clements's (1985a) own feature geometry.

Suppose, instead, that the class nodes {laryngeal} and {supralaryngeal} are incorporated into the representation and linked to a unique {root} node associated to two C slots, indeed the common interpretation of geminates (NB the tree in (34) includes {manner} and {place/manner} class nodes, in line with Clements's proposal):

(34)

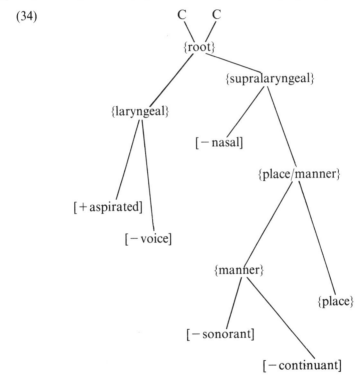

It is clear that the delinking of the supralaryngeal node from (34) will now result in the sequence [hh], rather than in the desired [h] + plosive. Alternatively, if we sever the connection between the root and the first C, such a position will become empty, rather than filled by [h].

On the basis of these and similar data, Hayes (1990) propounds direct access to the skeleton for all the features, indeed as embodied in Clements's analysis of Icelandic. In essence, therefore, Hayes advocates a return to the original autosegmental model, which in Chapter 1 we likened to a hub-and-spoke or open-book construction (Hayes's own analogy is that of a bottlebrush). If taken at face value, however, this step implies the dismissal of feature geometry and its attendant feature groupings, obviously an undesirable outcome.

In actual fact, however, Hayes attempts to have the best of both worlds by explicitly maintaining the hierarchisation of the features, while still allowing features to link directly to the skeleton. Thus, suppose that we represent all the relevant features of an Icelandic form, say, /feitt/, as literally autosegmental, along the lines we followed for Turkish vowel harmony in Chapter 1 (note that there is no crossing of lines in (35), as the features are on different planes):[14]

(35)

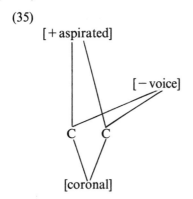

What we want is of course to sever the connection between the first C and [coronal], to derive the sequence [ht]. There will be no problem in formulating the appropriate rule on this configuration, but such a rule will operate exclusively on coronals, by definition. Therefore, we need to find a way of extending its applicability to all place features, given the fact that Icelandic preaspiration affects equally /pp/ (→ [hp]; cf. *ka*[hp]*i*) and /kk/ (→ [hk]; cf. *ba*[hk]*a*). The converse difficulty (which does not materialise in Icelandic, but does in, e.g. Thai, as discussed above) is that, on the representation in (35), there is no way of delinking [+aspirated] and [−voice] in one sole stroke, our old problem.

The solution is in fact quite straightforward, as represented in (36):

(36) [+ aspirated]$_L$

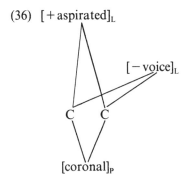

All we have done is to provide the features with information about their class membership in the feature geometry. In particular, we are now assuming that each feature will be subindexed for all the class nodes to which it is subordinated in the hierarchy (in the context of Sagey's geometry in (29) above, [coronal] would thus also be subindexed for S(upralaryngeal) and R(oot): [coronal]$_{PSR}$). This natural step renders the formulation of Icelandic Preaspiration maximally simple, as follows:

(37) Icelandic Preaspiration reformulated

[+ aspirated]$_L$

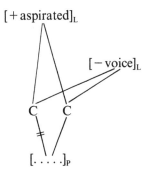

3.3.3.2 *Problems and answers*

Two aspects of this proposal must now be scrutinised. First, the class nodes (e.g. {place}) seem to have lost their autosegmental status, since they have now been reduced to the role of mere indices on features. Second, it is not clear how the noted dependency relations between the features themselves can be integrated into the new formalism.

Let us start with the issue of autosegmentalism. Arguably, the formal loss of autosegmental status for class nodes is a good result, their previous autosegmental rank being in fact spurious.

In order to substantiate this claim, we must briefly look back at the origins of autosegmental phonology. In a nutshell, the innovation embodied in autosegmental phonology concerns the formalisation of multiple timing, i.e. the abandonment of the assumption that each given feature is exclusively tied in to one segment. As expounded in Chapter 1, this idea found ready application in the area of tone, since tones often spread over several syllables, or move around them. The extension of this model to such areas as template morphology and vowel harmony is highly natural, both these phenomena also involving the relative timing of elements (skeletal slots and segments for template morphology; some selected feature(s) for vowel harmony).

Now, what is crucial for our present purposes is the fact that all such autosegmental elements are independently needed and justified: tones, features entering in the composition of segments, and so on. In the case of feature geometry, however, it can reasonably be argued that such entities as {place} or {laryngeal} have no reality independently of the features to which they refer, since their only apparent function is the expression of class membership for these features. If so, they should not be endowed with the power to engage in autosegmental behaviour, which is the exclusive reserve of autosegments.[15]

Turning now to the issue of cross-feature dependencies, there is no problem of principle. Thus, assuming that, e.g. [anterior] and [distributed] are dependents of [coronal], they will be connected to the skeleton through [coronal]:

(38)

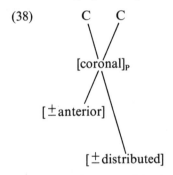

Note that the substance of the dependency relation is precisely the award of structural pre-eminence to the superordinate, as manifested in its placement between its dependents and the skeleton. Likewise, the (indirect) {place} class membership of $[\pm \text{anterior}]$ and $[\pm \text{distributed}]$ is correctly established via their superordinate [coronal].

A challenge to this interpretation of feature geometry is posed by McCarthy's (1988) decision to turn the {root} class node into a substantive feature bundle, $[\pm \text{consonant}, \pm \text{sonorant}]$. Within this proposal, only these two features have a direct link to the skeleton, thus apparently reopening the problem of Icelandic Preaspiration, as formalised in (34) above. However, in the present state of flux of the feature geometry, it is not clear what the overall import of this formulation will be. In particular, it is not inconceivable that McCarthy's root constitutes in fact the skeleton, the timing function of this tier being handed over to a new specialised structure (see the discussion on moras in Chapter 4). In this light, it would be unwise to assume that McCarthy's enriched root necessarily prevents the formal separation of the autosegmental and class membership aspects of feature geometry.

3.4 VALENCY

We have already seen the unqualified binarism of *SPE* dented by the postulation of monovalency for such superordinate features as [labial], [coronal], etc. In fact, as will be shown in this and the following sections, proposals exist for the extension of such unarism to non-superordinates. From an opposing perspective, binarism has come under fire by the postulation of multivalency for some features.

3.4.1 Multivalency

The phonetically gradual nature of some sound oppositions poses obvious problems for their description by means of binary features. One typical response to this challenge has been the postulation of n-ary values for the features in question (see e.g. Ladefoged 1971, 1975, Williamson 1977). In a current context, two approaches to the issue are worthy of notice: the construal of class nodes as multilateral features and the adoption of feature recursion.

3.4.1.1 Class nodes as multilateral features

McCarthy (1988) draws our attention to the correspondence between the only class nodes surviving his scrutiny ({laryngeal} and {place}) and the oppositions which are traditionally regarded as multilateral.

Thus, McCarthy reports, oppositions based on laryngeal activity range from binary to quaternary. In English the only contrast is one of presence vs absence of voice (or, perhaps more rigorously, short vs long time lag in voice onset). In Thai, voice oppositions are ternary, as discussed above. Finally, many Indo-Aryan languages (Hindi, Marathi, Bengali, Gujarati, and others) 'have a series of stops with murmured release, in addition to a three-way contrast between voiced, voiceless unaspirated, and (voiceless) aspirated stops' (Ladefoged 1971: 13).

Similarly, oppositions of place of articulation can be binary (rarely, as in Kitsai, which only has coronals and velars), more commonly ternary or quaternary (labials, coronals, velars, and perhaps palatals), and, rarely, even senary, as is the case with Malayalam nasals, which can be labial, dental, alveolar, postalveolar, palatal and velar (see Ladefoged 1971: 40).

The observation that class nodes act as superordinates (alternatively, subindices) of features standing in multilateral opposition leads McCarthy to construe feature geometry as 'a theory of nonbinary contrasts in binary terms' (McCarthy 1988: 94).

McCarthy constructs an argument for class nodes over multivalency (as in e.g. Ladefoged 1975 or Williamson 1977) on a constraint which limits to one the number of labial consonants permitted in Arabic roots. The crucial aspect of this prohibition is that it affects non-adjacent as well as adjacent positions. This situation is readily accounted for in a framework countenancing unary place features [labial], [coronal], etc. under a class node {place}, as shown in the (simplified) representation of *btf* in (39):[16]

(39)

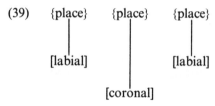

Given the autonomy of the [coronal] and [labial] tiers, the two instantiations of [labial] will occupy adjacent positions, with the consequent violation of the constraint, which can obviously be related to the OCP. By contrast, if a multivalued feature for place were adopted, no such contravention would occur:

(40)

The location of all the [place] values in the same tier is dictated by the very nature of the autosegmental geometry, where planes are defined by features, rather than by F-elements, as we have been seeing all along. It follows from this that the two occurrences of [1place] (the equivalent of the standard [labial]) will not be adjacent, and the Arabic root *btf* will illegitimately be let through. This gives a concrete advantage to the class node theory over its multivalent opponent.

In addition, the *n*-ary theory implicitly sanctions the possibility of incomplete assimilations in the direction of the triggering element, e.g. the change of /p/ to /t/ after /k/ to shorten the distance in place between the two segments. In as much as rules of this kind are unattested, the class node theory scores a further point over its rival.

3.4.1.2 Height levels as recursion

Laryngeal states and place of articulation zones do not exhaust the inventory of candidates to multivalency. In particular, vowels can have anything from two to five degrees of height (we are already familiar with the two-level height system of Turkish; the five-level height system of Kpokolo is discussed in Kaye *et al.* 1985).

The problems of the *SPE* approach to features with regard to vowel height are well known. In particular, the two binary features [high] and [low] can maximally define three degrees of height (again on the understanding that [+ high, + low] is functionally non-distinct from [− high, − low]). Yet, four-level vowel systems are not uncommon, and even five-level systems are attested, as noted.

The common strategy in the face of these facts has been to increase the number of features. Thus, the feature [ATR] (or its predecessor [tense]) automatically doubles the number of levels, each of the original three now being divisible into two sublevels with opposing [ATR] values. Now, while this move does solve the problem of accounting for richer inventories, a different, though connected, difficulty remains. In particular, as is again well known, languages abound in processes which systematically relate adjacent degrees of height. For instance, in the English Vowel Shift described in *SPE*, non-high long vowels undergo raising by one degree (and high vowels become [+ low], thereby occupying the only available slot left in the system). Similarly, in Lund Swedish the first half of all long vowels is lowered by one level (/iː/ → [ei], /eː/ → [ɛe], /ɛː/ → [æɛ]). While this type of change is still expressible within the standard system of features, the awkwardness and opacity of the formalisation exposes the system's inadequacy (the changes in (41) only refer to the first half of the vowel; all prosodic information has also been omitted for simplicity):

(41)

$$\begin{bmatrix} \alpha\text{high} \\ \langle -\text{ATR} \rangle \end{bmatrix} \rightarrow \begin{bmatrix} \alpha\text{ATR} \\ -\text{high} \\ \langle +\text{low} \rangle \end{bmatrix}$$

As formulated, the rule is highly unrevealing, and consequently unacceptable from the perspective of descriptive adequacy.

Hayes (1990) advances a solution making use of an alternative formalism, the rationale for which will be discussed in more detail in section 5 below (see in particular the discussion on Particle phonology in 5.2.1). The intuition captured by this formalism is simply that such multilateral oppositions as those concerning height betray the presence in the contrasting segments of different *amounts* of some common element. Suppose, for instance, that in the case of vowel height we construe the element in question as 'openness', and represent it by the symbol 'A', evocative of the vowel /a/, of maximum aperture. Adopting this approach, the height of the (front unrounded) vowels of the Lund system will be represented as follows:

(42) /i/
      /e/   A
      /ɛ/   AA
      /æ/   AAA

The lowering process in question can now be captured by the very simple and, more importantly, transparent rule in (43) (the notation is adapted from Hayes 1990).

(43)   V   V   CV tier
          ⋮
          ⋮
          A   Height tier

The unity of the process is now reflected in the notation, the rule simply increasing by one the number of A elements in the first segment.

3.4.2 Monovalency

Monovalency has recently been making some inroads into the terminal features of standard feature geometry, where they are commonly conceived of as binary, in direct contrast with their unary superordinates.

A good example is provided by the rounding harmony of Khalkha Mongolian, as discussed in Steriade (1987), which we illustrate in (44):

(44) a. tögl-ööd   'having played'   b. xür-eed   'having played'
          tör-öös   'from the state'   ger-ees   'from the house'
          odoo-g-oos 'from now on'   düliig-ees 'from the mute'

In (44a), the gerundive and origin suffixes show up with a rounded vowel (with additional, also harmonic, alternations in ATR-ness),[17] while in

(44b) they have a non-round vowel. Close scrutiny reveals that the suffix vowel is non-round whenever the root vowel also is (*gerees*), or when the root vowel is high, even if it is round (*xüreed*, etc.). Following on from these facts, we formulate the Khalkha rule of rounding harmony as in (45):

(45) Khalkha Mongolian rounding harmony

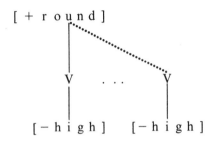

As is apparent in (45), Khalkha rounding harmony is parasitic on [−high]. We could perhaps fuse the two occurrences of [−high], in line with the OCP requirements discussed above. We could also perhaps formulate [+round] as a dependent of [−high], again following our previous discussion. We will however keep to the formulation in (45) in faithfulness to our source (the dots between the two Vs indicate optional non-adjacency).

As the data in (46) below show, /i/ is transparent to rounding harmony, but /u/ is not:

(46) a.   mol-ii-lg-ood   'having flattened'
      b.   oduul-aad   'having sent'

This creates a problem for Steriade's own theory of Contrast-based Underspecification, discussed in Chapter 2, which predicts /u/ as transparent for roundness, since this is the only Khalkha vowel for which roundness is not contrastive, as shown in (47):

(47) Khalkha vowel system

	[+high]		[−high]	
	[−ATR]	[+ATR]	[−ATR]	[+ATR]
[+round]	u	ü	o	ö
[−round]		i	a	e

Still in the context of CU, this will force us to order the redundancy rule providing the roundness value for /u/ before the rounding harmony rule (45) (remember that the Redundancy Rule Ordering Constraint (67) of Chapter 2 is orthogonal to CU), *contra* the common assumption that the ordering of redundancy rules cannnot be subject to language-specific stipulation. Moreover, in order to get the transparency of /i/, we must also assume that the distinctive value [−round] for /i/ has not yet been supplied at the stage where rounding harmony takes place. The resulting ordering is clearly unnatural, since, if anything, non-contrastive values ought to be filled in after contrastive values. If, on the other hand, [round] is a monovalent feature, as Steriade proposes, [−round] will simply be non-existent, and [round] will necessarily be lexical, the opacity of /u/ with respect to rounding harmony thus being automatically accounted for:

(48)

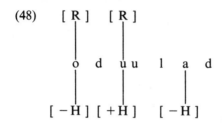

In (48), the adjacency of the two nonhigh vowels is broken by the also round (long) high vowel /u/, and consequently rule (45) will not apply.

The obvious implication of Steriade's strategy is that the set of non-round vowels does not constitute a natural class, and, as such, need not be identifiable by the phonology. To the extent that this implication holds up, the approach will be vindicated. Similar arguments would of course in principle be acceptable for the remaining features.

3.5 HOLISTIC ELEMENTS

The standard identification of the elementary particles of phonological analysis with distinctive features, inherited from the work of Trubetzkoy and Jakobson in the first half of the century, has recently been called into question. The alternative is the adoption as phonological primes of certain basic segments undivided, their combination giving then rise to more complex segments.

3.5.1 The vowel space

The starting point of all such holistic theories is the vowel space, which they divide by means of two axes, the vertical aperture axis, already referred to in connection with Lund Swedish vowel lowering, and the horizontal tonality parameter, which expresses front vs back/rounded polarity:

(49) Vowel space axes

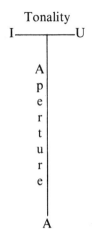

Holistic theories simply elevate the ends of these axes, namely I, U, and A (representing maximal palatality, labiality, and openness, respectively), to the rank of phonological primes. An analogy with colour will be apposite. In colour, red, blue and yellow (or perhaps green) are undecomposable, and thus the primary colours out of which all other colours are made up. Similarly with I, U, A for sound, according to holistic doctrine.

Phonetically, these three primes correspond to the three 'quantal' vowels of Stevens (1972, 1989). Stevens's discovery was the correspondence of each of the three vowels in question with an area where both the acoustic effect of articulatory variation and the perceptual effect of acoustic changes are negligible. By contrast, the boundaries between the three areas are quite sharp, i.e. catastrophic in the technical sense. Such simple facts of physics would accordingly explain the cross-linguistic robustness of the canonical three-vowel system.

3.5.2 Composite segments

The differences between the various holistic approaches hinge on such aspects as the role of recursion and the calculus of element combination. Three perspectives on these matters stand out, which we shall refer to by the labels 'Particle', 'Dependency' and 'Government', given to them by their respective practitioners.[18]

3.5.2.1 *Particle*

In the Particle approach, the simplest of the three, larger vowel inventories are constructed by means of recursive association of the three basic elements ('particles'), as shown in (50):

(50) /i:/:   I   /y/:   IU   /u/:   U   /ɨ/
      /e/:   AI   /ø/:   AIU   /o/:   AU   /ɤ/:   A
      /ɛ/:   AAI   /œ/:   AAIU   /ɔ/:   AAU   /ʌ/:   AA
      /æ/:   AAAI   /ɒ/: AAAU   /ɑ/:   AAA

The manipulation of vowel height will find a very natural and transparent formalisation within this machinery, as we already saw above in connection with Lund Swedish lowering. Let us now consider, as an additional example, such a common sound change as long vowel diphthongisation /e:/ → [ei], /o:/ → [ou], etc. This is accounted for in a maximally simple way in Schane (1984a):

(51) a.   AI   I   b.   AU   U   input
            AI   I   AU   U   output
              ⌒   ⌒

The doubling of the final particle of a complex expression (e.g. 'I I' in 'AI I') represents tenseness, and the space between two occurrences of a particle (ditto) stands for length. The top line in (51) thus corresponds to the vowels /e:/ and /o:/, respectively (NB not /ɛ:/, /ɔ:/, or /e/, /o/). From this configuration we obtain the diphthongal output [ei], [ou] by simple 'desyllabification' of the final element, an operation represented by the underscripting of the caret in the bottom line of (51) (the details of such 'desyllabification' operation are of no particular interest in the present context).

We shall not dwell on the obvious successes of this machinery for vowel description (see Schane 1984a, b for details). We will, however, point out a fundamental inadequacy that seriously undermines it. Thus, as revealed by the analysis of Lund Swedish lowering, there is no principled limit to the depth of recursion. The number of height levels is however universally restricted to five. Such a gross mismatch between the facts and the predictions of the theory thus seriously mars the proposal.

In addition, the high elements I, U are arbitrarily barred from undergoing recursion. Such a stance is indeed necessary, given the fact that the four tonality series can be derived through the combination of single elements (at least on the assumption that central vowels are not phonologically differentiated from back unrounded vowels). The contrast in the recursive power of the two sets of elements is however unprincipled, and thus also militates against this theory.

3.5.2.2 Dependency[19]

A more constrained holistic approach now to be examined imposes dependency relations between the elements which partake in the construction of composite segments. The advantage of this requirement is that it obviates the need for brute force recursion, thus putting a check on this source of overgeneration.

3.5.2.2.1 Basic elements and formalism

From a Dependency perspective, the eight canonical vowels included in (50) above will be represented as in (52) (the central, maximally open vowel /a/ will in turn formally correspond to the simple element A):[20]

(52) /i/:   I   /u/:   U
      /e/:   I ⇒ A   /o/:   I ⇒ A
      /ɛ/:   A ⇔ I   /ɔ/:   A ⇔ U
      /æ/:   A ⇒ I   /ɒ/:   A ⇒ U

The interpretation of these schemata is as follows. For each pair of elements, either one governs the other ('⇒'), or they both govern each other ('⇔'). Clearly, thus, five segments can be generated out of two elements, namely two simple segments, and the three composite segments corresponding to the three possible governing relations, as shown in each of the columns of (52) (in both cases the fifth segment will of course be /a/: A).[21]

This machinery provides a principled formalisation for many phenomena involving height. Consider by way of example the widely attested process of /ai/, /au/ monophthongisation:

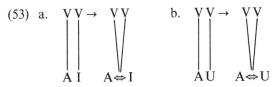

(53) a.   V V →   V V   b.   V V →   V V

           A I   A ⇔ I   A U   A ⇔ U

Simply, the elements A and I or U undergo fusion. These elements are thus mutually governing in the output, whereas in the input they were independent. The converse process, i.e. the diphthongisation of long mid vowels (see (51) above), can correspondingly be construed as element fission:

(54)

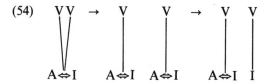

This process is however less straightforward than its monophthongisation counterpart. In particular, in (54) fission must be followed by a simplification of the structure associated with the second vowel. While this procedure obviously works, it clearly includes an element of arbitrariness, since, first, there is no apparent reason why such simplification should be so common, and, second, it is equally far from obvious why it is precisely the A element in the second vowel that must exit, and thus why the output /ɛi/ is preferred over /ɛa/, /iɛ/ or /aɛ/, all of which are likewise obtainable via deletion of one of the input elements.

3.5.2.2.2   Additional dependencies

The operations considered so far clearly fall short of yielding the total inventory of vowels present in the world's languages, and must therefore be augmented. Front rounded vowels are formalised as involving a mutual dependency of the elements I and U,[22] as we show in (55):

(55)   /y/:   I⇔U
       /ø/:   (I⇔U)⇒A
       /œ/:   I⇔U⇔A
       /Œ/:   A⇒(I⇔U)

These structures bring out a further property of the calculus, which can now be seen to allow for the embedding of dependencies. One question which immediately arises is whether such practice effectively opens the door to overgeneration through multiple embedding, along the lines of (I⇔U)⇒(I⇔U), ((I⇔U)⇒(I⇔U))⇒A, etc. The difference between these expressions and those in (55) lies in the presence in the former of multiple occurrences of the same element, in infringement of Anderson and Ewen's (1987: 32) principle that only one element per expression be permitted. While this principle is obviously stipulative, it is not algebraically unreasonable, and it clearly does its job. Unfortunately, however, the principle is relaxed in the case of the elements V and C,[23] defined as involving relative periodicity and periodic energy reduction, respectively (Anderson and Ewen 1987: 151), and which make up the 'phonatory subgesture' of the 'categorial gesture', related to sonority and manner of articulation.

We have just seen that the expression I⇔U (in effect the unordered combination I,U: see note 22 above) is made responsible for the set of front rounded vowels. In principle, there is no obvious reason why the additional dependencies I⇒U and U⇒I should not be generated. Indeed, it may be thought that the three different government relationships between these two elements could be made responsible for the three non-canonical sets of front round, mid, and back unrounded vowels, as represented in (56):

(56) /y/   I⇒U   /ɨ/   I⇔U   /ɯ/   U⇒I

There would still be the problem of differentiating a central unrounded /ɨ/ from its round counterpart /ʉ/, but this matter could perhaps be left to rules of phonetic implementation.

3.5.2.2.3 The centralisation element

The close allegiance of the Dependency approach to phonetics, however, prevents it from adopting the hypothetical formalisation in (56) ('no combination of |i|, |u| and |a| can account for the articulatory properties of central vowels'; 'any representation involving one or more of . . . the components of frontness, roundness and lowness . . . would appear to be unnatural' (Anderson and Ewen 1987: 218)). Instead, an additional element ə is introduced to represent centralisation (i.e. schwa likeness). The range of central vowels will therefore be formalised as in (57):

(57)   ə
     ə⇒A
     ə⇔A
     A⇒ə
     A

The new element ə is also made use of in the formalisation of non-round back vowels, on the grounds that they 'are acoustically similar to central vowels' (Anderson and Ewen 1987: 223). Non-round backness will thus be represented by means of the three elements ə, I and U, with A again brought in to differentiate degrees of height:

(58) /ɯ/:   ə⇔I⇔U
    /ɤ/:   (ə⇔I⇔U)⇒A
    /ʌ/:   ə⇔I⇔U⇔A
    /ɑ/:   A⇒(ə⇔I⇔U)

We must at this point make explicit two problems associated with the ə element. First, ə does not fit phonetically into the universe of the three quantal vowels, thereby weakening the metatheoretical basis for element selection. Second, the increase of the number of elements to four makes available no less than 75 vowel segments, a clear instance of over-generation. It is in fact far from obvious how the unwanted output can be blocked in a principled manner which accords with the general tenets of the Dependency model.

3.5.2.2.4 Labiality vs velarity

Another problem is posed by the element U, which is part of the basic stock. This element merges the phonetic properties of velarity and labiality, and consequently it embodies the prediction that these two traits will inevitably undergo simultaneous spreading and delinking. This prediction is clearly mistaken (cf. e.g. the discussions on Mongolian and Turkish above).

This difficulty is circumvented by Lass's (1984) proposal to replace U with two independent elements W and Ɯ, corresponding to labiality and backness, respectively. This move has however the undesirable consequence of formalising /Ɯ/ as less marked than /u/ (Ɯ vs Ɯ⇔W). While this result fails to disturb Lass ('segments ought to code only their own properties, not statistics of cross-language distribution' (Lass 1984: 279)), most other practitioners have remained faithful to the system in Anderson and Ewen (1987).

3.5.2.2.5 Tongue root activity

Anderson and Ewen also propose the utilisation of the element Ə in the composition of such lax vowels as /ɪ/ and /ʊ/, which they represent as I⇔Ə and U⇔Ə, respectively (or, possibly, I⇒Ə, U⇒Ə). These vowels have been approached as [−ATR] in other frameworks, and the question therefore arises of whether Ə also formalises ATR-ness in the Dependency framework.

In fact, Anderson and Ewen (1987: 243ff.) propose an independent component R to characterise tongue root retraction in pharyngeal consonants, which they argue A is insufficient to define. It would therefore appear that this new element can take over the characterisation of vowel ATR-ness, but Anderson and Ewen suggest that the dominance of the advanced tongue root set in harmonic vowel systems demands the postulation of an additional component α corresponding to the [+ATR] F-element of standard theory.

It is clear that this proposal is problematic on several accounts. Thus, on the one hand, it intensifies the overgeneration problem already mentioned in connection with ə, raising the number of possible vowels to 351.[24] Second, as was already the case with ə, α is a misfit in the world of quantal vowels. Third, the presence of both R and α in the same system constitutes a clear instance of concealed binarism, given the fact that R corresponds to [−ATR], and α to [+ATR]. Finally, the introduction of α creates an obvious indeterminacy in the description of such vowels as /ɪ/, /ʊ/ mentioned above, which goes unaddressed in Anderson and Ewen's treatise.

3.5.2.2.6 Form and content

The Dependency notation is geared to capturing the relative distance of each vowel with respect to the poles defined by the elements. For instance, both physically and phonologically, [e] is closer to [i] than [ɛ] is. This follows in Dependency notation from the fact that in [e] I governs A, while in [ɛ] the two elements are in a relationship of mutual dependency. From this perspective, therefore, the differences between vowels can be conceptualised as differences in the degree of tension exerted by the respective poles, strength of pull being formally defined as direction of government.

Such good purposes notwithstanding, the Dependency approach is in reality phonologically underdetermined. Thus, consider for instance the opposing pair I⇒A, A⇒I. While both dependency relations express a segment somewhere between I and A, the former is construed as being 'more like I', and the latter 'more like A'. What is lacking, however, is a precise specification of the degree of such likeness. Notice that the issue is far from academic. Thus, while in the Dependency literature the expressions I⇒A, I⇔A, and A⇒I are taken to correspond, respectively, to the vowels represented by the IPA symbols [e], [ɛ], and [æ], there is nothing obvious or natural about these correspondences. In particular, there is no a priori way of deriving precisely these symbols (more rigorously, the sounds for which these symbols stand) from the given Dependency representations.

Two strategies come to mind to resolve this problem. First, we could resort to simple brute force (e.g. I = [i], etc.). Alternatively, we could divide the corresponding spaces (namely the phonological space and the phonetic space) and assume a direct mapping across spaces as the null hypothesis. Crucially, however, either solution needs to be system specific, thus presupposing that the learner knows the number of phonological units present in the system prior to the formulation of the corresponding Dependency expressions. Consequently, as in Contrast-based Underspecification, discussed in Chapter 2, the learner must be assumed to have mastered the system before he can define its individual components, a learnability paradox.[25]

3.5.2.2.7 The negative operator

A further difficulty with the Dependency approach, which it shares with other unary frameworks, stems from its claim to (phonological) monovalency across the board. In particular, in order to disprove this claim, all we have to do is to show that the two values of one feature are made use of by phonological operations. One such case is provided by high vowels (/i/, /u/, etc.), which are undefinable as a class in the formalism as it stands (palatalisation of dental stops in Papago, for instance, takes place precisely in the environment of high vowels; see Halle and Clements 1983: 53).

The strategy adopted in Anderson and Ewen (1987) relies on the introduction of a 'negative operator'. Such an operator allows reference to both the absence of a given element and the presence of a given set of elements, as follows (see Anderson and Ewen 1987: 30, 127; NB Anderson and Ewen use braces to enclose material defining a segment; for the vertical bar notation see note 21 above):

(59) a. $\{|\sim a|\}$ a segment whose sole component element is not A
      b. $\{\sim a\}$ a segment which contains at least an element other than A (possibly in addition to A)

Clearly, the class of high (equivalently, non-low) vowels can now be formalised as $\{|\sim a|\}$.

There are two difficulties associated with the negative operator. First, its apparent success is clearly an artifact of the geometry of the quantal vowels, rather than a principled consequence of the theory. Thus, consider the centrality element ə, which we saw is used in the definition of both central and back unrounded vowels. The negation of this element defines a set made up of the canonical vowels (both front and back) *and* the front round vowels. The naturalness of this class is of course highly dubious. On the other hand, it is clear that, given a triangular system such as I, A, U, the exclusion of one term will define the set made up of the other two, namely the unrounded set {I, A}, the high set {I, U}, or the back set {A, U} (note, however, that this last prediction need not be welcome from the Dependency perspective that /a/ is central, rather than back).

The second difficulty concerns the status of the negative operator itself. In particular, it is far from clear how the complementary classes defined by such an operator differ from the complementary classes defined by binary features.

Conscious of this problem, Ewen and van der Hulst (1988) make the proposal that I and U are themselves subordinate to an element Y, which they define as relating to tongue body constriction. The proposed structure is displayed in (60):

(60)

Clearly, the characterisation of high vowels is now unproblematic, since there is no need to resort to the negative operator.

The introduction of this additional element, and its superordinate status with regard to I and U, creates problems of its own, however. Thus, first, Y, like ə and α before, is not quantal, and consequently the presence of this component further calls into question the supposed quantal foundations of the system. Moreover, if (60) is interpreted as embodying a dependency relation, such relation will be qualitatively different from all the previous ones. Specifically, up to this point, dependency has been used as a means of building composite objects out of the basic elements of the theory. Now, however, we would be faced with an intrinsic relation between two basic elements, in a manner akin to the configurations of standard feature geometry. Aware of this difficulty, Ewen and van der Hulst make the suggestion that I and U in (60) may in fact be values (i.e. values of Y), rather than full-fledged elements. Their chief motivation seems to be the inability of these two objects to occur as absolute governors of each other (remember that I⇒U and U⇒I were mentioned above as gaps), which property would remain unaccounted for otherwise. Such a proposal amounts, however, to a partial withdrawal from basic Dependency theory.

3.5.2.3 Government

The most elaborate of the three approaches under scrutiny is the Government approach, and it would not be unreasonable to regard it as a developed version of its two counterparts.

3.5.2.3.1 Phonetic base and phonological contrast

We have seen that one of the weak points of the Dependency framework concerns its translatability to phonetics. This is however not a problem for Government theory (see Kaye *et al.* 1985), where the feature composition of the holistic elements is made explicit along familiar lines (the significance of the emboldened features will become clear directly):

(61)   a. I:
$$\begin{bmatrix} -\text{round} \\ \mathbf{-back} \\ +\text{high} \\ -\text{ATR} \\ -\text{low} \end{bmatrix}$$
b. U:
$$\begin{bmatrix} \mathbf{+round} \\ +\text{back} \\ +\text{high} \\ -\text{ATR} \\ -\text{low} \end{bmatrix}$$
c. A:
$$\begin{bmatrix} -\text{round} \\ +\text{back} \\ \mathbf{-high} \\ -\text{ATR} \\ +\text{low} \end{bmatrix}$$

The theory is still rooted in the three quantal vowels I, A, U. Only these three elements are open to manipulation by the phonology, which is denied access to the internal features, provided only as a phonetic interpretation module. From this perspective, therefore, Government theory meets the requirement of phonetic answerability, while still remaining holistic.

Phonological contrast is effectively carried by the emboldened F-elements. As can be seen, the three matrices in (61) are identical except with respect to the emboldened features (the value of [low] is directly related to, and assumed to be derived from, the value of [high], which it complements). For reasons which will become better understood as we proceed, we shall construe and refer to such emboldened features as 'marked' (the term used in the Government literature is 'hot feature').

3.5.2.3.2 Combinatory calculus

We need of course to increase the number of segments generated. As in previous holistic approaches, this is done through the combination of the basic elements.

The Government calculus also represents an obvious improvement over its two counterparts. Combined elements are required to stand in a dependency relationship, with one element as the head or governor, and the other as the complement or dependent. The product of the combination (known as 'fusion' in Government jargon) is a matrix identical to that of its governor except for the marked feature of the dependent, which is carried over to the product. We illustrate in (62) (by a convention of dubious felicity, the governor *follows* the dependent in the graphic sequence; the dot indicates the combination operation, or 'fusion'):

(62)   a.   I   A   I   [ɛ]

$$\text{A} \quad \begin{bmatrix} -\text{round} \\ +\text{back} \\ \mathbf{-high} \\ -\text{ATR} \\ +\text{low} \end{bmatrix} \quad \cdot \quad \begin{bmatrix} -\text{round} \\ \mathbf{-back} \\ +\text{high} \\ -\text{ATR} \\ -\text{low} \end{bmatrix} \quad = \quad \begin{bmatrix} -\text{round} \\ -\text{back} \\ -\text{high} \\ -\text{ATR} \\ -\text{low} \end{bmatrix}$$

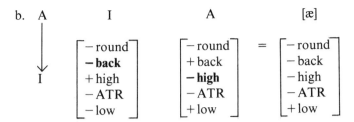

The dependency relations are displayed in a familiar format on the left. Specifically, in (62a) I governs A, and in (62b) A governs I. Correspondingly, the product matrix in (62a) equals the matrix of the head I in all but the value for [high], taken from the dependent A on account of its markedness. Likewise, in (62b) the values of the governor A are carried over to the product, with the exception of the value for [back], which is marked in the dependent I, and therefore passed on to the product matrix. The identification of the phonetic values of the two product matrices with [ɛ] and [æ], respectively, follows standard practice.

As noted, the obvious advantage of this procedure over its Dependency counterpart is that it spells out exactly what the output of each process will be, and how it is arrived at, in terms of independently defined, familiar features. In addition, the requirement of unidirectional government narrows down the output, thus going some way towards meeting the charge of overgeneration levelled against Dependency. Further constraining follows from the principles of 'charm', as will be seen below.

The difficulties faced by the Dependency account in blocking two of the operations involving the elements I, U are also circumvented by the Government calculus, where the desired result is automatic. In particular, the direction of dependency will be immaterial in this case, since, as transpires from the representations of I and U in (61), these elements differ only in the values of two features, namely [back] and [high], and so these and only these two features will appear with their marked values in the product of these two elements. By contrast, the combination of either I or U with A must take account of the direction of dependency, owing to the divergent value of [low] in A. In particular, while this value is initially derived from the value of [high], as noted, and is thus originally non-contrastive, it is carried over from the governor to the product matrix, where it becomes contrastive. This can be seen in (62), where a different product is obtained in (62a) and (62b), contingent on the status of A as a governor or a dependent.

3.5.2.3.3 Completing the matrix inventory

We pointed out above that the contrastive load of the basic matrices is carried by the marked feature, in the obvious way. Given the markedness characterisations in (61) above, the matrix in (63) will therefore be markedness-free:

(63)
$$\begin{bmatrix} - \text{round} \\ + \text{back} \\ + \text{high} \\ - \text{ATR} \\ - \text{low} \end{bmatrix}$$

Phonetically, this matrix corresponds to the high back non-round lax vowel [ɪ]. In Government terms, this vowel is consequently considered default (and referred to as the 'cold' vowel, since it completely lacks 'hot' features). As is now apparent, each of the basic elements in (61) differs from the unspecified matrix in (63) by exactly one value, notated here as emboldening. As already mentioned, [low] is considered non-contrastive, its value simply complementing the value of [high]. On the other hand, the fifth feature, [ATR], can be subject to marking:

(64)
$$\begin{bmatrix} - \text{round} \\ + \text{back} \\ + \text{high} \\ \mathbf{+ ATR} \\ - \text{low} \end{bmatrix}$$

The matrix in (64) defines the tense counterpart of [ɪ], i.e. [ɯ]. This completes the inventory of the basic elements of Government theory, namely I, U, A, ɪ, and ɯ (confusingly, ɯ is represented as ɪ, and ɪ as v, in Government notation). The advantage of this set over its Dependency counterpart is that its non-quantal section is derived by the logic of the theory itself. Consequently, it is not open to the charge of arbitrariness that we levelled against the Dependency elements ə and α (and Y, if applicable).

3.5.2.3.4 Some problems

Some obvious problems do however accrue to the Government system. First, as pointed out by Coleman (1990a, b), the set of basic elements (i.e.

minimally marked segments) is truly bizarre, as it includes four high vowels, of which three are back, two of them non-round. Clearly, this selection is significantly at odds with the findings of markedness research, and is thus in need of explicit empirical justification.[26]

The second difficulty concerns the default status of [ɨ], implicit in the approach. Thus, compare Government theory with Radical Under-specification, examined in Chapter 2. In RU, markedness is construed as partly universal (as encoded in the Default rules) and partly language-specific, since the underspecified segment, which determines the lexical values of features, is selected on language-particular grounds. In Government, by contrast, we are seeing that markedness is established on a purely universal basis, [ɨ] being therefore predicted to behave as default across the board. This prediction grossly misfires, since, as we saw in Chapter 2, languages vary considerably in their choice of default vowel. Faced with this fact, we could try to appeal to language differences in phonetic implementation, and thus interpret the attested variance as phonetic. It is however far from clear how, for instance, a default vowel [a] could be 'phonetically' derived from the matrix in (63), which corresponds to [ɨ] (remember that we are holding phonetic accountability as one of the virtues of Government theory).[27]

A third difficulty is associated with the definition of natural classes, as follows from the claim that only elements (NB *not* their component features) are accessible to the phonology. A problematic case concerns the high vowels, which (ironically, given their frequency in the basic set) are not definable as a class by the Government procedure (cf. e.g. (61) above). The existence of phonological processes making direct reference to this class thus poses a formidable challenge to Government theory. One could of course think up several strategies to eschew this predicament. For instance, one could deny that there are any such processes making reference to [+high]. If substantiated, this claim would obviously circumvent the problem. Another strategy would be to allow for a negative operator along the lines of Anderson and Ewen (1987). Such a device came under serious criticism in the previous subsection, and the failure of Government theorists to fall back on it is therefore to their credit. In the absence of a credible solution, however, the problem of high vowels (or any other such natural classes escaping the net of Government notation) stands as a substantial cloud on the Government horizon.

3.5.2.3.5 Segmental and systemic markedness: charm

As we are by now familiar, the set of Government basic elements contains the lax (i.e. [-ATR]) objects I, U. Obviously, however, the basic universal vowel triangle is made up of the [+ATR] vowels [i] and [u], alongside [a]. The prediction of the Government system is instead [ɪ], [ʊ], [a]. This again seems bizarre, if not outright erroneous.

In order to solve this puzzle, Kaye *et al.* (1985) draw a distinction between segmental and systemic markedness. Thus, from the point of view of the segment, they claim that [ɪ] and [ʊ] are indeed less marked than [i] and [u], since the former are primes, while the latter require fusion with the ATR element ɯ. Moreover, in languages with ATR harmony, it is precisely the ATR vowels that are marked (Archangeli and Pulleyblank's analysis of Yoruba ATR harmony as [−ATR] spread examined in Chapter 2 stands in the way of this interpretation). All this would thus suggest that the markedness hierarchy implicit in Government notation is correct.

Segmental unmarkedness is however no guarantee of systemic unmarkedness. In particular, in the absence of an ATR contrast, [+ATR] non-low vowels are vastly preferred, as noted. In order to derive this state of affairs, Kaye *et al.* take two complementary steps. First, they constrain the combinatory potential of the primes by means of a property they dub 'charm' (positive charm being intuitively related to 'voweliness', in turn characterised by the activation of a resonating cavity – oral for A and pharyngeal for ɯ),[28] which can be construed as a coarse sonority ranking (sonority will be discussed in detail in Chapter 4). Specifically, some elements will have positive charm, notated as a superscript '+', others will have negative charm (superscripted '−'), and a third category will be charmless ('º').[29] In the case of vowel elements, the charm assignments will be as follows:

$$(65) \qquad A^+ \qquad I^\circ$$
$$\qquad\qquad\quad \text{ɯ}^+ \qquad U^\circ$$
$$\qquad\qquad\qquad\qquad\quad I^\circ$$

The phonological significance of charm is that, as with magnetic and electric polarity, like charm repels, and unlike charm attracts. The obvious consequence of this for vowel elements is that the combination of A and ɯ will be barred, thus accounting for the apparent anomaly that [−ATR] [a] coexists with [+ATR] [i] and [u] in the canonical vowel system (charm will be further discussed in 4.6.3 in Chapter 4).

The [+ATR] specification of these two vowels is still in need of justification, in the face of its marked status. Kaye *et al.* (1985: 314) propose to derive their favoured status in simple vowel systems from the following universal principle, which we have brought into line with current Government theory (see note 29 above):

(66) Principle of charm markedness

> The presence of a segment with non-positive charm in a vowel system implies the presence of its positively charmed counterpart.

The provision of the ATR element Ш to the elements I, U to yield the desired segments [i], [u] in canonical vowel systems is interpreted as an automatic consequence of this principle.

While the procedure obviously works, two shortcomings must be noted. First, the principle in (66) is clearly stipulative. In particular, it does not fall out of the Government formalism, contrary to the stated aim of this and other holistic theories of phonological primes of doing away with the brute force element they attribute to standard feature theory. Second, it incurs the learnability paradox which we observed above in connection with the Particle and Dependency approaches, where we noted that the phonetic representation of the elements and operations is system-specific. In the case of principle (66), it makes the formal specification of the segments in question contingent on the characteristics of the system, which are in turn determined by the formal specification of its elements.

The introduction of charm further reduces the inventory space of composite elements, given the noted incompatibility of A and Ш (both in isolation and in complex expressions). This again places Government theory in a good stead relative to its rivals, for which we saw overgeneration to be a serious problem. Indeed, as emphasised by Kaye (1990a), Government theory is explicitly designed to avoid excessive output. The results of the computer quest reported in Coleman (1990a) suggest however that, as well as overgenerating in some areas, the Government machinery may undergenerate in others (in particular at the level of phonetic interpretation).

3.5.3 Features vs elements

We must at this point submit to specific scrutiny the claim made by holistic theories in general of the unary valency of their primes. This claim is of course rooted in the fact that, in these models, composite elements are built by accumulation of simple elements, rather than by changes in the polarity value of a fixed set of parameters, as in distinctive feature theory. We will in our discussion avail ourselves of the Government machinery, which, as mentioned above, represents the most advanced articulation of the holistic view, and this crucially includes the provision of a phonetic interface.

3.5.3.1 Government and Radical Underspecification

A comparison of Government with Radical Underspecification will be revealing. As will be remembered, in RU only one value of each feature is allowed in lexical representation. In particular, values which are predictable, either from the (language-particular) identity of the unspecified segment or from universal markedness rules, are omitted from the lexicon. Now, appearances notwithstanding, this is not a thousand miles away from the Government system. Thus, suppose we reformalise the Government basic elements as simply their marked features, as in (67):

(67) I: [−back]
      U: [+round]
      A: [−high]
      Ɯ: [+ATR]

The claim that elements, rather than features, are manipulated by the phonology can now be construed as a prohibition against the provision of the complementary values by redundancy rules prior to completion of the derivation. In this, therefore, the Government approach starkly contrasts with RU, where unmarked values must be supplied at various derivational stages, as follows from such universal ordering principles as the Redundancy Rule Ordering Constraint and the Elsewhere Condition. From this perspective, Government can be viewed as an extreme form of RU.

The maximally unmarked vowel [ɨ] is not included in (67), and yet this vowel fulfils a critical function in the system. Clearly, however, such a vowel corresponds to the empty vowel of RU, i.e. to the vowel with no lexical values. As in RU, therefore, this segment can be formalised as completely unspecified.

The next question concerns the mechanics of the mapping from the underlying underspecified representations onto their fully specified phonetic counterparts. As in standard redundancy theories, we can assume that such a mapping is effected by a set of structure-building rules providing the complements of the lexical values, as follows:

(68) [ ] →   [+back]
      [ ] →   [−round]
      [ ] →   [+high]
      [ ] →   [−ATR]

Besides their ordering outside the phonology proper, the rules in (68) differ from their RU analogues (but not from their equivalents in Kiparsky's version of underspecification, or in *SPE*'s markedness theory) in their universality. Thus, while RU allows for language-specific Complement and Learnt rules, Government theory aligns itself with universal markedness, therefore making itself liable to similar criticism (see Chapter 2).

The feature [low] is idiosyncratic in not being determined by Complement rule, unlike the rest of the features in (68). Instead, its value is a function of the value for [high], as already mentioned:

(69) $[\alpha \text{ high}] \rightarrow [-\alpha \text{ low}]$

A problem for our reinterpretation of the Government machinery now arises in composite segments (in our terms, segments containing more than one lexical feature), since, as we know, in standard Government theory the value of the redundant features in these segments is determined by the head element, rather than by the dependent. Importantly, however, such a dependency relationship only encodes the pre-eminence of the redundant values of the head (in particular, it does not encode differences in access to the skeleton, as it does in Mester's (1988) approach examined above). Now, the Government basic elements share in fact their redundant F-elements, with the noted exception of [low]. This provides the clue to the resolution of the outstanding problem, since it reveals that [low] does function as an underlying distinctive feature, contrary to the claims of standard Government theory. Consequently, [−low] must be included into the inventory of basic elements. The difference between, e.g. /ε/ and /æ/ will now be that the former element will be lexically [−low], but not so the latter, which will be redundantly assigned [+low] by rule (69) above.

3.5.3.2 Bivalency

Let us now address the issue of valency. In the light of our reinterpretation of elements, we can see that features are monovalent in the lexicon in the way they are monovalent in other underspecification theories examined in Chapter 2. They are not however unary at the phonetic level, where a conventional binary interpretation is provided. The difference between Government and standard underspecification theories lies therefore in the states mediating between the lexical and the phonetic levels: as already mentioned, features act as monovalent throughout the whole derivation in the Government system, but not necessarily so in the standard redundancy theories. This is of course a very important difference between the two systems, and one which could indeed have significant empirical consequences. Its bearings on monovalency are however far from obvious.

Curiously, under some circumstances Government features seem to be allowed to play a bivalent role also in the phonology. Thus, while, in the unmarked situation, features occupy their own autosegmental plane, or 'line', in Government parlance,[30] the possibility exists of plane merger (dubbed 'line fusion' in Kaye *et al.* 1985). The empirical consequences of this merger concern blocking and OCP effects (plane geometry is the object of specific attention in 5.6.3 below).

From our present perspective, plane merger can be interpreted as follows. Let us assume the canonical merging of the I and U planes. The desired implication is that these elements cannot combine, i.e. that the language in question lacks front rounded vowels. This is equivalent to saying that [round] is not contrastive in this system. If so, the opposition between /i/ and /u/ must be implemented in some other way. Total underspecification for one of these vowels will not do, since this would yield the unmarked segment /ɨ/ (the 'cold' vowel). Therefore, it appears that the opposition in question must be formalised by means of a lexical contrast [− back] vs [+ back], a clear instance of binarism. Once the two opposing values of [back] are allowed in the phonology, the noted blocking and OCP effects will follow automatically, in the obvious way.

3.6 CONCLUSION

There seems to be broad agreement on the need for a partial revision of the *SPE* feature inventory, carried out in different ways and to different degrees by different authors. There is also practical consensus on the existence of dependencies between features, although the details of these dependencies remain subject to wide discrepancy. The adoption of monovalent elements would meet with approval in all quarters, as witness the independently pursued lines of research of under-specification theory and holistic prime theory. The empirical feasibility of this desirable goal is however at present still far from obvious.

4 The sonority fabric

4.1 THE NEED FOR THE SYLLABLE

4.1.1 Syllables in *SPE*

As explained in Chapter 1, *SPE* representations exclusively consist of strings of distinctive feature matrices. Such matrices define segments or boundaries, the latter derived directly from the (morpho)syntax. No further phonological structure, such as that embodied in syllables or in the higher prosodic units to be examined in this and the next chapter, was countenanced by Chomsky and Halle.

The list of distinctive features first proposed in *SPE* includes [vocalic]. Sounds marked as [+vocalic] are said to be 'produced with an *oral cavity in which the most radical constriction does not exceed that found in the high vowels [i] and [u] and with vocal cords that are positioned so as to allow spontaneous voicing' (*SPE*: 302).[1] Further on in the book, however, this feature is abandoned in favour of [syllabic], on the basis of the oscillating behaviour of French high vocoids with regard to the triggering of schwa and consonant deletion (see *SPE*: 353ff. and Milner 1967 for discussion of the French case and its implications for feature theory). The new feature [syllabic] is taken to 'characterize all segments constituting a syllabic peak' (*SPE*: 354). In a nutshell, consonants and lexical glides will be [−syllabic], while vowels and derived glides will be underlyingly [+syllabic], the relevant data thus being satisfactorily accounted for.

The introduction of the feature [syllabic] is obviously paradoxical in a framework which does not accommodate syllables. In particular, the definition of [+syllabic] by reference to syllable peakness implies the formal reality of syllables, in the absence of which there clearly can be no syllable peaks, and [syllabic] cannot be defined.

The *SPE* omission of syllables is moreover truly puzzling from both a traditional and a current perspective. As will become obvious directly,

Chomsky and Halle's drive for formal economy ironically resulted in an increase in complexity in the rule apparatus, and in a concomitant decrease in rule transparency. In fact, as this and the following chapter will make abundantly clear, phonological atoms are glued together by a prosodic fabric which is abstract to the extent that it cannot be heard directly. The postulation of abstract structure in order to account for a body of otherwise unconnected empirical facts is of course the stock-in-trade of linguistics, and needs no special justification here.

4.1.2 Evidence for syllables

The main argument for the postulation of syllables hinges on the recurrence of the context $\begin{Bmatrix} C \\ \# \end{Bmatrix}$ in rules. Thus, for instance, many English dialects (RP among them) render *l*s velar (through a simultaneous raising of the back of the tongue) under certain conditions, as attested by the contrast between *mole* or *moulding*, where the *l* is velar, and *molar*, with a plain *l*. The common denominator for the velarisation context is thus the disjunction C or #, as specified in (1):

$$(1)\quad [+\text{lateral}] \rightarrow \begin{bmatrix} +\text{high} \\ +\text{back} \end{bmatrix} / \_\_\_ \begin{Bmatrix} C \\ \# \end{Bmatrix}$$

It has been observed since the early 1970s that this context reappears in rule after rule in languages of the most variegated typology (see Hooper 1972, Vennemann 1972, and Kahn 1976 for three influential studies). Thus, consider the following Turkish alternations (Clements and Keyser 1983: 59):

(2)		acc.	nom.	abl.	
	a.	hiss + i	his	his + ten	'feeling'
		hakk + i	hak	hak + tan	'right'
		zamm + i	zam	zam + dan	'price increase'
	b.	devr + i	devir	devir + den	'transfer'
		koyn + u	koyun	koyun + dan	'bosom'
		karn + i	karin	karin + dan	'abdomen'
	c.	zama:n + i	zaman	zaman + dan	'time'
		i:ka:z + i	i:kaz	i:kaz + dan	'warning'
		ispa:t + i	ispat	ispat + tan	'proof'
	d.	hara:b + i	harap	harap + tan	'ruined'

| ahmed + i | ahmet | ahmet + ten | Ahmed |
| reng + i | renk | renk + ten | 'colour' |

The following processes are exemplified: degemination (2a), epenthesis (2b), vowel shortening (2c), and obstruent final devoicing (2d). Examination of the conditions under which these disparate processes occur invariably leads to the environment in (3):

(3) /___ $\left\{\begin{matrix} C \\ \# \end{matrix}\right\}$

Clearly, the recurrence of this environment in what otherwise appear to be unrelated phenomena cannot be merely attributed to chance.

The adoption of syllables provides the desired answer to this challenge. Thus, suppose that we enrich phonological representation with syllable boundaries. The syllabification of some of the words we have been discussing is given in (4) (the dollar sign was common in the early generative literature on the subject):

(4) mol(e)
    $moul$ding$
    molar$
    $reng$
    $reng$ten$
    rengi$

We must reserve the justification for these particular parsings for further below, trusting at this point that they do not conflict with the reader's intuitions in any significant way. Assuming thus the structures in (4), the context for all the rules in question can now be simplified to (5):

(5) ___ $

Obviously, the advantage of (5) over (3) goes beyond simplicity and involves explanation.

4.1.3 Autosegmental syllables

The linear representation of syllables was soon abandoned for one of autosegmental flavour, along the lines of (6):

(6)   σ
       /|\
      a b c

We shall present two arguments in favour of (6). First, consider again *l* velarisation in *mole* and *moulding*, which we could now formalise as in (7):

(7) $[+ \text{lateral}] \rightarrow \begin{bmatrix} + \text{high} \\ + \text{back} \end{bmatrix} /\underline{\quad}\$$

In *mould*, however, *l* does not immediately precede the syllable boundary, but velarisation still takes place. With the autosegmental formalism, the syllabic conditioning becomes quite transparent:

(8)

In (8), *l* is shown to be tautosyllabic with V, and to follow it in the linear sequence of melodies, as required by velarisation.

The second argument for the autosegmental formalisation of syllables, brought to the fore by Kahn (1976), concerns the phenomenon of ambisyllabicity. Thus, English *t* is flapped in practically all American dialects in words like *city*, *sitting*, or *sitter*, but not in *sister*, *settee*, or *sit*.[2] The principal (though not the sole) criterion for flapping is, according to Kahn, the ambisyllabicity of the *t* in *city*, etc.:

(9)

In *settee*, by contrast, the *t* is only assigned to the second syllable:

(10)

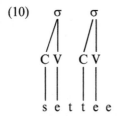

Similarly for *sister*, where the *s*, rather than the *t*, enjoys ambisyllabic status:

(11)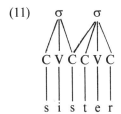

In *sit*, of course, the possibility of syllable sharing simply does not arise.

Ambisyllabicity is clearly incompatible with the boundary-inspired approach to syllables we have been examining. An also unilinear alternative involves the use of improper bracketing ([ₛci[ₛt]ᵢy]ⱼ, etc.; see Anderson and Jones 1974). As pointed out by Kahn, however, improper bracketing allows for multiple ambisyllabicity (e.g. [ₛsi[ₛst]ᵢer]ⱼ). Kahn contends that such a parsing runs counter to both speakers' intuitions and to phonological evidence, and consequently it must be disallowed. This result follows automatically if an autosegmental representation is adopted:

(12) *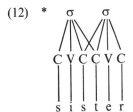

As can readily be seen, multiple ambisyllabicity would now involve the crossing of lines.

While the device of ambisyllabicity is not uncontroversial, the autosegmental construal of syllables runs through practically all the recent literature. A non-autosegmental conception of the syllable is however also possible, as will be seen below.

4.2 THE TIMING TIER

4.2.1 Problems with CV representations

Having established the phonological reality of syllables, we must now begin the detailed examination of their structure, starting off with the skeleton, the baseline of syllabic structure.

In Chapter 1 we pointed out the timing function of the skeleton, and in Chapter 3 the formal independence of this function was sanctioned with the introduction of a class node 'root' to express phonemic unity. Such a development makes questionable the formalisation of the skeleton by the symbols V and C, a shorthand for plus and minus [syllabic], respectively.[3]

Arguments against the inclusion of such information in the skeleton indeed exist. We pointed out in Chapter 1 that in Clements and Keyser's (1983) CV model it is not essential for vowels to associate with Vs, and for consonants with Cs. In particular, we analysed the (compensatory) lengthening of the Kinyarwanda word [kuːⁿgana] (from /kungana/) as involving the dissociation of /n/ from its lexical C slot and the subsequent association to this slot of the vowel /u/, already linked to a V in lexical representation. This clearly conflicts with the interpretation of C slots as [−syllabic].

In addition, Levin (1983) points out that the CV skeleton potentially includes an unwarranted amount of redundancy. In order to show how this is so, she traces the origin of this formal device back to McCarthy's early descriptions of Semitic, Arabic in particular (see McCarthy 1979, 1981). Now, as was mentioned in Chapter 1, in this type of language the vowels and consonants that make up a word are awarded separate lexical entries on account of their semantic independence. On composing the word, vowels and consonants are brought together with the help of a template made up of a sequence of CV slots. The differentiation between C and V slots thus fulfils the function of guiding the consonantal and vocalic melodies to their rightful skeletal association. However, in languages with non-templatic morphology (the majority of the world's languages), none of this machinery is necessary. In particular, in these languages there is no reason not to have the skeleton already associated to the melody in lexical representation (or to project it from the lexical melody, for greater economy). Clearly, thus, the presence of the [syllabic] specification implicit in the CV formalism serves no purpose in these cases. Moreover, as will be seen below, the availability of syllable structure obviates the need for CV information in non-concatenative morphology as well.

4.2.2 Skeletal slots as empty positions

Facts such as these led Levin (1983, 1985) to streamline the skeleton down to its timing function by giving all skeletal slots a uniform representation (a similar formalisation is advocated in Kaye and Lowenstamm 1986, albeit in the context of a different conception of the syllable). Thus, for the Kinyarwanda data mentioned above, the following structure will now be postulated:

(13)

As can be seen, the skeletal elements have been stripped of all intrinsic content and reduced to the role of time place-holders. On this representation, changes in association can take place without incurring feature clash:

(14)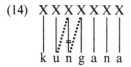

The formalisation of skeletal slots as pure timing elements raises an obvious question with regard to Semitic-type templates, since, within this novel conception, the distinction between slots to be associated to vowel melodies and slots to be linked to consonantal melodies is no longer carried by the skeleton. Clearly, therefore, some structural enrichment will be in order. Levin's (1985) proposal relies on the provision of rudimentary syllabic structure to the skeletally impoverished templates. By making reference to this structure, the association rules will implement the desired bifurcation between vocalic and consonantal association. Full understanding of this proposal presupposes familiarity with the internal structure of the syllable, a matter to which we turn next.

4.3 SYLLABLE STRUCTURE

4.3.1 Syllable typology

As a backdrop to our investigation, we shall first briefly survey the basic syllable types available cross-linguistically (see Clements and Keyser 1983).

The most basic syllable is unanimously recognised to be made up of a consonant followed by a vowel (cf. Chomsky and Halle's comment that 'reduced to the most rudimentary terms, the behavior of the vocal tract in speech can be described as an alternation of closing and opening' (*SPE*: 301)). The fundamental syllable can thus be represented as in (15) (the lower case letters c and v will be used hereafter as an informal representation of consonant and vowel melodies, respectively):

(15) Basic syllable

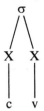

A language whose syllable inventory is limited to (15) is reportedly Senufo (Clements and Keyser 1983: 29). More commonly, however, the pool of syllables is augmented by the action on (15) of one of two elementary operations, involving the deletion of the prevocalic consonant or the addition of a consonant after the vowel, respectively. The resulting structures are given in (16):

(16) a.   b.

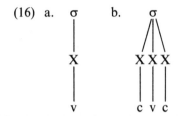

If both options are taken, the result will be as in (17):

(17)

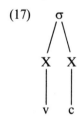

As Clements and Keyser point out, these procedures implicitly contain the prediction that the presence of the more complex types in any one language implies the presence of their simpler counterparts.

Syllable structures of greater complexity are of course also attested cross-linguistically. Aware of this fact, Clements and Keyser allow for the expansion of the core inventory on a language-particular basis, as follows:

(18) Expanded syllable inventory

$C^n V^m C^p$

for *n, m, p* to be fixed language-specifically

A language like English (with forms like *spray* or *twelfths*) must clearly avail itself of the formula in (18) in order to build its syllables.

4.3.2 Subsyllabic constituents

We can now proceed to the examination of the internal composition of syllables.

So far in the exposition, no internal structure has been postulated, in line with the theories of Kahn (1976) and Clements and Keyser (1983). In traditional accounts of the syllable, however, a structure essentially as in (19) is suggested (cf. e.g. Trubetzkoy 1939, Pike and Pike 1947, Kuryłowicz 1948, Hockett 1955, Haugen 1956):

(19)

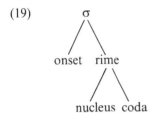

The syllabic parsing of *pen* will accordingly be as in (20):

(20)

Evidence for such constituency will now be presented, focusing on the onset–rime divide.

We have already assigned an autosegmental interpretation to the strikingly common environment $\left\{ {C \atop \#} \right\}$. Clearly, however, σ daughterhood is not a sufficient defining criterion, for the simple reason that, in the flat representations of syllables we have been using up to this point, the onset consonants are likewise σ daughters. The solution we adopted in (8) above involved the incorporation in the rule's structural description of the requirement of right adjacency to the nucleus for the segment under focus.

Now, such a requirement is clearly too strong. For instance, German obstruent devoicing (with similar effects to the Turkish one exemplified in (2d) above) takes place in *Bun*[t] 'federation' (cf. *Bunde* 'federations'), alongside *Ta*[k] 'day' (cf. *Tage* 'days'). Characteristically, the distance between the nucleus and the focused segment is not significant: all that matters is that the segment be part of the rime rather than the onset. The simplest expression of this condition is as in (21):

(21)

This formulation would not be possible in the absence of a constituent 'rime'.

The English language game 'Pig Latin', discussed in *SPE* (pp. 342–3), is mentioned by Steriade (1982) as contributing evidence for an 'onset' constituent. In this ludling, a word like *Latin* comes out as *atinl*[eɪ], and *day* as *ayd*[eɪ]. The *SPE* rule accounting for the change is as in (22):

(22)   ##C$_o$VX## → ##VXC$_o$[eɪ]##

The inclusion of a C$_o$ variable makes the rule unwarrantedly unconstrained, however. In particular, the generalisation is missed that the movement affects precisely the material in the onset. Indeed, the C$_o$ formalisation implies that *any* string of consonants could be similarly moved, regardless of syllabic (sub)constituency, as reflected in rule (23), which differs minimally from (22):

(23)   ##XC$_o$VX## → ##XVXC$_o$[eɪ]##

Here, C$_o$ will include all the consonants from the immediately preceding rime as well as from the onset. On the assumption that such rules do not exist, an onset-based formalisation of Pig Latin is consequently to be preferred.

Besides its role in rule formulation, the proposed internal structure of the syllable is supported by the fact that lexical cooccurrence restrictions between segments typically affect only subconstituent mates. Thus, in English,[4] as in many other languages, onsets can be maximally bisegmental (apparent trisegmental onsets are however possible if the first segment is *s*; we shall put aside all *s* + consonant combinations, for reasons which will be explained in 4.5 below). In bisegmental English onsets, there appear to be no constraints on the identity of the first segment, while the second segment must necessarily be drawn from the set of liquids and glides. Crucially, the source of this restriction is the preceding onset segment, and not the vowel that follows, as attested by the fact that in monosegmental onsets the choice of consonant is practically unrestricted, but this could obviously not be so if the vowel exerted an influence. The conclusion to draw is that there are strong cooccurrence restrictions within the onset, but none (or only negligible ones) between the nucleus vowel and the onset consonants. This situation is nicely encapsulated in the formal separation of the onset from the rime, but would be cumbersome to express otherwise.

Similar arguments support the rime constituent. Consider, for instance, the phenomenon of vowel shortening in such alternants as *abstention* (cf. *abstain*), *abundant* (vs *abound*), *deceptive* (vs *deceive*), and so on. This change can be interpreted as the consequence of a preference for a rime length of two segments (the exceptions almost inevitably involving coronals and/or occurring on the word edge). Obviously, here too, the size of the onset is irrelevant (cf. e.g. *scribe* ~ *scripture*, with a similar alternation after a complex onset, and *eight, rate, trait, straight*, where there is no change in the vowel to balance out the onset increments).

The evidence for the subsyllabic constituents in (19) above is therefore quite robust. Some weaker correlations may also be observed across constituents, namely across the onset and the nucleus, or even across the onset and the coda. This has indeed provided the main ammunition for the defence of a structurally flat syllable, along the lines of (6) above (see e.g. Kahn 1976, Clements and Keyser 1983, Davis 1984, 1985). While a final decision on this matter is beyond the scope of the present work, we must register the fact that the proponents of the flat syllable find themselves in a clear minority. This must not be taken to imply that the structure in (19) has received unanimous approval elsewhere, since there are important differences between authors with regard both to the number of constituents they allow for and to the explicit labelling of nodes.

4.4 SYLLABIFICATION PROCEDURES

Clearly, the distribution of segments between syllables and between subsyllabic constituents, is far from arbitrary. As we shall now see, there are both universal principles and language-specific constraints guiding the syllabification procedure.

The common assumption is indeed that lexical representations are unsyllabified. Two construals of the syllabification procedure are in existence, namely as a set of rules or as a well-formedness template. For each of these, two interpretations are also available. Thus, rule-based syllabification is compatible both with persistent rules of the kind examined in Chapter 2 in connection with lexical regularities, and with rules similar to ordinary phonological rules, notably capable of extrinsic ordering. If, on the other hand, syllabification involves template matching, the template positions can be interpreted as mandatory or optional.

4.4.1 Syllabification by rule

4.4.1.1 Procedure

Syllabification by rule will be unproblematic for a sequence (c)v(c), on the working assumption that the vowel corresponds to the syllable nucleus (see below for further refinement). In particular, the consonant(s) preceding the vowel will be gathered in the onset, and the consonant(s) following it in the coda:

(24) a. Onset formation b. Coda formation

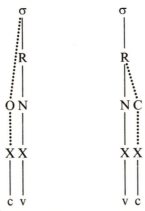

In the case of complex onsets or codas (i.e. onsets or codas with more than one consonant) the rules in (24) will simply apply in an unbounded mode.

Intervocalic consonants can in principle be parsed in the coda of the first syllable or in the onset of the second. As will be remembered, however, the string cv corresponds to the least marked syllable, and consequently onset formation must be given priority over coda formation.[5]

Different formal devices have been proposed to capture such onset preponderance, prominent among them the 'CV rule' (Steriade 1982) and the 'Maximal Onset Principle' (Selkirk 1982: 359). Cutting through terminological variation, we shall recast these principles as in (25) and (26), respectively:

(25) Minimal Onset Satisfaction Principle
Onsetless syllables are disallowed (in the presence of suitable melodic material).

(26) Maximal Onset Realisation Parameter
Onset construction must be completed prior to coda formation.

The Minimal Onset Satisfaction (MOS) Principle in (25) is assumed to be universal (modulo such languages as mentioned in note 5 above), while the Maximal Onset Realisation (MOR) Parameter obviously needs language-specific setting. The unmarked setting is however positive, in line with the cross-linguistic tendency to maximise onsets.

Notice that the MOS Principle amounts to the bounded incarnation of the onset formation rule (24a) above. For completeness, Steriade's formalisation of this rule is now provided (Steriade's skeletal CV notation is of course readily translatable into X-slot formalism):

(27) Steriade's CV Rule

Steriade (1984) proposes that this rule be universally applied iteratively from left to right.[6]

4.4.1.2 *Justification*

An obvious advantage of rule-based over template-based syllabification resides in the possibility it affords of interspersing ordinary phonological rules between the rules responsible for syllable formation. A situation of this type is claimed by Steriade (1982) to be in existence in ancient Attic Greek.

Of direct relevance to the argument is the assimilation rule in (28) (Steriade's formulation has been slightly modified to bring it into line with the present exposition):

(28) Labial Nasalisation

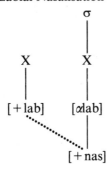

Crucially for our present purposes, the two segments engaged in the rule are not included in the same syllable (i.e. they are heterosyllabic).

Compare now the two sets of forms in (29):

(29) a. semnos   'venerable'   (/seb-nos/; cf. sebomai 'to worship')
         eremnos   'murky'   (/ereb-nos/; cf. Erebos)

     b. pneō   'I breathe'   (*[mneō])
        dapʰnē   'bay tree'   (*[damnē])

Only the forms in (29a) have been affected by Labial Nasalisation (28), notwithstanding the similarity of the underlying segmental sequence in the two sets.

The source of this difference is seen by Steriade in the respective derivation of syllable structure. Consider first the non-assimilating set (29b). All we have to assume is that the sequences *pn* and *pʰn* are incorporated into the onset prior to the activation of (28). The assimilation rule will consequently be blocked by the tautosyllabicity of the segments.

The clusters in the assimilating set include a voiced plosive *b*, and it can be independently shown that, in Attic, such voiced plosives may not form complex onsets with nasals. This obviously paves the way for the application of Labial Nasalisation (28), since the heterosyllabicity requirement is now met.

The obvious question at this point is why the input non-nasals cannot be incorporated into the previous coda before assimilation takes place. This ordering would of course still be consistent with the heterosyllabicity requirement. Moreover, and crucially for us here, it would allow all syllabification to take place in one fell swoop, a situation which would be compatible with syllabification by template.

As independently shown by Steriade, however, Attic obstruents can only be incorporated into the coda if they share some feature with the following (onset) segment. This means that coda formation must be fed by Labial Nasalisation (28), in turn fed by onset formation, since (28) stipulates that the trigger consonant must be part of a syllable.

The upshot of this discussion is that, at least in Steriade's analysis of Attic Greek, a non-syllabification rule (Labial Nasalisation) must interrupt the syllabification procedure. This implies that syllabification rules must be endowed with the same properties as the other rules of the phonology, notable among them the possibility of engaging in ordering relations. This result obviously cannot be obtained from syllabification by template matching (for persistent syllabification by rule see e.g. Rubach and Booij 1990, 1992).

4.4.2 Syllable templates

4.4.2.1 *Templatic morphology*

We still have pending the problem of formalising skeletal templates (as used in Semitic morphology and in reduplicating languages) without specifying slots for the feature [syllabic]. As was already hinted at, the solution will involve the use of an (embryonic) syllable template.

Consider the Arabic form *katab*, which McCarthy (1979) derived from the junction of the consonantal root *ktb* and the vowel melody *a* to the skeletal template CVCVC, as represented in (30):

(30)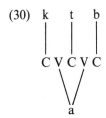

As will be recalled, the outstanding problem concerns the distribution of consonants and vowels across the skeleton when the CV slots are replaced with pure timing units 'X'. Levin's (1983, 1985) solution consists in having the slots designated for vowel association lexically marked as syllable nuclei, as follows:

(31)

In essence, the template in (31) is but an underspecified version of the one in (30). Thus, on the interpretation of V as [+ syllabic], the information contained in the symbol 'V' is equivalent to having an X slot associated with a syllabic nucleus 'N', while lack of association with syllable structure simply amounts to lack of specification for [syllabic].

The advantages of the new formalism are substantial. First, it allows us to definitely dispense with the spurious distinctive feature [± syllabic]. Second, it directly incorporates into lexical representation that portion of syllable structure which is unpredictable. Third, it makes available free slots onto which either consonants or vowels can associate without incurring any melody–skeleton mismatches.

The application of the association procedure to *katab* is shown in (32) (NB naturally, the syllable plane is geometrically orthogonal to the melodic planes, as suggested by the graphic arrangement):

(32)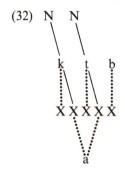

On the assumption that, in Arabic, association to syllable nuclei is restricted to vowels (reasons for this restriction will be given in section 4.5), the desired result follows automatically from the conventions on autosegmental association and the general principles of syllabification.

4.4.2.2 *Syllabification as template matching*

A cogent case for the extension of template syllable construction outside non-concatenative morphology is made in Itô (1986). According to Itô, syllabification is based on essentially three universal principles, namely locality, prosodic licensing, and structure preservation, and on one parameter, directionality, all of which lead to a formalisation in terms of template matching.

Itô's locality requirement is geared to defining syllable well-formedness within the syllable itself, without reference to outside elements. The demonstration that this constraint can only be met in the context of template syllabification is as follows.

Take a language like Japanese, with only nasals in the coda in non-geminate contexts. A rule-based framework would express this fact by means of the coda formation rule in (33) (for simplicity of presentation, we follow Itô's practice and represent slots associated with the syllable nucleus as 'V', and others as 'C'):

(33) Japanese coda rule

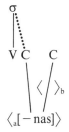

Condition: if a, then b

This rule violates the locality requirement, since the second C is not incorporated into the specified syllable. It also makes use of the angled bracket notation, an unwarrantedly powerful mechanism.

Both these difficulties are circumvented in a templatic formalism, where the following (negative) condition will be solely responsible for the observed restrictions:

(34)   *   C]$_\sigma$
           |
      [$-$nas]

The scope of this remarkably simple condition is not immediately apparent. Clearly, the condition will be inapplicable to nasals, which will accordingly be accepted in the Japanese coda. At first blush, it also appears to block the incorporation of non-nasals across the board, geminates included. The condition must however be interpreted in the context of Hayes's (1986) universal '[Exhaustiveness of] Linking Constraint':

(35) Exhaustiveness of Linking Constraint
     Association lines in structural descriptions are interpreted as exhaustive.

(Hayes 1986: 331)

This principle imposes a literal interpretation of the uniqueness of association between the non-nasal melody and the skeleton in (34). In particular, the condition will not be operative where the melody is linked to two skeletal slots (as it obviously must be for geminates). This means that (34) indeed captures all the restrictions on Japanese coda formation.

Let us next consider prosodic licensing and its import for template syllabification. The principle of Prosodic Licensing is proposed as a universal Well-formedness Condition on phonological representations:

(36) Principle of Prosodic Licensing
       All phonological units must be part of prosodic structure.[7]

The effect of (36) is that, in order to achieve phonetic realisation, melodic elements need to be incorporated into syllable structure (additional prosodic structure will be presented and discussed below, especially in Chapter 5). In a rule-based approach, prosodic association must be specified rule by rule, in a piecemeal manner, with the concomitant loss of generality. By contrast, in its templatic counterpart, Japanese syllabification will simply fall out of prosodic licensing, given the presence in the grammar of this language of the (maximal) syllable template in (37) (complemented, of course, with the negative condition in (34)):

(37)

The last of the three general principles in Itô's (1986) syllabification procedure is the principle of Structure Preservation (Kiparsky 1985), to which we shall only refer briefly here (further discussion is included in Chapter 5). The aspect of this principle relevant to syllabification concerns the fact that the application of word-bounded phonological rules must be consistent with the various syllabification conditions active in any one language (some violations are however tolerated phrasally, on a language-specific basis). Crucially, the infringement of any such condition by a word-bounded rule will automatically trigger desyllabification. Now, this machinery obviously presupposes a prior definition of the structure to be preserved, Itô's claim being that this is only viable if syllabification is effected by templates.

The final piece in the model is a directionality parameter, by which the direction of association is determined parametrically (in contrast with Steriade's (1984) universal left-to-right syllabification), in the manner of the autosegmental association conventions examined in Chapter 1. This flexibility affords a simple account for such facts as the contrast in *i* epenthesis site between the Cairene form [ʔultilu] (/ʔul-t-l-u/ 'I said to him') and its Iraqi counterpart [gilitla] (/gil-t-l-a/ 'I said to him'), as follows (the direction of syllabification is informally indicated by the arrows):

(38) a.

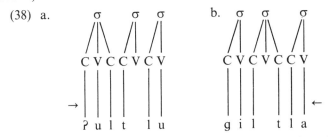

Both Arabic dialects share the syllable template CV(C). Associating the melody to this template left to right in (38a), we incorporate *t* into the onset of the second syllable. At this point there is no lexical vowel available for the next V slot, which is consequently automatically provided with an epenthetic *i*. By contrast, in (38b) the association takes place from right to left, and thus the *t* is parsed in the coda of the second syllable, after which the by now familiar processes will complete the derivation.

The undoubted appeal of Itô's arguments for a template-based syllabification procedure needs weighing against the fact that they are grounded in some not entirely uncontroversial assumptions. Thus, the unbridled adoption of the Exhaustiveness of Linking Constraint would require a reinterpretation of a substantial body of rules as proposed in the literature (see Schein and Steriade 1986: 730ff. for specific criticism). In turn, the principle of Structure Preservation has been found to be too strong and weakened to a 'Strong Domain Hypothesis' (Kiparsky 1984), by which the only legitimate global constraint on rule application concerns the possibility of (idiosyncratic) rule deactivation (but, crucially, not activation) at some morphological layer (see Chapter 5 for some additional discussion).

4.5 SONORITY

For ease of presentation, we have been systematically overlooking one fundamental aspect of syllabification, namely the relationship between the intrinsic content of the segments and their respective distribution throughout syllabic structure. We turn to this basic issue now.

4.5.1 Sonority sequencing

In Chapter 1 we referred to a hypothetical language *L* with a vocabulary of three phonological elements {p, e, n}, and pointed out that the free combination of these elements yields the following sequences:

(39)   a.   pen
       b.   pne
       c.   enp
       d.   epn
       e.   nep
       f.   npe

It is interesting that, although English does contain the three phonemes in question, only (39a) and (39e) qualify as words of this language ((39a) is of course a real English word, while (39e), although at present non-existent, is a possible word of English). Granted that English licenses complex onsets and complex codas, as has already been hinted at, it is unclear why the other forms in (39) should be disallowed.

Throughout the preceding discussion we have conveniently operated under the assumption of a clear-cut division of syllabic labour between vowels and consonants, such that only the former qualify as syllable nuclei. This assumption is of course factually incorrect, as attested by such English words as *little* and *button*, the second syllable of which is vowelless. Moreover, even when it does match the data (as it does for the majority of words in English, and across the board in most of the world's languages), it falls short of explaining the reasons for this distribution.

It has long been observed that speech sounds can be ranked on grounds of relative 'sonority' (see e.g. Whitney 1865, Sievers 1881, Jespersen 1904, Saussure 1916, Grammont 1933, and, more recently, Hooper 1972, 1976, Vennemann 1972, Kiparsky 1979, Selkirk 1982, and many others thereafter). While a precise phonetic measurement of sonority has still not been achieved (and is perhaps unobtainable on principle), the general interpretation of the notion is reasonably straightforward: simply, 'sonority' refers to the amount of sound let out as the segment is pronounced. Obviously, the narrower the stricture, the lower the sonority level, and conversely. It follows from this simple definition that the various sound classes can be graded on the basis of their respective sonority, as follows (numerical values are given for expository convenience only):[8]

(40)   1   (oral) stops   Least sonority
       2   fricatives
       3   nasals
       4   liquids
       5   glides
       6   vowels   Most sonority

The favoured position of vowels as syllable heads can now be seen to follow from their high sonority ranking. In the sequence *npe*, for instance, *e* will qualify as a syllable nucleus in a language like English, but the initial *n* will not (*p* will of course form the onset of *e* by the Minimal Onset Satisfaction Principle (25)), since liquids and nasals are only allowed as syllable peaks in English under a rather special set of circumstances (see Chapter 5 for discussion of a similar situation in German). As a consequence, in this sequence, *n* would only be syllabifiable as the first element of a complex onset *np*. This interpretation stands however in violation of the Sonority Sequencing Principle in (41):

(41) Sonority Sequencing Principle
    The sonority profile of the syllable must slope outwards from the peak.

The import of (41) is that the level of sonority must rise as we proceed from the beginning of the syllable to the syllable peak, and fall as we advance from the peak to the end of the syllable.[9] Equivalently, a syllable may not contain sonority troughs, as a putative syllable *npe* indeed would:

(42)

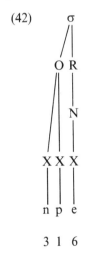

3 1 6

The nucleus of this syllable is the vowel *e*, as noted. The inclusion of both *n* and *p* in the onset would create a sonority trough on *p*, as shown in the informal digit line, in violation of the Sonority Sequencing Principle (SSP) (41). As a consequence, it will not be possible to assign this sequence to the onset, and therefore *npe* will not be licensed as a syllable (although *pe* of course will). The same reasoning will clearly apply to *epn*, whose sonority arrangement mirrors that of *npe*.

The sequences *pne* and *enp* contrast with *npe* and *epn*, respectively, in that they do not contain violations of the Sonority Sequencing Principle (41). Accordingly, they ought to be legitimate in English, following our reasoning so far. Clearly, however, besides universal principles, such as the SSP, the syllabification procedure contains language-particular parametrised constraints. One such parameter in English (and, interestingly, in many other languages) limits the second member of a complex onset to a liquid (or a glide). This parameter is commonly interpreted as a requirement of minimal sonority distance:

(43) Minimal Sonority Distance Parameter
      The difference in sonority value between sisters in constituent C
      must not be less than x.

Given our scale in (40), we can account for the ungrammaticality of *pne* in English by setting x in (43) as 3 in onsets (see Borowsky 1986: 173). This will allow the sequence stop + liquid (or glide), but not stop + nasal (or, *a fortiori*, fricative), in the obvious way.

This analysis creates a new problem, however. Simply, if the sonority difference between C_1 and C_2 must not be less than 3 in English, then the sequence fricative + liquid ought to be ungrammatical (NB $4 - 2 = 2$; $2 < 3$), in conflict with the grammaticality of *fr, fl* (cf. *free, flee*), and *thr* (cf. *three*).

We could attempt to overcome this difficulty by reformulating the sonority scale in (40). In particular, were we to assess fricatives on a par with stops by merging (oral) stops and fricatives at the lowest end of the scale and resetting x to 2, the problem would disappear. Different versions of the scale are indeed in existence to meet the challenge of the corresponding languages (see e.g. Steriade 1982). Clearly, such flexibility results in a less constrained, and thus less desirable, theory, but it is far from obvious how a tighter hypothesis can be reconciled with the cross-linguistic facts.

In the English case under scrutiny, the merger of the stop and fricative classes would not take us very far, however. Specifically, while it would indeed solve the problem of both *f* + liquid and *thr*, it would give rise to new difficulties, since it would predict the possibility of such onsets as *vr*, *vl* and *thl*, as well as of *s*, *z*, or *sh* + liquid. Of these, only *sl* and *shr* are legitimate, and probably amenable to independent analysis (*s* can, in some way, be incorporated at the start of *any* English onset, as attested by *spray*, *stray*, *scrape*, while *shr* can be derived from underlying /sr/, which corresponds to a systematic surface gap). It would thus appear that we have no alternative but to admit that, while sonority undoubtedly plays an important role in determining syllable structure, additional factors still to be discovered may be in existence.[10]

We must finally turn our attention to the mirror image of *pne*, namely *enp*, which is also disallowed in English. The reasons for this rejection cannot however be the same as those just considered for *pne*, since a sequence nasal + plosive (or fricative) is clearly permitted in English codas, as demonstrated by such words as *hemp* or *dent*. The reason for the starring of **enp* obviously lies in the lack of agreement in place of articulation between *n* and *p*. This suggests that, while English codas are not constrained for sonority distance, they are subject to conditions arising from feature agreement. For ease of exposition, we shall ignore them and continue pursuing the main thread of the argument.

4.5.2 Sonority and syllabification

We are now in a position to examine the role of sonority in syllable formation. We are assuming syllables not to be specified in the lexicon, at least in languages with non-concatenative morphology in the unmarked case.

We shall start with the hypothetical form *penpen*. In (44), we provide the correct segmental ordering and the sonority index corresponding to each phoneme:

(44)   p e n p e n
     1 6 3 1 6 3

Let us assume that segments associating to N in English need in the first instance a sonority index of 6 in the scale in (40) (i.e. they must be vowels). This implies that the string in (44) may only contain two syllables, with the nuclei on the two *e* vowels, as shown in (45), where we assume that the skeleton has been automatically projected from the melodies:

(45)

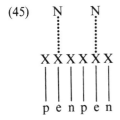

Notice that it is now possible to construe the nuclear nodes 'N' as simply first-level projections of the vowels on the syllable plane.

Nucleus projection must obviously be followed by the construction of a minimal onset, in compliance with the principle of Minimal Onset Satisfaction in (25) above:

(46)

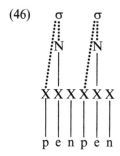

There now remain the two *n*s to be syllabified. The final *n* can obviously only be parsed in the rime, since it is not followed by any further syllabic material. For the middle *n* there are in principle two possibilities, namely also as a coda or as a member of a complex onset *np*. The latter analysis would indeed follow from the positive setting of the Maximal Onset Realisation Parameter (26). Such a complex onset would however violate the Sonority Sequencing Principle (41), and consequently this *n* must be allotted to the coda of the preceding syllable, as specified in (47):

(47)

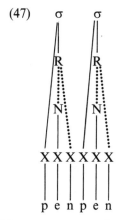

This outcome constitutes a possible word in some languages (e.g. Chinese). In English, however, the medial *n* must undergo place of articulation assimilation with the following *p*, as noted, to yield a final form *pempen*, a possible English word (cf. e.g. *pamper*, *dampen*).

4.5.3 X-bar structure

If we pay close attention to the configuration in (47), we shall notice its strong resemblance to that of syntactic phrases. In particular, the nucleus node is dominated by precisely two nodes, associated with segmental material respectively on the right- and left-hand sides. Such a parallel led Levin (1985) to formally interpret syllables as instantiations of X-bar structure, as (48) makes explicit:

(48)

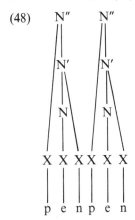

As can be seen, the rime has become the X′ projection of N, and the onset its X″ projection. Correspondingly, the onset material is interpreted as the specifier of the nucleus, and the coda material as its complement.

From this perspective, syllables can be viewed as an explicit formalisation of the sonority relations obtaining between the (ordered) melodic elements. Importantly, this interpretation is compatible with a non-autosegmental construal of the construct. In particular, the arboreal structure in (48) is in all equivalent to a formulation in terms of paired brackets, as in (49):

(49) $(p((e)_N n)_{N'})_{N''} (p((e)_N n)_{N'})_{N''}$

The representation in (49) still expresses constituency, but it does not contain an autosegmental syllabic level.

Levin's (1985) X-bar analysis of syllables gives rise to a number of technical difficulties, on which we shall now comment.

First, the Minimal Onset Satisfaction Principle (25) enforces the activation of the maximal projection N″ prior to that of the intermediate projection N′. This clearly runs against the grain of X-bar machinery, in that it introduces an element of ordering in the projection mechanism, thus weakening the parallel between syllable structure and syntactic phrase structure.

Also problematic is the analysis of additional melodic material. Thus, consider the structure of a word like *flounce*:

(50)

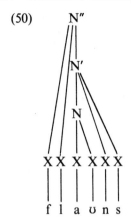

f l a ʊ n s

All the constituents in (50) are complex: the nucleus [aʊ], the onset [fl] and the coda [ns]. Clearly, thus, the model must be enriched with constituent 'incorporation' rules along the lines of (51) (similar rules are included in Steriade's 1982 account):

(51) Levin's Incorporation Rules

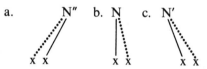

The rules in (51) add extra material to the onset, nucleus and coda, respectively. At least two aspects of these rules are questionable. First, the rules appear to be liable to specific directionality requirements, since the locus of incorporation lies on opposite sides for the onset and the two other constituents. One possible solution would be to make directionality follow from the respective position of the constituents being acted on *vis-à-vis* the nucleus, on the assumption that syllable construction proceeds outwards from the nucleus, as is seemingly implicit in Levin's approach. This still does not resolve the dilemma posed by the nucleus, however, which could in principle incorporate in either direction.

The second issue concerns recursion. In particular, were the rules in (51) to apply only once, all constituents would be maximally binary.[11] Levin does not impose this constraint on the procedure, and allows instead for parametric unbounded application, along the lines of Steriade (1982). The implicit prediction is that in languages with such a setting there will be no a priori limit on recursion, modulo the Sonority Sequencing Principle (41). Thus, assuming that English incorporation is unbounded (cf. e.g. the onset in *flew* and the coda in *twelfths*), words like *pfnliaurnst* are predicted to be possible in principle, although perhaps filtered out by the minimal sonority distance constraints of the language. Now, in Polish, sonority plateaux are allowed for obstruents (see Rubach and Booij 1990: 123). This means that Polish ought to tolerate very complex syllables in any position, but in fact long syllables are only found at word edges, and even here there is a limit to the degree of consonant accumulation: words like *ptfsnlarfstp*, which manifestly comply with all the sonority requirements of the language, are ominously absent from Polish, and are rejected as a possibility by Polish speakers.

Facts like these suggest that it is necessary to constrain unbounded incorporation in some way, but it is unclear how this can be accomplished within Levin's (1985) framework. Worse still, some languages, including English and Polish, exhibit violations of the Sonority Sequencing Principle (41) (cf. e.g. the *s* + stop clusters word-initially or their mirror image word-finally in English).[12] As an answer to this further challenge, Levin appeals to a second syllable augmentation procedure, which she formalises as Chomsky-adjunction. Crucially, such 'syllable adjunction' is declared free of the strictures of the SSP. This amounts to a substantial removal of constraints on syllable formation, with the obvious adverse consequences for the theory.

4.6 GOVERNMENT AND CHARM

A proposal directly aimed at meeting such challenges has been emerging from the work of Kaye, Lowenstamm, Vergnaud, and their collaborators in the Government and Charm (GC) framework, introduced in the previous chapter in the context of distinctive feature theory.[13] There are both formal and substantive differences between this framework and the standard approaches. In themselves, the formal mismatches are of course ultimately trivial. They are however closely interlocked with the more substantive aspects of the proposal, and must therefore be presented together.

4.6.1 Constituents

In this subsection we examine the basic syllabic structure countenanced by GC. The main innovations concern the abolition of the syllable constituent and the requirement of maximal binarity in the onset and in the rime (NB no coda constituent is recognised). In addition, we shall commence the exploration of the role of empty constituents.

4.6.1.1   *The abolition of the syllable*

Let us consider a word like *pray*, which includes a complex onset (*pr*) and a complex nucleus (*ay*). The representation of this form in Levin's (1985) X-bar syllable theory would be as in (52):

(52)

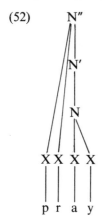

Its GC equivalent is given in (53):

(53)

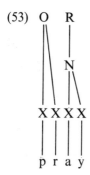

The superficial differences between the two representations must not be allowed to obscure their underlying unity.

The most obvious contrast concerns the absence of a syllable node from (53), and the concomitant graphic autonomy granted to the onset and the rime. The suggested reason for the abolition of the syllable constituent concerns the supposed lack of specific evidence for any such constituent universally. Leaving aside the controversial nature of this assertion,[14] the independence of the onset from the rime ought to translate as freedom of cooccurrence. In GC theory, however, an implicational relationship is stipulated between these two constituents (see Kaye *et al.* 1990: 200–1). Such stipulation (to be integrated formally in the system in 4.6.2.1) appears equivalent to the more usual stance of interpreting these two elements as syllabic subconstituents.[15]

4.6.1.2 Binarism

A more substantial difference between the two theories concerns the requirement of (maximal) binarism imposed on GC constituents. Thus, consider the analysis of *sprout* in Levin's X-bar model:

(54)

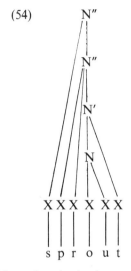

Note that both the onset and the rime crucially encompass three melodies. Compare now the GC analogue:

(55)

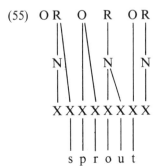

The binary limit on constituent membership prevents the incorporation of the *s* and the *t* into the onset and the rime of *prou*, respectively. These segments must however still be syllabified, since they are clearly part of the phonetic makeup of the word. Consequently, additional structure must be brought in, crucially including nodes empty of melodic, and possibly also skeletal, material, as shown.

The positive aspect of this analysis concerns the obviation of the need to resort to such ancillary devices as incorporation and adjunction, which we saw above to be necessary part and parcel of X-bar syllable theory. As pointed out at the time, these devices are by their very nature unconstrained, and therefore undesirable.

The replacement of the syllable by an implicational relationship between the two surviving constituents, and the requirement of maximal binarism on such constituents, lead to the (maximal) syllabic template in (56) (NB the final X will be attached to N or R depending on the identity of its melodic material):

(56) GC syllabic template

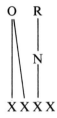

This template thus encapsulates the GC conception of the syllable,[16] and can profitably be compared with its analogues in Itô (1986), from which it additionally differs in its universality.

4.6.1.3 *Empty constituents*

The presence of empty constituents in (55) must be the object of special attention, since the unchecked proliferation of such elements would obviously result in arbitrariness.

Note that empty constituents are effectively also countenanced in X-bar syllable theory. Thus, consider the syllabic representation of the form *about* in this framework:

(57)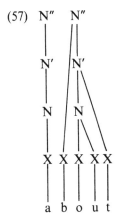

The first syllable, *a*, has no onset or coda. From this perspective, therefore, the respective nodes N″ and N′ are devoid of skeletal (and a fortiori melodic) material (these nodes are in fact mere projections of N, as pointed out at the time). N″ nodes can also dominate skeletal slots unassociated to melodies, as we have already seen and illustrate now in (58) for greater clarity:

(58)

Such a configuration could for instance correspond to the first syllable of the French word *haricot* 'bean', with 'h aspiré': *l*[ə a]*ricot* 'the bean' (cf. *l'habit* 'the habit': *l*[a]*bit*).

This possibility does not however extend to the N node (nor effectively to the N′ node, a point of agreement between the two theories), since in the X-bar framework N is simply a projection of the appropriate melodic material.[17] By contrast, in the GC approach, as in Itô (1986), N enjoys a degree of structural autonomy, independent of melodic substance, as brought out by (55) above.

The various cases of empty subsyllabic material accommodated for in GC are now listed for greater clarity:

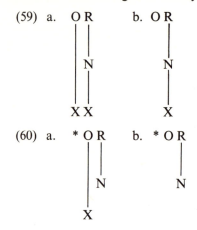

Note that, while onsets need not dominate either melodic or skeletal material (see (59a) and (59b), respectively), skeletonless nuclei, as in (60), are disallowed (pace Kaye 1986–7; Charette p.c.). Such asymmetry is suggestive of a more central role for the nucleus, the gap with X-bar syllable theory being concomitantly reduced.

4.6.2 Justifying the structures

GC theory endeavours to make explicit the principles responsible for all aspects of the proposed structures, and we must now review such principles.

4.6.2.1 *Licensing*

At the core of the system is the following Licensing Principle:

(61) Licensing Principle
All phonological positions save one must be licensed within a domain. The unlicensed position is the head of this domain.
(Kaye 1990b: 306)

As can be seen, GC licensing differs from Itô's (1986) in allowing one element in each (morphophonological) domain to remain unlicensed. Such an element will act as the head of the overall domain, the licensing of all other elements ultimately originating in it through a dependency chain. As will be seen, domain licensing necessarily emanates from a realised nucleus (effectively from a vowel).

In GC, licensing can be direct, or take place via a structural relation termed 'government'. For clarity of exposition, we shall refer to the former procedure as D-licensing, and to the latter as G-licensing. The operative difference between the two types of licensing is that the various instances of D-licensing are simply stipulated, whereas G-licensing is made to fall out of a specific set of principles, which we shall discuss directly.

We have already come across the stipulation that the presence of a nucleus implies the presence of an onset. Within the formal framework we are proposing this stipulation can be naturally interpreted as a case of D-licensing (Charette p.c.). Thus, remember that in GC all elements of syllabic structure are subject to licensing (see the Licensing Principle (61) above), the ultimate licensor (the domain licensor) being a vowel (note however that R is effectively treated as a projection of N, and as such enters no special licensing relations). It follows from this that O will need external licensing, the suggestion thus being that such licensing takes place from its right adjacent N.

4.6.2.2 *Principles of government*

The most common form of licensing (G-licensing) involves government. 'Government' is a relation between skeletal elements equivalent to dependency, in the familiar sense (see Chapter 3 for a discussion of dependency in the context of distinctive features). What is particular to GC, however, is the imposition of the following two constraints on government (see e.g. Kaye 1990b: 306):

(62) Adjacency Principle
The governor (= head) must be linearly adjacent to the governee(s) (= dependent(s)).

(63) Directionality Principle
Government is strictly directional:
a. left-to-right within constituents;
b. right-to-left across constituents.

The Adjacency Principle (62)[18] enforces contiguity between the governor and its dependent, while the Directionality Principle (63) establishes the respective identity of the dependent and the head. It will be useful to remind the reader that the intended terms of the government relation as defined are the skeletal slots (melodically filled or empty).

Let us illustrate briefly, drawing on the discussion in Kaye *et al.* (1990: 210, and *passim*). In (64) below, a nucleus slot is shown to engage in a government relation both intraconstituently (it governs its nuclear sister in (64a), and its rimal sister in (64b)), and transconstituently (it governs its antecedent onset in (64c)) (as will be seen below, the government relationship is further constrained in the absence of melodic association, and therefore we must assume that the relevant skeletal positions in (64) are associated to melodies, which we omit from the representation for simplicity; also, it is not necessary for the slots not partaking in government to be present, in line with the discussion above):

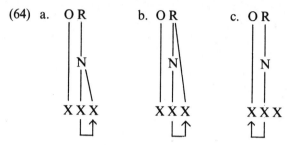

Next, in (65), the onset slot governs both its intraconstituent mate (in (65a)) and the preceding 'coda' slot (in (65b)):

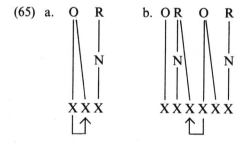

All but one of the skeletal slots dominated by nuclei must obviously also be licensed (the unlicensed nucleus slot acting as the domain head, as already mentioned). Not unexpectedly, adjacent nucleus slots are subject to standard government:

Note the right-to-left direction of government, as corresponds to the transconstituent nature of the relation.

We must now consider the case where other skeletal positions intervene between the two incumbent nuclear slots, as in (67):

(67)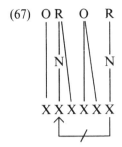

Any such government would obviously infringe the Adjacency Principle (62). Consequently, an alternative source must be sought for the required licensing.

The answer given to this problem in GC relies on the notion of projection, with which we are already familiar. In particular, a distinction is drawn between 'strict locality', which indeed requires skeletal adjacency, and 'locality' *tout court*, where adjacency is defined at some other level (in particular, a level derived via projection), as illustrated in (68), which is proposed as an alternative to (67):

(68)

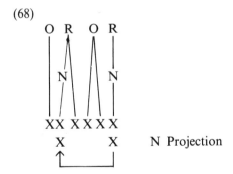

N Projection

Besides being exempt from the requirement of strict adjacency, such higher level internuclear government is assumed to be parametrically directional, rather than universally right-to-left, as is the case with ordinary transconstituent government. This flexibility makes it possible to interpret such bidirectional phenomena as stress and harmony as concrete manifestations of nucleus-to-nucleus government. The same flexibility, however, also calls into question the wisdom of formalising the nucleus-to-nucleus relationship as government. In particular, it is far from self-evident that this relationship shares in any of the properties which characterise government, as defined in (62) and (63) above, and thus would probably be better construed as D-licensing. Such D-licensing alternative is further supported by the fact that a G-licensing interpretation results in loss of formal unity for nucleus-to-nucleus government (cf. (68) vs (66)).

In (68), the slot associated to the last nucleus remains unlicensed. This slot thus constitutes the domain head (cf. (61) above), the remainder of the slots being G-licensed by the corresponding government relations, in the manner discussed.

At this point, we can return to the issue of the binary ceiling on constituent branching pending from 4.6.1.2 (see note 16), which we can now see is directly derived from principles (62) and (63). In particular, a ternary constituent would stand in violation of either of these two principles, as illustrated in (69) for a hypothetical ternary onset:

(69)   * O

    a b c

In this structure, the government relations can only be exhausted if b is the head, since otherwise the Adjacency Principle (62) would be violated. The postulation of b as the head of a and c is however incompatible with the Directionality Principle (63), according to which government is strictly directional, and applies from left to right inside constituents. Such a principle will obviously predict a as the head, but now c becomes ungovernable, by (62).

4.6.2.3 Proper government

As anticipated above, G-licensing of slots unassociated to melodies is subject to additional constraints. Thus, consider by way of example the hypothetical representations of *pray* in (70), where the contrast between empty and filled slots has been made explicit (for ease of reference, we have subscripted the nuclei on a scale down to 1, on the assumption of a right-to-left directionality setting):

(70)

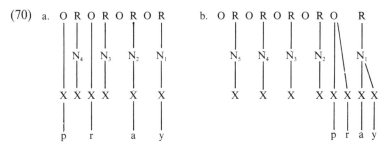

Let us examine the structure in (70a) with a view to determining the reasons for its dismissal. On the given right-to-left setting, the network of internuclear dependencies will be $N_1 \rightarrow N_2$, and $N_3 \rightarrow N_4$, for '$\rightarrow$' = 'governs', and $N_1 \rightarrow N_3$ at a second level of projection. Now, if this was the end of the story, the structure in (70a) would indeed be legitimate. As it happens, however, the principles in (62) and (63) simply define canonical structural paths. Once such paths are established, additional conditions are imposed on the identity of the corresponding melodic elements. Directly relevant to the case at hand is the phonological counterpart of the 'Empty Category Principle' (ECP), which we formulate in (71) (see Kaye *et al.* 1990: 219):

(71) Empty Category Principle
Melodically empty slots must be 'properly governed'.

'Proper government' is a specially rigorous form of government, which requires compliance with two additional conditions. First, the head must be melodically filled.[19] Following on from this, the empty nucleus N_3 cannot be a proper governor of N_4, since N_3 is melodically empty. The second condition prohibits the presence of a further government relation between the two terms of the dependency in question. Thus, in (70b), N_1 cannot proper-govern N_2, given the intervention of a complex onset between the two nuclei, since this onset constitutes the domain of a government relation (between the onset head and its complement).

One particularly common way of salvaging unlicensed structures is by means of melodic epenthesis, essentially along the same lines as in Itô (1986). Clearly, however, English does not exhibit epenthesis in the word in question, its phonetic form being [preɪ], rather than, say, [pəreɪ], as would follow from (70a) (cf. [pəreɪd] *parade*). Consequently, the hypothesis embodied in the representation in (70a) cannot be upheld (a similar argument applies of course to (70b), *mutatis mutandis*).

4.6.2.4 Coda licensing

In (65b) above we showed the government of the skeletal slot daughter to R by the onset slot that follows it (remember that such effective coda has no official status in GC). Such government will obviously fail to affect a word-final coda element, which will simply be governed from its nucleus, intraconstituently.

Consider our familiar word *pen*. At first blush, the GC analysis of this form ought to be as in (72):

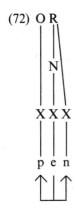

(72)

Note in particular that all its constituting elements are governed (and thus licensed), as shown underneath for convenience (the government relation of course affects the skeletal slots, not the melodies). This notwithstanding, the structure falls foul of an additional principle that requires codas to be licensed by a phonetically realised onset, as encapsulated in the following Coda G-Licensing Principle:

(73) Coda G-Licensing Principle
      Post-nuclear rhymal positions must be licensed [through government, IMR] by a following onset.[20]

(Kaye 1990b: 311)

The coda (= 'post-nuclear rhymal') skeletal position in (72) cannot be G-licensed by the following onset position, for the simple reason that no such onset is available. Consequently, the structure in (74) must substitute for its (72) analogue:

(74)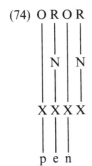

While consistent with the Coda G-Licensing Principle in (73), the structure in (74) raises the question of the licensing of the empty skeletal slot in its final nucleus. In particular, the domain-final location of such a nucleus prevents it from being properly governed, as the Empty Category Principle (71) would require it to be.[21] This dilemma is resolved by the postulation of the additional parameter in (75):

(75) Final Empty Nucleus D-Licensing Parameter
A domain-final empty nucleus is licensed (yes/no).

English is obviously set positively for this parameter, while a language with a (c)v structure, such as Desano or Hawaian (or, more weakly, Italian), is not. This accounts for the viability of (74), as desired.

4.6.2.5 *Empty onsets*

We must finally examine empty onsets. As pointed out above, there are two different degrees of onset emptiness, involving melodic emptiness (cf. (59a)) and melodic and skeletal emptiness (cf. (59b)). For ease of exposition, we shall refer to them as empty and superempty onsets, respectively.

As we have seen, the licensing of melody-free slots is generally implemented by proper government, and therefore empty onsets also come under the remit of the ECP (71). Superempty onsets, however, cannot be G-licensed, since the government relation exclusively concerns skeletal points, as we know. Consequently, superempty onsets are only D-licensed from the nucleus.

The general availability of onset D-licensing from the nucleus allows us to circumvent a difficulty associated with government of filled complex onsets from the nucleus. In particular, such government would infringe the Adjacency Principle (62) above, as we show in (76):

(76) O   R

The postulation of D-licensing from the nucleus thus provides the appropriate licensing machinery, since D-licensing is not constrained by strict adjacency (i.e. skeletal adjacency). Consequently, it must indeed be assumed that all onsets are subject to D-licensing by their respective nuclei. In addition, empty onsets (but not, of course, superempty onsets) must be properly governed, also from the nucleus.

4.6.2.6 *Interpretation of the GC formalism*

We have now reached a position from where it is possible to assess the import of the obviously rather complex GC machinery. This is best achieved through a comparison with X-bar syllable theory. In both approaches, syllables are effectively construed (and formalised) as projections of a 'syllabic' segment (usually a vowel). In X-bar theory this is done directly through X-bar projection, while in GC it is done indirectly, via the various licensing principles. Significantly, though, the ultimate licensor of GC syllabic structure must also be a lexical vowel, as shown (see 4.6.3.1 for further details).

The essential difference between the two approaches concerns the issue of complex constituents. As we saw above, X-bar theory basically places no limit on the number of elements included in each such constituent. In GC, by contrast, they are explicitly constrained by the licensing principles, in particular the G-licensing principles of government and proper government. In essence, these principles allow a (realised) nucleus to license an additional degenerate syllable (i.e. a syllable without an overt nucleus) under certain conditions, geared to keeping structural complexity under check. From this perspective, therefore, it is possible to interpret GC syllable theory as an enriched version of X-bar theory, one in particular that imposes specific constraints on syllable expansion.

4.6.3 Charm

4.6.3.1 Charm requirements

No restrictions on the melodic identity of the various elements have as yet been proposed. Consideration of the pair *pray*, **rpay* indeed reveals the need for such restrictions. In particular, the latter form is in all respects consistent with the principles given so far:

(77)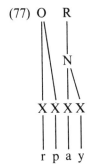

The structure in (77) is identical to that in (53) above, which was declared legitimate. The two representations differ however in the ordering of the respective onset melodies, *pr* in (53), but *rp* in (77). Note that, in both cases, we must assume that the constituent-initial segment governs its adjacent mate, given the left-to-right directionality of constituent-internal government.

In mainstream syllable theory, the illegitimacy of (77) will be attributed to the fact that the onset *rp* contains a violation of the Sonority Sequencing Principle (41). Clearly, GC theory must also avail itself of sonority scaling and of the ordering constraints which follow from it (in accordance with such principles as the SSP and the Sonority Distance Parameter (43)). As already referred to in Chapter 3, it does so by means of a tripartite 'charm' classification of segments into positively charmed, negatively charmed, and charmless (see e.g. Kaye 1990a, b). As pointed out at the time, this amounts to a coarse sonority taxonomy along the lines of (78) (for ease of reference, we maintain the informal numbering of (40)):

(78) 1 (oral) stops   Negative Charm
      2a non-sibilant fricatives

    2b sibilant fricatives   Neutral Charm
    3 nasals
    4 liquids

5 glides and lax non-low oral vowels

---

6 tense vowels, nasal vowels,
      and lax low oral vowels   Positive Charm

The following charm (i.e. sonority) requirements are now imposed on constituent membership (see Kaye *et al.* 1990: 202):

(79)   Charm Requirements on Constituent Membership
        a. an onset element must not have positive charm;
        b. a nucleus element must not have negative charm.

Following on from (79a), therefore, positively charmed vowels cannot be part of the onset, while by (79b) stops and non-sibilant fricatives are banned from the nucleus.[22]

The conditions in (79) apply in both simple and complex constituents. Complex constituents constitute of course government domains, and are therefore additionally subject to the general charm constraints on government, as follows (see Kaye *et al.* 1990: 202):[23]

(80)   Charm Constraints on Government[24]
        a. governors must be charmed (i.e. have positive or negative charm);
        b. governees must not be charmed (i.e. they must have neutral charm).

Given (80), the class of governors and the class of governees will be in complementary distribution.

The conjunction of (79) and (80) implies that the structural distribution of the various segmental classes in complex constituents will be severely limited. Thus, complex onsets only admit an (oral) stop or a (non-sibilant) fricative in their governing position, while the identity of the governor of complex rimes is confined to tense, nasal, or lax low oral vowels. In both cases, the melody associated to the governee position must be a lax non-low oral vowel, a liquid, or a sibilant fricative, since only these segments are charmless.[25]

Note, importantly, that the government principles just stated apply beyond the boundaries of the syllable. In particular, they also obtain across constituents. An instantiation of the latter case is the governing relationship between an onset head and the preceding coda. Specifically, the principles in (80) will restrict the segmental collocations straddling these two positions, such that, for instance, a heterosyllabic sequence *p.r* will be disallowed, since the putative governor, *r*, is not charmed, and the putative governee, *p*, is not charmless (remember that transconstituent government operates from right to left at the skeletal level). Such fine detail of transyllabic accountability is notoriously absent from the standard theories of syllabification (see however the Syllable Contact Law in Murray and Vennemann 1983). As we shall now further sample, however, the greater strictness inherent to GC theory inevitably gives rise to a number of weaknesses which cast a shadow of doubt on the adequacy of the approach.

4.6.4.2 Further machinery

It is in fact not infrequent for the predictions of GC theory to be at odds with the facts, which can be extraordinarily complex and even idiosyncratic. Consider for instance the existence in (rhotic) English of such heterosyllabic sequences as *rl, rn, rm, lm, ln*, while their converses (*lr*, etc.) are systematically banned (at least from the common vocabulary). Crucially, principle (80a), which requires governors to be charmed, is violated in either case. Faced with this fact, the proposal has been made that the internal complexity of segments (where internal complexity is to be defined in the context of the GC analysis of segment composition presented in Chapter 3) also plays a role in government, as encapsulated in the principle in (81):

(81) Complex Governor Principle
     A neutral segment may govern if it has a complexity greater than
     its governee.

                                                    (Kaye *et al.* 1990: 218)

Note however that this principle appears to condone the converse sequences (*lr*, etc.) in the onset, for the simple reason that, if *l* is a good transconstituent governor, and *r* a good transconstituent governee, the same relation ought to be applicable constituent-internally.

A similar problem concerns the absence from English of such complex onsets as *pn*, *vr*, and others, which seemingly comply with all the requirements presented so far, while *shr* and *sl* are allowed, despite the charmless nature of their governor (remember that sibilants are assigned neutral charm; see (78) above). In fact, according to recent proposals (e.g. Kaye *et al.* 1990: 204ff., and Kaye 1991–2), *s* + consonant sequences do not constitute complex onsets, in English and in other languages alike, so that the structure of *sprout* in (55) above will carry over to, e.g. *spout*, or, for that matter, *slouch*.[26] If so, however, it is not clear why a similar analysis should not be available for the other sequences concerned, and therefore why, e.g. *pn* cannot occur word-initially in English, on the following representation:

(82)

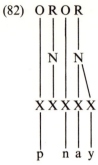

The empty nucleus in (82) is properly governed by the following filled nucleus, and therefore it is G-licensed. Such a licensed empty nucleus in turn D-licenses the preceding onset *p*, and therefore a word like [pneɪ] ought to be possible, contrary to fact (such structures are of course legitimate in other languages: see French *pneu* [pnφ] 'tyre', Greek *pnéuma* [pnevma] 'spirit', etc.; it is interesting, however, that the analogous sequences [tn], [kn] are banned from French, and correspondingly for other languages).

English does allow the sequence /pn/ heterosyllabically (cf. *hypnosis*), and this creates a new problem, since, by (80) above, governors, but not governees, must be charmed, but this relationship is reversed here. More common is /pt/ (e.g. *captive*, *opt*), where the governor is indeed charmed, but the governee, again, is not charmless. The problem of charmed governees is addressed in Kaye *et al.* (1990: 216), among other sources. The proposal there is that onset *p* and coda *p* are in effect different segments, only the former supposedly being marked for vocal cord stiffness (represented by the element H, evocative of high tone, in GC theory). This structural difference must however be supplemented with the following additional principle if the right result is to be achieved:

(83) Negative charm is a property of elements whose hot feature involves the state of the vocal cords.

(Kaye *et al.* 1990: 216)

Following on from this, the *p* of *captive*, *opt*, etc. will now be charmless, and thus qualify for governee status. It is of course still unclear what makes the *n* in *hypnotic* (a charmless segment) a legitimate governor, since by (80a) governors must be charmed. Doubtlessly, a variety of strategies are open to the analyst (among them to view /n/ as more complex than /p/, or to declare *hyp* a prefix, thus dispensing with the governing relationship), but at this point we decline to explore the matter any further, and bring to a close the discussion on GC syllable theory.

4.7 MORA THEORY

4.7.1 Problems for the skeleton

4.7.1.1 Syllable weight

One important function of syllable structure has been left out of the discussion so far. This concerns the fact that stress mechanisms (to be examined in detail in Chapter 5) frequently differentiate between two types of syllables, commonly referred to as light and heavy. Thus consider the stress patterns of the following English nouns (stress is indicated by a mark ´ on the stressed vowel):

(84) a. América   b. agénda   Arizóna
       cínnamon   conúndrum cicáda
       Cánada   appéndix   balaláika
       Ágatha   Matílda   Therésa

In (84a) stress is antepenultimate, while in (84b) it is penultimate. Observation of the respective syllable structures will reveal a principled reason for this difference. Specifically, in (84b) the penultimate syllable either is closed or contains a long vowel or a diphthong, while in (84a) none of these conditions is met. Syllables of the (84a) type (i.e. open syllables with a lax vowel) are known as light syllables, whereas syllables of type (84b) are called heavy syllables. Clearly, thus, syllable heaviness can act as a barrier to the progression of stress towards the left (in some way to be made precise in Chapter 5). Consequently, stress rules must have access to syllable structure.

The situation just reviewed is of course not exclusive to English, although there are also many languages where syllable weight does not influence stress assignment. Syllable weight can also be determined on a different basis than in English. For instance, as noted in Hyman (1985), it is not uncommon for languages to treat as heavy only syllables with long vowels (and, where appropriate, diphthongs), all syllables with short vowels, whether open or closed, being consequently light. Examples of this include Huasteco and Khalkha Mongolian. In other cases, specific information about the consonant closing the syllable may be necessary in order to establish weight. For instance, in Cayapa, while closed syllables are generally considered heavy, syllables closed with a glottal stop are treated as light. By contrast, in Dagur Mongolian closed syllables count as light except if they are closed by [ŋ]. Finally, the identity of the vowel may also play a role in the determination of weight, and in some languages (e.g. Chitimacha, Chuvash, Cheremis) syllables with schwas do not count as heavy, even if they are closed.

We must now find an adequate formal representation for such varied configurations. The common attitude has been simply to stipulate that the onset does not count for weight (see however Davis 1985, 1988 for a different opinion), and that the rime must branch in order for the syllable to be heavy. One problem with this approach is that, under most accounts (including, of course, the GC account), closed syllables and open syllables with a complex vowel receive different representations:

(85) a.   b.

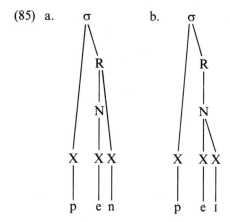

In (85a), the rime is branching, whereas in (85b) the nucleus branches. The obvious strategy for the determination of weight in the face of this variety would be to stipulate that 'branching' can be computed at any level within the rime, be it on the rime node itself or below. As pointed out by Hyman (1985: 7ff.), however, this procedure runs into difficulties. Thus, consider the representation of a 'light' diphthong in (86):

(86)

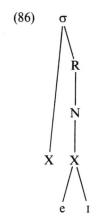

The existence of light diphthongs (in effect, contour vowels, akin to such contour consonants as affricates, which we discussed in Chapter 1) has been reported in the literature (see e.g. Anderson 1984 for Icelandic, and Kaye 1982, 1985 for Vata). Now, if rime branchingness can be computed at any level inside the rime, syllables containing such diphthongs ought to be counted as heavy, a conclusion which conflicts with their behaviour. An additional difficulty with the purely geometrical approach to weight concerns the segmental conditions which we have seen can enter in the computation of weight, since such conditions are clearly not geometrical.

4.7.1.2 Further questions

Hyman (1985) also draws attention to the fact that the projection relevant to syllable weight is basically identical to the projection necessary for other prosodic processes, notably for tone association. In particular, onset elements are not tone carriers, and in the rime it is usually only vowels and syllabic consonants that qualify as tone bearers, although sometimes also sonorants (e.g. Lithuanian), and exceptionally obstruents (e.g. Hausa). The tendency to isomorphy of the weight and tone-bearing elements is however not captured by the projection approach, since there is no reason for both projections to coincide.

Another problematic aspect of the standard formalisation concerns the asymmetrical consequences of melody deletion in the coda and in the onset. In particular, the former, but not the latter, potentially triggers the lengthening of the adjacent (vowel) segment. This can be illustrated with the process of *s* deletion before anterior sonorants in Latin, as in *casnus* → *caːnus* 'grey' (Hayes 1989a):

(87)

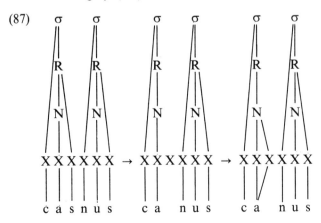

The problem is that the standard skeletal representation makes available a similar change upon deletion of onset melodies, as exemplified in (88) for the hypothetical input forms /sa/ and /osa/:

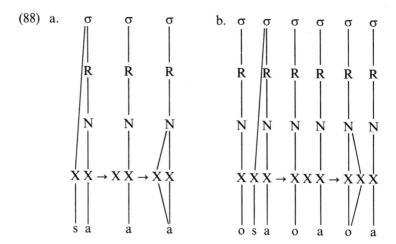

The respective outputs would be [aː] and [oːa]. This type of process appears however to be unattested.

4.7.2 Skeleton–melody mismatches

Difficulties such as these are circumvented in Hyman (1985) through the unification of the weight and tone-bearing elements. In addition, he takes the step of identifying the resulting units with the 'moras' of some traditional descriptions.

Hyman's point of departure, like Levin's (1985) and GC's, is a skeleton stripped of all featural information. According to this view, the representation of *pen* will be as in (89) after projection of the slots from the segments:

(89) X X X
      | | |
      | | |
      p e n

Hyman's innovation consists in submitting the initial X slot associations to various modifications prior to the building of syllable structure above the X tier. These modifications are brought about by both universal and language-particular rules.

The first such rule is the Onset Creation Rule (OCR), which he formulates as follows:

(90) Onset Creation Rule

[+cons][−cons]

The effect of this rule on *pen* is shown in (91):

(91)

On the identification of Xs with weight units (i.e. 'moras'), the failure of the onset to contribute weight now follows directly from the representation, without resort to stipulation. Notice, importantly, that the function of the OCR (90) is similar to Steriade's CV Rule (27), or to our Minimal Onset Satisfaction Principle (25), thus being independently motivated by the facts of syllabification. Like these procedures, the OCR is assumed to have universal scope, and consequently its effect on weight computation comes cost-free.

Consider now the contribution of the penultimate rime to weight, illustrated by the English triad *América, agénda, Therésa*:

(92)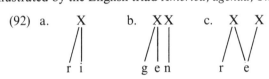

Simply, heavy syllables contain two X slots, while light syllables only have one. The approach accordingly provides a geometry for the principled computation of syllable weight.

We must obviously also account for the fact that not all languages make use of the contrast between light and heavy syllables. Hyman's move involves the postulation of a parametric Margin Creation Rule (MCR) attaching a further consonant to the nuclear vowel's mora:

(93) Margin Creation Rule

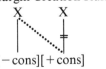

[−cons][+cons]

Application of this rule would change the representation of *pen* from (91) above to (94):

(94)

The MCR is of course inoperative in English, where we have seen stress to be sensitive to weight, but it will be active in weight-insensitive languages. Note, importantly, that the rule can be subject to further restrictions, and can thus take account of all the idiosyncrasies mentioned above.

As set out in the programme, the procedure also yields the desired results for tone mapping. Thus, consider the Gokana word *téèrài* (as in the verbal expression *ò téèrài* 'you-pl. run'), which contains an assortment of vowels and consonants, of which only the former are tone bearing. Assuming that the relevant lexical tones are H and L, the following mapping will result (Hyman 1985: 16):

(95)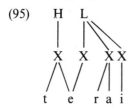

In (95), the melodies have associated to the available X elements in accordance with the given principles, in particular the Onset Creation Rule (90) and the Obligatory Contour Principle, which we first mentioned in Chapter 2 (see note 4 in Chapter 3 for specific discussion). As can be seen, the derivation of the correct tonal associations needs no further stipulations. Finally, the observed asymmetry in compensatory lengthening between onset and coda falls out of the fact that onsets have been deprived of their own skeletal slot by the OCR, whereas codas preserve theirs (modulo the Margin Creation Rule (93)).

Hyman's account is undoubtedly appealing, but it leaves a number of questions unanswered. First, it is far from obvious how syllable formation on the X tier will proceed. Thus, consider the representations in (96), which Hyman (1985: 17) presents as the most common syllable types:

(96) a.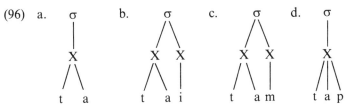

Given the fact that syllables can contain two segments specified as [−consonantal] (cf. (96b)), it is not clear how the procedure can be prevented from generating the configuration in (97):

(97)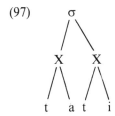

Obviously, we could impose the appropriate conditions on syllable formation (namely that the second daughter not be branching, etc.). It is doubtful, however, that these conditions would go beyond a mere restatement of the facts.

A further, less tractable problem arises in connection with the existence of more complex types of syllables, in particular syllables with complex onsets and complex codas, for which 'additional rules will be needed' (Hyman 1985: 18). As we have already seen, however, the postulation of such rules is by no means a straightforward matter, and various proposals, some of them remarkably elaborate, are in existence precisely to achieve this end. Clearly, therefore, the details of such rules cannot be left to common sense or to the initiative of the reader, and it is not beyond expectation that they are simply unworkable within the confines of Hyman's theory.

4.7.3 Lexical moras

4.7.3.1 The model

Hyman's (1985) skeletal slots are licensed by the melody in as much as, under normal circumstances, such slots are not lexical, but simply projected from the melody in the course of the derivation (the exceptions involve gemination and affrication, as expected).

An alternative conception is offered in Hayes (1989b). Hayes notes that vowels can be monomoraic (the usual case), bimoraic (long vowels) or non-moraic (glides). He represents these three distinct possibilities in the lexicon as follows (as before, 'v' = any vowel, and 'c' = any consonant; 'μ' = mora):

(98)   a.   μ   b.   μ   μ   c.

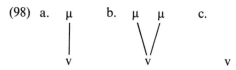

In (98a) we see an ordinary vowel associated to one mora. In (98b), vowel length is encoded as association to two moras. Finally, the vocalic melody in (98c) has no mora associated to it, and therefore corresponds to what is usually (but not unambiguously) known as a 'glide'.

Similar representations are available for consonants:

(99)   a.   μ   b.   μ   μ   c.

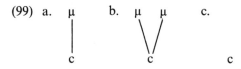

By contrast with vowels, ordinary consonants are not lexically associated to any mora (99c). Linking to one mora (99a) corresponds to a geminate consonant, as we shall see directly, and linking to two moras (99b) to a double geminate, a rare occurrence, although reported in Kimatuumbi (Odden 1981) and Gokana (Hyman 1985).

We shall now illustrate how the various syllabic structures are derived from these lexical representations. The most general case is given in (100):

(100)

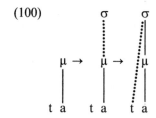

The input contains a moraic vowel and a non-moraic consonant, the unmarked situation. In the first step, a syllable node is projected from the mora, and in the second the consonant associates (directly) to the syllable node. This last process is equivalent to Hyman's Onset Creation Rule (90) in giving rise to a non-moraic onset. It differs from it, however, in that the melody associates to the syllable node, rather than to the lower level mora (represented as a skeleton slot in Hyman's account).

We next exemplify the case of consonant gemination:

(101)

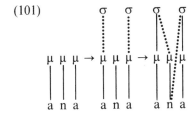

The relevant step is the last one, which encompasses in fact two processes: the association of the consonant-linked mora to the preceding syllable node, of which it will therefore effectively become the coda, and the association of the consonantal melody to the following σ to form the onset. These two processes are assumed to be an automatic part of the syllabification procedure.

In the absence of a following syllable node, non-moraic consonants obviously cannot form an onset, and therefore associate directly to the preceding mora:

(102)

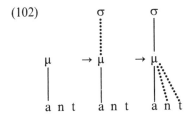

In languages where cvc syllables are treated as heavy by their stress systems, however, a 'Weight by Position' parameter comes into play:

(103) Weight by Position

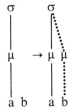   (for the input σ dominating only one μ)

As can be seen, Weight by Position projects an additional mora, duly incorporated into the syllable, which it renders heavy. The condition on the domination of a single μ by the input σ limits syllables to a maximum of two moras (the data discussed in section 7 of Hayes's paper, involving trimoraic syllables, suggest however that this condition needs to be relaxed).

For completeness, we now provide three possible mora structures for the string *apta*:

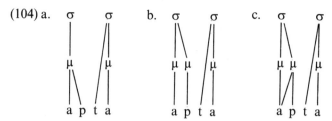

The simplest alternative is represented in (104a), with only the vowels moraic, the consonants being incorporated into the adjacent structure by the universal principles mentioned above. In (104b) the *p* has been provided with its own mora by Weight by Position (103). Finally, in (104c) the first *a* is assumed to be long, and is thus lexically endowed with two moras, the second of which will also receive the (mora-less) consonant *p* by the general procedure. Note, crucially, that Weight by Position could not apply to a representation such as that in (104c) if the noted constraint of two moras per syllable is upheld.

4.7.3.2 Evaluation

We shall now compare Hyman's and Hayes's frameworks, in an attempt to apportion merit.

Consider first the fact that in Hayes's account the onset melody attaches directly to the σ node, rather than to the adjacent skeletal slot. The obvious claim implicit in this formalism is that onsets can never be moraic. Under Hyman's, however, circumstances could arise where an onset melody could indeed become moraic, following the deletion of the nucleus melody. An illustration is provided by the English historical change [talə] → [taːl] (eventually [teɪl] *tale*), analysed in Hayes (1989a) as in (105):

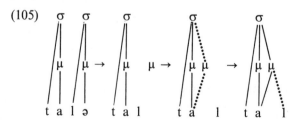

As can be noticed, the deletion of [ə] is accompanied by the simultaneous erasure of the corresponding syllable structure, an automatic result of the interpretation of syllable structure as a layered projection of the nuclear vowel, along the lines of Levin (1985). On the other hand, the mora initially associated to [ə] is preserved upon deletion of this melody, in keeping with the independent status of Hayes's moras. The remainder of the process is also highly natural, and involves the association of the vacant mora to the nuclear vowel, and the incorporation of the stray consonant into the structure by the standard procedure.

Consider now the equivalent derivation on Hyman's mora theory:

(106)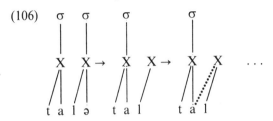

In the second step the melody [ə] is deleted. Because of the original multiple association of the corresponding skeletal slot, it is reasonable to assume that this slot will survive the deletion of the nucleus. If so, there simply is no pressure for the third step to take place, in the absence of which the incorrect output [tal] will be derived, after syllable incorporation:

(107)

Further problems for Hyman's approach stem from its effective lack of mora autosegmentality. Thus, consider the 'double flop' historical change which took place in the East Ionic dialect of Ancient Greek, exemplified by the form *[odwos] → [oːdos]. Under Hayes's account, this change is straightforward:

(108)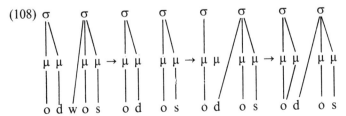

Compare now this derivation with its equivalent under Hyman:

(109)
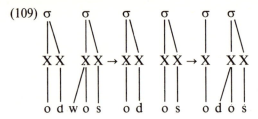

The crucial difference concerns the third step. Specifically, as noted above, Hyman's Onset Creation Rule (90) is accompanied by the deletion of the corresponding skeletal slot. Clearly, if this slot is deleted, no compensatory lengthening will take place. By contrast, Hayes's moras survive melody deletion. As a result, the adjacent vowel can lengthen, following the usual procedure.

Problematic areas also exist for Hayes's approach, however. One problem concerns the representation of glides, which is carried exclusively by the moraic level, as noted (in Hyman's approach, by contrast, glides must necessarily be marked [−consonantal] at the melodic level). Now, a purely vocalic interpretation of glides manifestly leads to a violation of the Obligatory Contour Principle, as shown in (110):

(110)
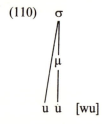

Such a violation can only be avoided by a merging of the melodies, as in (111):

(111)
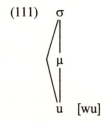

The problem now is that this representation needs to be lexicalised, since, clearly, it must be kept separate from its vowel-only counterpart:

(112)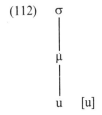

The lexicalisation of (111), however, entails the presence of syllables in the lexicon, explicitly argued against by Hayes on the grounds that syllable division is predictable cross-linguistically.

Additional problems for Hayes's mora theory are pointed out in Sloan's (1991) detailed study of Southern Sierra Miwok syllabification and template patterns. Drastically summarising for reasons of space, Southern Sierra Miwok geminate consonants occur in positions other than preceding a vowel (a convenient test case is provided by the morpheme /ʔynː-/ in the pair /ʔynː-eH-Nko?/ 'I'll come while . . . ' vs /ʔynː-jak-te-ʔ/ 'I'm from . . .', the gemination persisting through to the surface in both cases: [ʔynneNko?], [ʔynnyjakteʔ]). Moreover, SSM suffix-supplied stem templates differentiate the sequences VC, VV, and VX, for 'X' = C or V (VC: *wyks-* 'to go' → *wykys-kuH-* 'someone evidently went' and *lot* 'to catch' → *lotuʔ-kuH-* 'captive', with ʔ supplied by default; VV: *helj* → *hela:-t-poksu-* 'to be scared', with *j* loss and vowel lengthening; CX: *kojow-na-* 'to tell for someone' and *heka:-na* 'to clean for someone', with preservation of the original C or V). Finally, Hayes's moraic model is powerless to accommodate (morpheme-initial) floating phonemes (cf. *palal-ci-* 'people from near Palona' vs *ʔawo-:ni-* ʔci-* 'Yosemite people', the latter with syllabification of ʔ in *ʔci* after the vowel).

4.8 CONCLUSION

The principle of Prosodic Licensing, whether implicit or explicit under whatever incarnation, imposes a requirement of prosodic constituency on all melodic (and skeletal) elements at some level of representation (typically, the phonetic level, or, more stringently, the output of each cycle). The lowest rung of prosodic structure is occupied by the syllable (or perhaps the mora, if this construct is countenanced), typically broken down into subconstituents.

A number of principles, some purely geometric and some related to sonority, govern the formation of syllable structure. Reduced to their essentials, these principles ensure that, both numerically and from the standpoint of sonority, the fabric of the syllable and its subconstituents obeys the dictates of both universal and parochial grammar. While the core structure of syllables is fairly straightforward and well understood, a striking range of added complexities shows up in many of the world's languages. Such complexities provide the acid test for the available theories of the syllable, none of which can be declared free of challenge. This result obviously points to the need for further research in the area, undoubtedly to benefit from a terminological and formal *rapprochement* between its various practitioners.

5 Domains and modes of application

5.1 PROSODIC STRUCTURE

In the preceding chapter we presented a substantial body of evidence in support of the prosodic construct 'syllable'. The thrust of the argument hinged on the identification of this construct and its subconstituents as the domain of a variety of phonological processes and phonotactic constraints. The question which now arises is whether the inventory of prosodic constituents is exhausted by the syllable.

5.1.1 Direct relation to syntactic constituency

5.1.1.1 Phonological boundaries

In both *SPE* and Selkirk (1972), a pioneer work on prosodic phonology, the interface between (morpho)syntax and phonology was formalised as a direct mapping of syntactic constituent brackets on to phonological boundaries (see also McCawley 1968).

In a subsequent work (Selkirk 1980), the same author points out some false predictions implicit in this approach to prosodic phenomena. Consider for instance the following Sanskrit process of regressive voice assimilation (Selkirk 1980: 114):

(1) a. ad + si   →   atsi
         ad + thas   →   atthas

     b. ap – jaḥ   →   ab-jaḥ
         dik – gadaḥ   →   dig-gadaḥ

     c. jyok jīva   →   jyog jīva
         parivrāṭ gacchati → parivrād gacchati

Within the *SPE* model, rules that apply irrespective of the presence of (any type of) boundaries internally require the parenthesisation of such boundaries, as generally illustrated in (2) (Selkirk 1980: 126ff.):

(2) a. A → B / C(#(#))D(#(#))____(#(#))E(#(#))F
    b. A → B / C(#)D(#)____(#)E(#)F

The *SPE* boundaries '##' and '#' are taken by Selkirk to define the phonological phrase and the phonological word, respectively (see below for specific discussion of these constructs). Now, given the present formalism, as represented in (2), nothing prevents the formulation of rules mixing up different types of boundaries, as in (3): (NB the direction of the context is irrelevant):

(3) A → B / C(#(#))E(#)F

What is characteristic of (3) is the simultaneous inclusion of boundaries of diverse levels (cf. '##' = phonological phrase vs '#' = phonological word; these constructs will be examined below). According to Selkirk, rules of this kind are not found in natural languages.

A further, important argument against this type of approach, also made in Hayes (1989b), concerns the existence of a strength hierarchy between the different boundaries, such that if a rule R is not blocked by boundary B, then it is not blocked by any boundary in the set $\{B - 1, \ldots, B - n\}$ either, where the negative scaling 1 to n represents progressively lower degrees of strength. Conversely, if a rule applies in the neighbourhood of B, then it also applies in the neighbourhood of any boundary in the set $\{B + 1, \ldots, B + n\}$, i.e. in the context of boundaries of greater strength. Now, crucially, by itself, a theory of prosody based on phonological boundaries leaves these implications unaccounted for. Both this result and the previous one are clear hints that a different approach to prosody is called for.

5.1.1.2 C-command in phonology

In one such approach, Kaisse (1985) argues for direct reference to the 'c-command' relation in phonological rules. Consider for instance the following data from Italian (Napoli and Nespor 1979: 20, Nespor and Vogel 1986: 167):

(4) a. Maria è più [k:]*alda* che mai   'Maria is hotter than ever'
        ho visto tre [k:]*ani*   'I've seen three dogs'
        Mario ha [f:]*atto* tutto   'Mario has done everything'

b.   la gabbia era dipinta di già [k]*ompletamente*
     'the cage was already completely painted'
     l'entrata allo zoo costa di più [p]*er* i turisti
     'the entrance to the zoo is more expensive for tourists'
     ne aveva soltanto tre [d]*i* bassotti
       '(s)he had only three dachshunds'

The phonological conditioning required for consonant gemination (namely the presence of a final stressed vowel in the immediately preceding word) is met by all the highlighted words in the two groups. This notwithstanding, only those in (4a) undergo the process, as shown.

Kaisse's account relies on the imposition of two structural conditions on the application of this rule (commonly known as 'Raddoppiamento Sintattico', i.e. 'Syntactic Doubling'): (i) c-command: the first word of the pair (e.g. *più* in *più calda*) must c-command the second word (*calda*); (ii) edge: the first word must occupy the left edge in the c-commanding domain. For clarity, we provide the configurations of two contrasting examples:

(5)   a.   b.

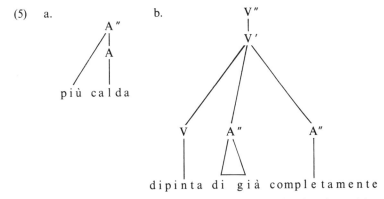

In (5a), the c-command requirement is met, since the first branching node dominating *più* also dominates *calda*. This is however not the case for *già* with regard to *completamente* in (5b). According to Kaisse, this structural difference is responsible for the contrasting behaviour of the two phrases with regard to the rule in question.

While Kaisse (1985) provides abundant exemplification and argumentation for her syntactic approach to phonological sandhi processes, this theory is faced with a number of empirical problems. Thus, for instance, it cannot account for the application of Raddoppiamento Sintattico in *Mario ha di già* [f:]*atto tutto* (see its counterpart in (4a)), since here the relevant form is not c-commanded by the trigger:

(6)

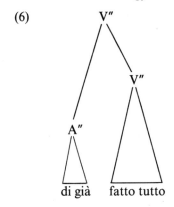

di già   fatto tutto

There are also general considerations against direct access to syntax by phonological rules (see Hayes 1989b). First, the actual use of syntactic information by phonological rules is very sparing across the board (for example, a rule limiting nasal assimilation to noun phrases is well-nigh unthinkable). Indeed, phonological rules typically apply irrespective of syntactic categorisation. Second, there is specific evidence that syntactic constituency cannot just be taken over by prosody. For instance, the phonological phrasing of the phrase *this is the cat* || *that caught the rat* || *that stole the cheese* is clearly at variance with its semantico-syntactic constituency *this is* [*the cat that caught* [*the rat that stole* [*the cheese*]]], as was already pointed out in *SPE* (p. 372). Third, a purely syntactic approach to prosody predicts the existence of overlapping prosodic domains, such that, given the sequence ABC, with the syntactic parsing A[B[C . . . , it would be possible for a prosodic rule to focus on the AB domain, and for some other rule on BC. Such a prediction has however not been backed up by facts. Finally, it is possible for several phonological rules to apply in the same (often complex) syntactic domain. Now, if the mapping were direct from the syntax, such a domain would have to be defined individually for each rule, an uneconomical strategy.

5.1.2 The Prosodic Hierarchy model

All the difficulties mentioned are directly addressed by the Prosodic Hierarchy model (for several useful papers bearing on these and related issues see *Phonology Yearbook* 4 (1987)). Like its boundary predecessor, this model includes a mapping procedure from the syntax to the (prosodic) phonology. As in the direct syntax approach, however, the representations in the Prosodic Hierarchy model are hierarchical. Several incarnations of the prosodic hierarchy are in existence (e.g.

Selkirk 1981, 1984b, 1990, Nespor and Vogel 1982, 1986, Hayes 1989b), mainly differentiated by the omission of some constituents from some of the inventories. The list in (7) can be considered maximal, disregarding levels below the syllable (NB we are deliberately using 'P' as systematically ambiguous between 'phonological' and 'prosodic', both of which labels are used in the literature):

(7)

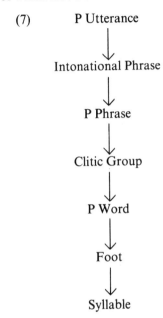

P Utterance

↓

Intonational Phrase

↓

P Phrase

↓

Clitic Group

↓

P Word

↓

Foot

↓

Syllable

The direction of domination is as given.

An important property attributed by some to the prosodic hierarchy concerns the exhaustive domination of each level by the node(s) of the immediately higher level, as embodied in the following 'Strict Layer Hypothesis' (SLH) (the formulation here is from Selkirk 1990: 180):

(8) Strict Layer Hypothesis
$P^n \rightarrow P^{n-1}*$ (where $X* = $ 'one or more Xs')

The product of the SLH (8) and the prosodic hierarchy in (7) is the set of layered structures in (9):

(9)

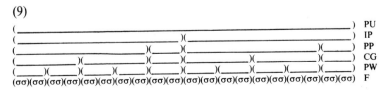

As can be seen, the string undergoes successive parsings at different levels of the hierarchy, each level obeying the SLH (8) (for arguments against the SLH see e.g. Hyman *et al.* 1987). The SLH has two obvious consequences. First, it does not allow the skipping of levels, or of material within levels. Second, it is incompatible with improper parsing. If extended to all levels, the latter implication would obviously rule out ambisyllabicity.

The amount of research which has gone into each of the proposed prosodic constituents is very uneven. For instance, while the Intonational Phrase has been the object of attention for several decades now, the Clitic Group is not very well documented prosodically, and indeed some authors omit it from their lists altogether. Of particular importance for our present purposes is the foot constituent, for reasons which will become clear as we proceed. Before turning to the foot, however, we shall provide a definition and a minimum of justification for each of the other levels in (7) above. For expository convenience, we shall present the domains from top to bottom, although it must be borne in mind that prosodic constituent construction proceeds in fact from bottom to top, in line with the SLH (8).

5.2 INVENTORY OF PROSODIC CONSTITUENTS

5.2.1 The P Utterance

According to Nespor and Vogel (1986), the P Utterance (PU) constitutes the domain for the phenomenon of r-Insertion in RP English, which they exemplify as follows (pp. 228, 238–9):

(10) neve[r] again
      . . . saw[r] Ellen
      we're trying to teach our Siamese cat not to claw[r] at the furniture
      the giant Panda[r], as you know, is an endangered species
      it's Anna[r]: open the door
      that's a nice ca[r]: is it yours?
      where's the saw[r]?: I need it!

In order for the process to take place, the appropriate phonological environment must be present in a given prosodic domain. The phonological environment consists of two adjacent vowels (the first of which non-high) straddling two words, while the domain of application of this rule is obviously larger than the syntactic phrase or even the sentence. Specifically, as well as phrase-internally (*never* a*gain*), the process applies between phrases (*saw* E*llen*; *claw* a*t the furniture*) or even sentences (. . . *car: is* . . .). On these grounds, it would appear that a strictly syntactic definition of the domain of this rule is out of the question. Indeed, Nespor and Vogel's proposal is for a specifically prosodic constituent PU, the highest in the prosodic hierarchy.[1]

The conditions on the construction of PUs are not simple, and are thus best approached in stages. First, given the Strict Layer Hypothesis (8), the PU must dominate an uninterrupted sequence of Intonational Phrases, the next level down constituent in the prosodic hierarchy. Second, such a string of Intonational Phrases is required to be dominated by a single syntactic label. Third, no phonetic pause can intervene inside a PU (but, significantly, pure performance interruptions have no effect on prosodic constituency). Formulaically, the core conditions on PU formation can therefore be stated as follows:

(11)   Core conditions on PU formation
       $[_X [\ldots]^*_{IP}]_X$ where X is a syntactic label, and
                                    IP = Intonational Phrase
       Condition: no deliberate internal pause

Once the basic PUs have been erected, they can optionally undergo merger, provided that the following (rather heterogeneous) set of conditions on the component PUs be met:

(12)   Conditions on PU merger
       a.   pragmatic:
            i. utterer identity
            ii. addressee identity

       b.   phonological:
            i. relative shortness
            ii. no pause in the delivery

       c.   *either* (syntactic):   i. a relation of ellipsis or anaphora
            or (semantic):   ii. a relation of the type encapsulated
                                   in 'and', 'therefore', or 'because'.

These conditions thus differentiate the set of data in (10) above from alleged cases of non-occurrence of r-Insertion, such as *stop fidgeting, dear*; *I'll leave otherwise* ('or' relation, not included in (12cii)); *that's a nice sofa*; *it's five o'clock!* (no ellipsis or anaphora); *I have always made a handsome living without transgressing the limits of the* law *and my brother's businesses are also blameless from that point of view* (excessive length: cf. the expression *law*[r] *and order*), etc.

It would of course be rewarding to find the rationale for each and all of the conditions in (12), and some tentative discussion can be found in Nespor and Vogel (1986). Here, however, we shall proceed to the exposition of the next lower prosodic constituent in the hierarchy in (7), namely the Intonational Phrase.

5.2.2 The Intonational Phrase

Besides constituting the domain for the association of intonational melodies (in essence sequences of tones subject to autosegmental linking, in the mode expounded in Chapter 1),[2] as obviously suggested by its name,[3] the Intonational Phrase (IP) plays host to such phonological rules as the (Tuscan) Italian 'Gorgia Toscana', by which intervocalic voiceless stops become fricatives (thus, *ponte* → *i* [ɸ]*onti* '(the) bridge(s)', [t]*orta* → *la* [θ]*orta* '(the) cake', and [k]*asa* → *la* [h]*asa* '(the) house', with a glottal, rather than a velar, fricative).

Consider the following data (Nespor and Vogel 1986: 206):

(13) Gorgia Toscana
a. i *c*anarini *c*ongolesi *c*ostano molto *c*ari
'Congolese canaries are very expensive'

b. i *c*anarini *c*ongolesi, come sai, costano molto *c*ari
'Congolese canaries, as you know, are very expensive'

c. i *c*anarini, congolesi o no, costano molto *c*ari
'canaries, whether or not Congolese, are very expensive'

The italicised orthographic *c*s have all undergone GT (→ [h]), the others receiving a plosive interpretation ([k]). As can be seen, the insertion of parenthetic material (*come sai, congolesi o no*) blocks the application of GT. According to Nespor and Vogel (1986), this suggests that the domain of application of this process is smaller than the PU, of which each of the sequences in (13) would indeed constitute one. The domain in question is in fact the IP, which they define as follows (p. 189):

(14) IP constituency
1 a (sequence of) P Phrase(s) structurally unattached to the sentence tree;
2 any (sequence of) P Phrase(s) remaining inside a root sentence.

The criteria given in (14) are exclusively syntactic, but it has commonly been noticed that both semantic and phonological criteria often also play a central role in the delimitation of IPs. As an example of a semantic factor we shall mention the favoured location of an IP boundary between the sentence subject and its predicate (the weight of semantics in IP parsing is emphasised by some authors, e.g. Selkirk 1984b: 290ff.). A typical phonological parameter interfering with IP formation is length (perhaps in tandem with certain syntactic conditions). In particular, long IPs tend to be broken up into smaller ones (the resulting IPs must of course still comply with (14)), as exemplified in (15) (Nespor and Vogel 1986: 194):

(15) $[_{IP}$ my friend's baby hamster always looks for food in the corners of its cage$]_{IP}$
   → $[_{IP}$ my friend's baby hamster$]_{IP}$ $[_{IP}$ always looks for food in the corners of its cage$]_{IP}$
   → $[_{IP}$ my friend's baby hamster$]_{IP}$ $[_{IP}$ always looks for food$]_{IP}$ $[_{IP}$ in the corners of its cage$]_{IP}$

IP restructuring also takes place under non-phonological conditions. For instance, in (16) we show that a list is best intonated with an independent IP for each of its component parts:

(16) $[_{IP}$ that mountain road is long narrow windy and bumpy$]_{IP}$
   → $[_{IP}$ that mountain road is long$]_{IP}$ $[_{IP}$ narrow$]_{IP}$ $[_{IP}$ windy$]_{IP}$ $[_{IP}$ and bumpy$]_{IP}$

Before leaving the IP, it is worth highlighting the important role played in its delimitation by non-structural factors (i.e. phonetic or semantic factors). The same consideration applies to the PU, both these constituents being correspondingly less easy to pin down than their lower rank counterparts, which we now proceed to present.

5.2.3 The P Phrase

The prosodic constituent underlying the IP in the hierarchy is the P Phrase (PP), which can be schematically defined thus (see Hayes 1989b, who follows Nespor and Vogel 1982):

(17) Definition of PP
   In $[_{X''}\ldots X^\circ\ Y''\ldots]$, where '$\ldots X^\circ$' stands for the non-recursive side of X,

   a. $[\ldots X^\circ]$ obligatorily forms a PP, and
   b. $[\ldots X^\circ\ Y'']$ parametrically (and perhaps optionally) forms a PP, provided that Y'' does not branch.
   Clitic Groups unaffected by this procedure form their own PPs.

(17) as stated is applicable to languages with right-bound (syntactic) recursion, like Italian and English. For languages with left-bound

recursion (e.g. Japanese), the formulation will be mirror image. Note that X in (17) effectively stands for N, V or A, but not for P, since, as is well known, prepositions and other function words tend to exhibit clitic-like behaviour, and therefore cannot constitute nuclei for the formation of PPs.

An example of the PP as a rule domain is provided by the phenomenon of stress retraction in (particularly American) English, exemplified in (18) (see Hayes 1989b: 216):

(18) a. N″: [A″N]   hórizontal líne (cf. horizóntal)
                          Jápanese ráilways (cf. Japanése)
             [N″N]   Tóscanini's íce cream (cf. Toscaníni)
                          Ténnessee's pólitics (cf. Tennesseé)
      b. A″: [Adv″A]   évidently trúe (cf. evidéntly)
      c. V″: [Adv″V]   he'll ábsolutely flíp (cf. absolútely)

The reason for the movement of the stress must be sought in the avoidance of clash with the stress carried by the initial syllable of the following word (cf. by contrast *horizóntal tabulátion, evidéntly incorréct,* etc.). A formal analysis of such a phenomenon is offered in 5.4.3.1 below, and here we simply assume its reality.

The following sentences (from Nespor and Vogel 1986: 178) forcefully bring out the confinement of English stress retraction to the PP:

(19) a.   John pérseveres gládly
      a′. John persevéres gládly and diligently

      b.   rabbits réproduce quíckly
      b′. rabbits reprodúce quíckly enough

In both cases retraction has failed to take place in the primed sentences, which consequently retain the clash (*persevéres gládly, reprodúce quíckly*). The reason for this contrast lies in the respective distribution of PPs, assuming of course that this is indeed the domain for stress retraction. We illustrate with the (19a/a′) pair:

(20) a.   [PP John]PP [PP pérseveres gládly]PP
      a′. [PP John]PP [PP persevéres]PP [PP gládly and diligently]PP

In (20a), the adverb *gladly*, placed on the recursive side of *perseveres*, has been incorporated by clause (17b) into the adjacent PP headed by this word. In (20a′), however, *gladly* is contained in a branching syntactic constituent (*gladly and diligently*), and incorporation is therefore blocked. Consequently, the clash is not encompassed in the domain of the stress retraction rule and cannot be corrected.

5.2.4 The Clitic Group

Evidence for the prosodic Clitic Group (CG) is provided by two English rules of assimilation first discussed in Selkirk (1972: 90ff.), who in turn acknowledges unpublished work by Zwicky as her source. The first such rule deletes a word-final [v] before a consonant, and the second palatalises [s] and [z] before [ʃ] and [ʒ].

The *v*-Deletion rule is lexically conditioned and applies only in fast speech:

(21) a. give me some   [gɪmiː]
      b. leave them alone   [liː ðm̩]
      c. will he save them a seat? [seɪ ðm̩]
      d. you'll forgive me my intrusion?[. . . gɪː miː]

This rule fails to apply in the superficially similar sentences in (22):

(22) a. give Maureen some
      b. leave Thelma alone
      c. will he save those people a seat?
      d. will you forgive my intrusion?

The Coronal Assimilation rule applies obligatorily in a sentence like *is Sheila here?* (*i*[ʒ] [ʃ]*eila* . . .), but only optionally (in fast or sloppy speech) in *Laura's shadow* (normally *Laura* [z] [ʃ]*adow*) (cf. Selkirk 1972: 128–9; Nespor and Vogel 1986: 150; Hayes 1989b: 209).

All the facts fall into place on the assumption that the (ordinary) domain of both rules is the CG, the noted contrasts being therefore attributable to differences in the CG membership of the relevant forms:

(23) a.
          [cg leav̸(e) them]cg [cg alone]cg

      b. [cg leave]cg [cg Thelma]cg [cg alone]cg

As can be seen, the context of the rule is only met in the first of the two cases.

Similarly revealing of the existence of the CG as a separate prosodic domain is the distribution of Latin stress, which can be penultimate or antepenultimate in ordinary words, but is invariably penultimate after the addition of a clitic (e.g. *que* 'and'):

(24) a. amícus   'friend'   b. amicúsque 'and friend'
          fémina   'woman'   femináque 'and woman'

Striking minimal pairs arise as a result:

(25) a. ítaque   'therefore'   b. itáque   'and so'
         úndique   'everywhere'   undíque   'and from there'

In our terms here, this means that, in Latin, the CG constitutes a different domain for stress than the word, since the stress pattern exhibited by the two constituents is different (it is also a different domain than the PP, which has no influence on stress in Latin).

At this point, we shall specify the details of CG construction, as follows (see Nespor and Vogel 1986; Hayes 1989b):

(26) CG construction
      1   each non-clitic P Word belongs to a separate CG;
      2   clitics are incorporated into the adjacent CG where they
          share a greater number of category memberships with the
          host;[4]
          where: 'category membership share' is established on the
          basis of a common dominating node

It can now be seen that in (21d) *me* will be incorporated into the preceding CG *forgive*, while in (22d) *my* will be assigned to *intrusion*. This difference in CG constituency thus accounts for the difference in the application of the rule of *v*-Deletion.

5.2.5 The P Word

We turn now to the description of the P Word (PW). As would be expected, in the unmarked case the PW corresponds to the morphological and syntactic object 'word', the output of the morphological derivation and the terminal element of the syntax. In marked situations, however, the PW can be smaller than its morphosyntactic counterpart (see Nespor and Vogel 1986: 141):

(27) Marked PW
      1   a stem;
      2   any element identified by specific phonological or
          morphological criteria;
      3   any element marked diacritically;
      4   any elements of the syntactic word left over which cannot be
          attached to an adjacent PW closest to the stem.

As an example of isomorphism between the PW and the morphosyntactic word, Nespor and Vogel mention Greek. For instance, in this language, stress is assigned on one of the last three syllables of the word:

(28) áloγos   'horse'
     patéras   'father'
     piθanós   'probable'

This principle also applies in compounds, and therefore such forms must also be assumed to constitute PW domains:

(29) ksilókola   'wood glue'   (ksílos + kóla)
     spirtokúti   'matchbox'   (spírton + kutí)
     ksiloθimonyá   'wood stack'   (ksílos + θimonyá)

By contrast, CGs preserve the original stress of their host:

(30) γrápse to   'write it'   (γrápse)
     to spíti mu   'my house'   (spíti)

In cases where, as the result of cliticisation, primary stress falls more than three syllables from the end of the CG, a secondary stress is inserted in penultimate position (here and henceforth we represent secondary stress by means of a grave accent):

(31) γrápse mù to   'write me it' (γrápse)
     ðyávasè to   'read it'   (ðyávase)

Such facts as mentioned attest to the existence of the PW and the CG as separate prosodic domains, the former crucially including in Greek all instances of morphosyntactic words, compounds included.

As specified in (27), the PW can also parametrically be smaller than the morphosyntactic word. Thus, consider Turkish, where stress is usually word-final, regardless of the number of suffixes:

(32) odá   'room'
     odadá   'in the room'
     odadakí   'that which is in the room'
     odadakilér   'those who are in the room'
     odadakilerdén   'from those who are in the room'

In compounds, however, each component word maintains its original stress locus (NB the stress of the second member becomes secondary):

(33) a. düğün   'of yesterday'   çiçegí   'flower'
             düğúnçiçegì   'butter cup'
     b. çáy   'tea'   eví   'house'
             çáyevì   'tea house'

Likewise, the normal principles of Turkish vowel harmony (cf. Chapter 1) do not apply across the two members of compounds (cf. e.g. *bu* 'this'

+ *gün* 'day' = *bugün* 'today'), thus suggesting that each of them constitutes a separate PW, the manifest domain of harmony and stress.

The PW can also correspond to morphemes below the (non-compound) word. In Yidin^y, for instance, words with an odd number of syllables undergo lengthening in their penultimate vowel, as illustrated in (34) (NB '^y' signals palatalisation):

(34) a. guda:ga   'dog-abs.'   b. mud^yam   'mother-abs.'
        mad^yi:ndaŋ 'walk up-pres.'   galiŋ   'go-pres.'

Suffixation brings about the expected changes:

(35) a. gudagagu   'dog-purp.'
     b. mud^ya:mgu   'mother-purp.'

Consider however the forms in (36):

(36) a. guma:ri   'red'
     b. guma:ridaga:n^yu   'to become red'

The form in (36b), from the base in (36a), is anomalous on two accounts. First, it exhibits vowel lengthening despite the fact that it contains an even number of syllables. Second, it inherits the lengthening of the base *guma:ri*. Nespor and Vogel's solution rests on two twin assumptions, namely that the domain of application of lengthening is the PW, and that only monosyllabic suffixes can be prosodically incorporated into a PW, as follows:

(37) a. [_{PW} gudaga + gu]_{PW}
     b. [_{PW} gumari]_{PW} [_{PW}daga + n^yu]_{PW}

The inchoative suffix *daga* does not meet the monosyllabic requirement, and consequently it must be assigned to an independent PW, to which the monosyllabic past suffix *n^yu* can now be added. The application of Vowel Lengthening to these representations yields precisely the data in (36).

5.2.6 The foot

5.2.6.1 Segmental evidence

The last of the novel prosodic constituents in (7) above is the foot (F), and we shall now provide some evidence for this constituent by examining the distribution of aspiration in English voiceless stops attested by the pronunciation of *t* as [t^h], as discussed in Nespor and Vogel (1986: 90ff.).

Consider first such data as in (38) (aspiration is informally represented in the data by means of italicisation):

(38) a.   *t*ime
              *t*alisman
              *T*amerlane
              *t*elegraph

        b.   *t*elegraphic
              *t*ombola
              *t*uxedo
              *T*anganyika
              *t*ambourine
              *t*errain

All aspirated *t*s in (38) are word-initial. Clearly, however, this is not the only context for aspiration:

(39) de*t*ain
      de*t*ention
      en*t*ire
      repu*t*ation

Here, non-word-initial *t*s are likewise aspirated. By contrast, those in (40) are not:

(40) alter
      satyr
      shatter
      hospital

The obvious difference between (39) and (40) is that, in the former, the syllable of which *t* is the onset carries the word stress. In this, the data in (39) agree with those in (38a). The problem now is (38b), where the stress falls elsewhere and yet the *t* aspirates.

Consider now (41):

(41) sa*t*ire
      rep*t*ile
      infan*t*ile
      longi*t*ude

Here, again, the word primary stress falls outside the syllable containing the aspirated *t*. Interestingly, however, this syllable carries a secondary stress, as an examination of the minimal pair *sa*[t^h]*ire* : *satyr* will reveal. In view of this development, it would appear that the strongest criterion on which to base aspiration is stress.

At this point we could (perhaps ought to) ask the question of what exactly stress is, but we shall postpone the discussion of this issue until later in the chapter. More pressing is the existence of the data in (38b), which will remain unaccounted for if aspiration is made contingent on stress. We could of course accommodate them by supplying the rule with a disjunctive environment, but we know such environments to be suspect, in fact a strong hint that a generalisation is being missed. Consider in addition the data in (42):

(42) Stanley
      stoppage
      abstain
      austere

Here the *t* is also unaspirated, even though it is clearly in the onset of the stressed syllable, which we shall assume shares with *s* (perhaps ambisyllabic when word-medial).

All the elements for a solution are in fact now at hand. Suppose that we postulate for the forms considered a prosodic constituency along the lines sampled in (43):

(43) a.   (talisman)   (38a)
           (tambou)(rine)   (38b)
           (repu)(tation)   (39)
           (rep)(tile)   (41)

      b.   (hospital)   (40)
           (ₐau(ₛs)ₜtere)ⱼ   (42)

As can be seen, stressed syllables signal the beginning of this new constituent. Crucially, however, because of the Strict Layer Hypothesis (8), any material left over will constitute an additional such constituent.

A generalisation now emerges. Simply, aspiration takes place when the appropriate segment occupies the (strictly) initial position in the constituent in question, as it does in (43a). In (43b), by contrast, *t* is not constituent-initial, and consequently there is no aspiration. The constituent at hand is in fact the foot.

F has also been called in to account for such English processes as *l*-Devoicing (cf. *eye-slip* vs *ice-lip*), Diphthong Shortening (in *ice-lip*, but not in *eye-slip*), *n*-Velarisation (*increment* vs *increase*), and *kr*-Assimilation (*crew* or *increment* vs *back-rub* or *cock-roach*), as well as for Chinese Tone Deletion, Gaelic Nasalisation, etc. (see Nespor and Vogel 1986: 93ff. for some discussion). It appears therefore that the existence of such a constituent as a domain of segmental processes is reasonably well substantiated.

5.2.6.2 Feet, rhythm, and stress

An additional, and central, role for the foot is as a basic unit of rhythm. Indeed, the word 'foot' itself (generalised in generative phonology since Liberman and Prince 1977) is taken over from classical metrics, where it precisely designates one such rhythmic measure.

The rhythm of languages like English has traditionally been based on stress, while the rhythm of another group of languages, typified by Spanish, has been considered grounded on syllabic organisation (see e.g. Pike 1944, Abercrombie 1967). The appropriateness of this dichotomy has however been questioned by recent research, which singles out stress as the sole overall source of linguistic rhythm (see Nespor 1990 for useful discussion and summary), hence its importance for us here.

A previously influential, now discredited, tradition identified stress with acoustic intensity (cf. e.g. the statement in Bloomfield (1933: 110) that 'stress – that is intensity or loudness – consists in greater amplitude of sound waves', and correspondingly in Jones (1950: 134) that 'force of utterance, abstracted from the other attributes of speech sounds, is termed *stress*'). The experimental evidence militates however against such a unique, direct physical correlate of stress. Specifically, as pointed out by Lehiste (1970: 153), stress is perceived on the basis of other phonetic properties besides intensity, such as duration, vowel quality and, above all, fundamental frequency. Chomsky and Halle (1968) explicitly distance themselves from a purely physicalist interpretation of the stress patterns generated by their rules, postulating instead a psychological basis for the stress hierarchies. The following quote is revealing (*SPE*: 25):

> There is little reason to suppose that the perceived stress contour must represent some physical property of the utterance in a point-by-point fashion; a speaker . . . should 'hear' the stress contour of the utterance that he perceives and understands, whether or not it is physically present in any detail. In fact, there is no evidence from experimental phonetics to suggest that these contours are actually present as physical properties of utterances in anything like the detail with which they are perceived.

This is in line with the Chomskyan programme, which regards linguistics and language as properly pertaining in the domain of cognitive psychology.[5]

Chomsky and Halle's stress rules are paradoxically expressed by means of numerical indices on (effectively) syllables. Thus, in their terms, the stress contour of the American place name *Apalachicola* will essentially be represented as in (44):

(44)   2   3   1
A p a l a c h i c o l a

The digits associated with the first, third and fifth syllables of this word conventionally correspond to a secondary (2), tertiary (3), and primary (1) degree of stress, respectively.[6] Such ranking would match well the interpretation of stress as pure phonetic intensity, but its adoption by Chomsky and Halle follows instead from their selection as stress data of the numerological contours of Kenyon and Knott's (1944) pronunciation dictionary, which are intended to represent different degrees of 'prominence', in a general sense.

In *SPE*, stress is formalised on a par with the other distinctive features. In particular, the defining matrix of each segment is postulated to include a feature [stress]. The problem with this stance is that the properties of stress are strikingly at variance with those of *bona fide SPE* distinctive features (DFS), as we now summarise in (45) (see Liberman and Prince 1977: 262–3):

(45) Stress	Other DFS
n-ary valency	binary valency
syntagmatic definition	paradigmatic definition
global effects	local effects
derivationally preserved	derivationally affected
disjunctive application	conjunctive application

Thus, as explained in Chapter 3 above, *SPE* features are characteristically binary throughout the phonology. By contrast, the stress feature is treated as multivalent from the start, in order to make it fit in with Kenyon and Knott's multifigure representation. Second, all non-primary values of stress are defined in relation to the primary value, i.e. syntagmatically, while the value of all other features is defined paradigmatically, i.e. in opposition to the value that the same feature could have taken in the same environment. Third, the phonetic effects of rules affecting ordinary distinctive features are usually local, i.e. manifested in the immediate neighbourhood of the feature itself. The effects of stress changes are however felt throughout the whole domain, irrespective of distance from the focus. Formally, this implies the use of variables effectively sanctioning an infinite distance between the trigger and the target(s), in contrast with the locality restrictions operative on rules manipulating other features. Next, relative stress prominence is typically preserved throughout the morphological derivation, at least in the *SPE* analysis of English (cf. e.g. *thèatre* → *thèátrical* → *thèátricálity*), contrary to what is the case with the other features.

Finally, stress rules must be ordered disjunctively with each other more often than rules affecting other features.

Faced with this impressive range of contrasts,[7] Liberman and Prince (1977) conclude that stress is in fact not a distinctive feature at all, but rather the attribute of being the strong term in a syllabic binomial. From this perspective, the opposition stressed–stressless in *Apalachicola* can be represented as in (46) (NB the notation is not strictly Liberman and Prince's; see note 8 below):

(46)
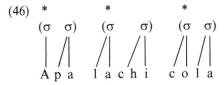

Two aspects of the prosody of the word have been written into this schema. First, the extension of each of the domains of the stress relationship: (*Apa*), etc. Second, the distribution of prosodic strength within each domain (the strong element carries the asterisk).

Higher-order strength relations between syllables can be represented by means of additional asterisk lines. For instance, in *Apalachicola*, *A* has greater prominence than *la*:

(47)
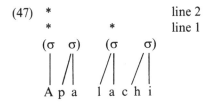

Likewise the location of the word's greatest prominence point in *co*, is represented as in (48), which gives the overall prominence pattern of the word, thus fulfilling the same function as the digits in (44) above:

(48)
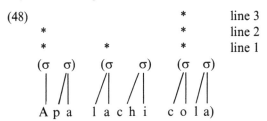

The asterisk-based structure superimposed on the line of syllables is technically known as the 'metrical grid',[8] the configuration and mechanics of which will become familiar as we proceed. At this point we must simply highlight the appropriateness of the device for the formalisation of rhythm, each graphic level representing a regular succession of beats (symbolised by the asterisks) and silences (simply left blank).

5.3 RHYTHM-BASED FEET

As mentioned, the basic domains of stress are typically identified with the feet of the prosodic hierarchy (the extension of the metrical grid to all prosodic levels is made explicit in Nespor and Vogel 1989). Notice that we are still to specify the mechanism responsible for the configuration of such feet, a task to which we now turn.

5.3.1 Foot configuration

There are, as noted, two basic ingredients to a metrical constituent, namely the extension of the constituent (in terms, e.g. of number of syllables) and the position occupied by the constituent head. We shall now investigate the determination of these variables.

5.3.1.1 The basic bounded foot

Consider the following forms from Maranungku (ng = [ŋ], ny = [ɲ], y = [j]):

(49)   Maranungku stress pattern

pán	'friend'
tíralk	'saliva'
mérepét	'beard'
ngúrinymín	'blackhead'
yángarmáta	'the Pleiades'
wóngowútanáwany	'thunderhead'

All odd syllables from the beginning carry stress. This pattern is of course reminiscent of the word *Apalachicola* in English. Contrary to what is the case in English, however (cf. e.g. *húllabaloó, páraphernália, hýpóthenúse, incántátion*, etc.), all Maranungku words are claimed to exhibit the same alternating pattern (see Tryon 1970), hence their heuristic value for us here.

The data in (49) carry the suggestion that Maranungku feet are binary, with the left term as the head, as captured in (50) below for the form *wongowutanawany* (following Halle and Vergnaud's 1987 practice, we include a grid baseline to represent the stress bearing elements, syllable heads as things stand at the moment):

(50)   *   *   *   line 1
      (*   *) (*   *) (*   *)   line 0
      w o n g o   w u t a   n a w a n y

The scope of the foot is represented within parentheses in line 0, and the head is identified by means of a superimposed line 1 asterisk. A pattern such as that of Maranungku can therefore be given the abstract representation in (51), where the dots informally stand for the (indefinite) repetition of the pattern, and the curly brackets indicate optionality:

(51)   *   line 1
      (* {*})   . . .   line 0

Such metrical constituents must be construed as maximal, in as much as the material enclosed by the curly braces need not be present (see the last foot in *(mére)(pét)*). The template in (51) can thus be readily interpreted as a set of conditions on head expansion, i.e. as a statement that dependents must be head-adjacent and placed on the head's right flank. Clearly, any such conditions are neutral as to the existence of dependents.

5.3.1.2 *A first set of parameters*

Halle and Vergnaud (1987) assume that metrical structures are the product of a small set of universal principles and parameters. Of immediate relevance are the Adjacency, Edge, and Flank parameters,[9] all of which relate to properties of the head, as follows:

(52) Head-related parameters
    a. Adjacency: adjacency between head and dependent(s) (yes/ no)
    b. Edge: head on edge of constituent (yes/no)
    c. Flank: constituent's flank where head is positioned (left/ right)

The Maranungku settings for these parameters are thus as in (53):

(53) Maranungku Head Parameter settings
    a. Adjacency: yes
    b. Edge: yes
    c. Flank: left

The machinery being proposed will now be further illustrated and explained.

5.3.1.2.1 Flank

We shall start with the Flank parameter. The data in (54) are from Yidin[y]:

(54) wawá:d[y]inú   'see-antipass.-past'
      gudá:ga   'dog-abs.'
      galbí: 'catfish-abs.'
      yabú:lam   'loya cane-abs.'
      mad[y]í:ndaŋ   'walk up-pers.'
      wayí:l   'red bream-abs.'
      gulúgulú:y   'black bream-com.'
      burwá:liŋá:lna   'jump-GOING-transitiviser-purp.'
      mad[y]índaŋá:d[y]iŋ   'walk up-transitiviser-antipass.-pers.'

The feet of these forms patently differ from those of Maranungku in being rightheaded, instead of leftheaded (in addition, final monosyllabic feet are stressless; see 5.3.2.3 below). The range of variation in the Flank parameter is therefore quite simple: the head can be located on the constituent's left or right flank. Crucially, the settings of this and other parameters are assumed to be uniform throughout the derivation, a pattern like that in (55) being therefore disallowed (O = head; o = dependent):

(55) (oO)(Oo)(oO)(Oo) . . .

Here the first foot would be rightheaded, the second leftheaded, and so on, in contravention of the uniformity of the setting. Note that such uniformity of parsing must be distinguished from the uniformity of parameter setting across the lexicon, which is also usually assumed. While highly desirable, some empirical difficulties for lexical uniformity of setting are pinpointed in Roca (1988, 1992a).

The following parameter settings account for the noted stress patterns of Yidin[y]:

(56) Yidin[y] Head settings
      a. Adjacency: yes
      b. Edge: yes
      c. Flank: right

5.3.1.2.2 Extrametricality

Consider now the forms in (57), from Winnebago:

(57) hochichínik   'boy'
  hakirújikshána 'he pulls taut'
  waghighí   'ball'
  haakítujík   'I pull it taut' (plain)
  haakítujíkshaná 'I pull it taut' (declined)
  naaná?a   'you weigh'

If we ignore the initial syllable, which is stressless throughout in Winnebago, and on the assumption that vowel sequences are bisyllabic in this language, the stress contours in (57) are construable as identical to those in (54) for Yidin^y.

In order to extend the procedure in (56) to Winnebago, we first need to account for the stresslessness of its initial syllable. This can readily be done by appeal to extraprosodicity, a device which enforces invisibility on a peripheral element, as already mentioned in Chapter 2. The extraprosodicity of the initial syllable (or, more rigorously, of the line 0 asterisk projected from the head of this syllable), yields the desired formal identity between the Winnebago and Yidin^y stress algorithms (NB '$\langle \rangle$' = extraprosodic):

(58)
```
              *           *           *      line 1
   ⟨ * ⟩ ( *    * ) ( *    * )   ( *    * )  line 0
   h a    a k i    t u j i k s h a n a
```

The origin of the extraprosodicity device can in fact be traced back to metrical theory, in particular to the work of Liberman and Prince (1977) (see also Nanni 1977). For this reason it is often referred to as 'extrametricality', even when put to use in a different module of the phonology (for some discussion of the history and uses of extrametricality see Roca 1992a).

For explicitness, the Extrametricality parameter and its attendant Peripherality Condition are now formally stated:

(59) Extrametricality parameter
  Mark element *e* on the (left/right)hand side as extrametrical (yes/no).

(60) Peripherality Condition
  Extrametrical elements must be peripheral in their domain.

5.3.1.2.3 Edge

We can now proceed to investigate the Edge parameter, which we will see allows for the expansion of the present foot inventory.

Consider the Cayuvava data in (61):

(61) maráhahaéiki   'their blankets'
      kihíBere   'I ran'

Such forms as in (61) are analysed in Halle and Vergnaud (1987: 25ff.) by means of trisyllabic feet. We assume once more that abutting vowels are heterosyllabic, and declare the final Cayuvava syllable extrametrical (notice that, being domain final, this syllable crucially complies with the Peripherality Condition).

We illustrate the analysis with the form *marahahaeiki*:

(62)   *   *   line 1
      (*   *   *) (* * *) 〈 * 〉   line 0
       m a r a h a   h a e i   k i

As can be seen, the head now occupies the central position in the foot. Feet of this kind still need to be marked positively for Adjacency, since clearly the head is adjacent to each of its two complements. They are however negatively set for the Edge parameter, since the head no longer obligatorily occupies the foot periphery. Note that, given these two settings, the setting of the Flank parameter becomes irrelevant:

(63) Cayuvava settings
      a. Adjacency: yes
      b. Edge: no
      c. Flank: n/a

5.3.2 Foot construction

5.3.2.1 Directionality

So far, we have implicitly assumed that foot structure is determined from left to right. Consider however the following forms from Warao:

(64) a. yápurúkitánehása
          náhoróahákutái
      b. yiwáranáe
          enáhoróahákutái

The contours in (64a) are similar to those of Maranungku. This identity is however deceptive, the forms in (64b) revealing the true nature of the Warao stress pattern. In prose, all even-numbered syllables from the end are stressed (abutting vowels are again heterosyllabic). This result will be achieved if, in addition to setting the three familiar parameters as in (53) above, we apply the foot construction algorithm from right to left, in contrast to Maranungku, where it must be applied from left to right (cf. again *mérepét*). This additional parameter thus affects construction, and is known as 'Directionality':

(65) Directionality parameter
  Constituent construction proceeds iteratively from the (left/right) edge.

Crucially, this parameter rules out such structures as in (66):

(66)

a. (*) (* *) (* *)   ←(* *)→   (* *) (* *)

b. →(* *) (* *) (*) (* *) (* *) ←(* *)

c. →(* *) (* *) (* *) (*) (* *) ←(* *)

As informally indicated by the arrows, foot construction has operated outwards from the middle in (66a), while in (66b) and (66c) it has applied inwards, simultaneously from both edges.[10]

5.3.2.2 *Maximality and Exhaustivity*

We pointed out above that metrical templates like the one in (51) must be construed as maximal, since the presence of the non-head material (enclosed in curly brackets for explicitness) is not necessary.

Faced with such optionality, the algorithm needs to be informed of the precise size of the target constituent. Halle and Vergnaud (1987) enforce maximal expansion by means of the following 'Maximality Condition':

(67) Maximality Condition
  Each constituent constructed by a rule of boundary construction must incorporate the maximal substring, provided that other requirements on constituent structure are satisfied.
                          (Halle and Vergnaud 1987: 15)

The Maximality Condition still falls short of guaranteeing the desired output, since nothing so far excludes such structures as in (68):

(68)   *   *

a. (* *) (* *) * * . . .

       *

    (*   *) * * * *

b. w o n g o w u t a n a w a n y = *wóngowutanawany

In (68), the input domains remain partly unparsed. This result is prevented by the following 'Exhaustivity Condition' on constituent construction:

(69) Exhaustivity Condition
> The rules of constituent boundary construction . . . apply exhaustively.

(Halle and Vergnaud 1987: 15)

The Maximality and Exhaustivity conditions are considered ultimately to fall out of a metaprinciple of determinism which Halle and Vergnaud claim underpins language competence just as much as language performance (some aspects of this principle will become clearer as we proceed):

(70) Procedural determinism
> The procedure for constructing the metrical constituent structure is the simplest possible deterministic procedure. The constituent demarcations are those licensed by the extremities of the input string, by the intrinsic heads, and, in the case of bounded constituents, by the iterative application of the construction rule, and only those.

(Halle and Vergnaud 1987: 135)

5.3.2.3 *Asterisk deletion*

The existence of the Exhaustivity Condition (69) raises a question of legitimacy for such forms as ⟨*ha*⟩*kirújikshána* (Winnebago) or *enáhoróahákutái* (Warao), since in both cases construction seems not to have affected the syllable parsed last by the algorithm (the rightmost and leftmost syllable, respectively). Had this syllable been incorporated into the grid, the corresponding structures would instead have been as follows:

(71) a.   *   * *   b. * *   *   *   *

     ⟨ * ⟩(* *)(*   *)(*)   (*)(* *)(* *)(* *)(* *)

     h a k i r u j i k s h a n a   e n a h o r o a h a k u t a i

Both the peripheral feet we have additionally constructed in (71) are 'degenerate', in that they fall short of the maximal number of elements (two in the present case). Moreover, in both cases the construction of the degenerate foot has brought about a stress clash. While such a situation is indeed compatible with the procedure (cf. again the curly brackets in the template in (51) above), the metrical weakness of degenerate feet makes them liable to deletion under language-particular conditions. One such rule is postulated in Halle and Vergnaud (1987) to delete the second of the two adjacent stresses generated by the Winnebago algorithm (NB '.' is intended to represent metrical weakness):

(72)   * *   * . line 1
        * * → * *   line 0

The mirror-image output will obviously dispose of the corresponding Warao degenerate foot in (71b). Deletion rules such as the one in (72) are commonly made use of as a clash resolution strategy in Halle and Vergnaud (1987) (in Prince 1983, the emergence of clash is instead parametrically prevented by a principle of Clash Avoidance).

5.3.3 Interferences with the algorithm

The pattern of alternating stresses we have been referring to so far can be considered 'metrical', in as much as the algorithm responsible for its creation divides up the input string strictly in accordance with the given measure. Such patterning does not however exhaust the range of possible stress contours, as we shall now see.

5.3.3.1 *Quantity Sensitivity*

Consider the following data from Odawa (a dialect of Ojibwa):

(73) ninágamómín   'we sing'
      ninágám   'I sing'
      niníbá   'I sleep'
      nagámó   'he sings'
      nibím(i)bátó   'I run'

The alternating stress on the even-numbered syllables from the beginning suggests the same head settings as in Yidin^y in (56) above, and a left-to-right setting for Directionality (consecutive stresses on the right edge are of course the product of degenerate foot construction on the last syllable; notice the persistence here of the clash thus created).

All the vowels in (73) are short. The inventory of this language also includes long vowels, however, as illustrated in (74):

(74) niwí:ndigó:wimín   'we are monsters'
      niwí:ndigó:w   'I'm a monster'
      nibímosé:mín   'we walk'
      bimósé: 'he walks'
      nigí:namádáp   'I sat'
      nigí:namádabímín   'we sat'
      bimíbató: 'he runs'

In (74), stress assignment is unaffected by differences in vowel length. In the additional forms in (75), however, the long vowels are placed in positions predicted as weak by the algorithm as given:

(75) niníbá:mín   'we sleep'
      kitó:wé:wikámikóm   'your store'
      niwí:pimítakkóná:n   'I'll carry it along'

As can be seen, long vowels are automatically stressed in this language, irrespective of their linear position. Such sensitivity to the light–heavy syllable distinction (Odawa long vowels obviously make syllables heavy) is encapsulated in the following parameter (see the related discussion in Chapter 4):

(76) Quantity Sensitivity parameter
      Heavy syllables (where 'heavy' can be defined on a language-particular basis) are obligatory constituent heads (yes/no).

All we have to assume in order to obtain the correct Odawa contours is a positive setting for this parameter in this language. The derivation in (77) thus ensues:

(77)
```
                              *              *   *   *
   *   *   *    *      *   *   *    *      ( *   *) (*) (*)
 n i n i b a : m i n → n i n i b a : m i n →  n i n i  b a : m i n
```

The effect of the originally constituentless asterisk mark on the construction algorithm follows from an additional condition on constituent construction, the 'Faithfulness Condition':

(78) Faithfulness Condition
      The output metrical structure respects the distribution of heads (accented elements), in the sense that each head is associated with constituent boundaries in the output structure, and that these are located at the appropriate positions in the sequence. Constituent

boundaries are erased in the output when none of the elements enclosed by the boundaries is marked as head.

(Halle and Vergnaud 1987: 16)

In essence, the Faithfulness Condition simply makes explicit the definitory complementarity of heads and constituents. In particular, a head is the head *of* a constituent, and a constituent is but the projection of a head.

5.3.3.2 Lexical accent

The net effect of the Quantity Sensititivy parameter is the licensing of heads of non-metrical origin, i.e. heads not created by the counting algorithm.

The introduction of this machinery makes possible the utilisation of lexical 'accent' (i.e. lexicalised metrical structure; in this technical use, accent is therefore quite distinct from stress) for the formalisation of stress idiosyncrasies. For instance, the basic stress contours of Aklan partially overlap with those of Odawa above, Aklan feet also being binary and rightheaded. On the other hand, Aklan contrasts with Odawa in the setting of Directionality, which is right-to-left, and in limiting syllable heaviness to closed syllables (long vowels are in fact reportedly absent from the Aklan inventory):

(79) (pitú)   'seven'
      (suɣúd)   'room'
      (bisá)   'kiss'
      (bí)(sahí)   'kiss-ref.-imp.'
      (gás)(tahún)   'spend-Goal-fut.'
      (suɣú)(guʔún)   'servant'
      (ʔatú)(baŋán)   'genitals'
      (kiná)(putús)   'wrap-Instrument focus-past posterior'
      (má)(tiná)(marún) 'being lazy'
      (asír)(tár)   'lucky'

In the last form, the accented heavy syllable *sir* prevents the maximal expansion of the foot headed by *tar*, which consequently remains degenerate.

Consider now the form *nagápánabún* 'go soaping-Actor pres.'. Clearly, our procedure would predict *(*ná*)(*gapá*)(*nabún*). The deviation in the contours predicted by the algorithm can be accounted for straightforwardly by assuming that the morpheme *-ga-*, signifying verbal progressive, carries a lexical line 1 mark (an 'accent'), the derivation proceeding otherwise as expected:

(80)
```
         *                      *   *      *
  *   *   *   *   *     ( *   *)( *)  ( *  *)
na-ga-pa-n-abu n → na-ga-pa-n-abu n
```

Such a simple and natural strategy allows us to preserve the general theory at a minimum cost.

Lexical accent marks are not confined to whole morphemes, and can in principle also be assigned to phonological material. Thus, for instance, the stress pattern of Tübatulabal parallels that of Aklan, but with long vowels now as heavy (see Prince 1983: 63):

(81) witáŋhatál   'the Tejon Indians'
      wítaŋhátalá:bacú   'away from the Tejon Indians'
      haní:lá   'the house-obj.'
      wašá:gáhajá   'it might flame up'
      ánaŋí:nínimút   'he is crying wherever he goes-DISTR'
      yú:dú:yú:dát   'the fruit is mashing'

Contraventions of the pattern are however found, as in the form *tíkapí ganáyín*, which ought to have been **tíkápígánayín*. All we have to assume is that the final stress bearer of the recent past agentive morpheme /pigana/ carries a lexical accent:

(82)
```
                *                  *      *     *   *
  *   *   *   *   *     *     ( *)( *   *)( *  *)( *)
t i ka-p i gana-y i n →  t i  ka-p i  gana-y i n
```

5.3.4 Stress algorithms and stress typology

The above procedures (essentially those propounded by Halle and Vergnaud 1987, building on antecedent work) are reported as vitiated by a fundamental flaw in Hayes (1985, 1987, 1991), as we shall now explain.

The parameters reviewed make available four distinct types of binary foot patterns, as follows ('X' = accented grid position; 'x' = plain grid position):

(83) a. Quantity Insensitive

```
                      x            x            x
  i. leftheaded     ...( x x )  ( x x )  ( x x )...
                         x            x            x
  ii. rightheaded   ...( x x )  ( x x )  ( x x )...
```

b. Quantity Sensitive

	x	x	x
i. leftheaded	... (X x)	(X)	(X x) ...

	x	x	x
ii. rightheaded	... (x X)	(X)	(x X) ...

The natural expectation is for a more or less even distribution of these patterns throughout the world's languages. Hayes's investigations have however revealed that iterative rightheaded systems are all quantity sensitive, while the majority of their leftheaded counterparts are quantity insensitive. This suggests that the patterns in (83aii) and (83bi) ought not to be freely generated by the system, but this restriction cannot be obtained on Halle and Vergnaud's account in any principled way.

A functional reason for this typological reduction is tentatively sought by Hayes in the principles of human rhythm perception. Specifically, binary feet of uneven internal length (. . . duh duhhh duh duhhh duh . . .) are commonly perceived as rightheaded, while binary feet of even internal length but uneven intensity (. . . duh DUH duh DUH duh . . .) are perceived as leftheaded (see Woodrow 1951 and Bell 1977 for reviews of the appropriate experimental evidence).

Hayes's proposal involves the replacement of Halle and Vergnaud's parametric construction procedure with a fixed foot inventory, as follows (NB the degenerate structures following the semicolon are only adopted upon failure of their predecessors; as before, 'X' represents an accented grid position, and 'x' its plain counterpart; 'σ' stands for a grid position irrespective of weight):

(84) a. Quantity Insensitive

	x		line 1
leftheaded	(σ σ) ;	(σ)	line 0

b. Quantity Sensitive

	x	x	line 1
i. leftheaded	(x x) ;	(X) ; (x)	line 0
	x	x	line 1
ii. rightheaded	(x σ) ;	(X) ; (x)	line 0

A reasonable interpretation of this inventory is as a set of conditions on foot well-formedness. Crucially, the observed weight restrictions are already built into the shape of the foot. An important aspect of the proposal concerns the inclusion by Hayes of headless feet. Such feet are clearly incompatible with Halle and Vergnaud's system, central to which is the construal of metrical constituents as the domain that corresponds to a head, as we have already seen (cf. the Faithfulness Condition in (78) above).[11]

The advantages of Hayes's proposal are brought out by the stress system of Cairene Arabic. In (85) we summarise the conditions for the placement of Cairene rightmost stress (see Langendoen 1968: 102, McCarthy 1979: 105, Halle and Vergnaud 1987: 61, Hayes 1991: 56ff.), ultimately to surface as the word's primary stress (as will be seen below, the remaining stresses are automatically derived by the same procedure):

(85) a. last syllable if superheavy;
     b. penult if heavy;
     c. penult or antepenult separated by an even number of syllables (NB nil is even) from:
         i. the immediately preceding heavy syllable;
         ii. the beginning of the word.

The clauses in (85) are all disjunctive and must be applied in the order given. Superheavy syllables are heavy syllables which contain an extra rimal consonant.

Some examples are now provided (see Halle and Vergnaud 1987:61, Hayes 1991:57):

(86) a.   katábt   'I wrote'
            sakakí:n   'knives'
     b.   Ýamálti   'you-f.-sg. did'
            haðá:ni   'these-f.-dual'
     c. i. martába   'mattress'
            mudarrísit   'teacher-f.-CONSTRUCT'
            Ýadwiyatúhu   'his drugs'
            Ýadwiyatúhuma: 'their drugs'
        ii. búxala   'misers'
            kátaba   'he wrote'
            katabítu   'they wrote'
            šajarátun   'tree'
            šajarátuhu   'his tree'

The facts just reviewed carry a number of implications concerning the setting of the parameters, as summed up in (87):

(87) Cairo Arabic parameter settings
     Head
     a. Adjacency: yes
     b. Edge: yes
     c. Flank: left

Construction
d.   Directionality: left to right
e.   Accent: all heavy syllables
f.   Extrametricality: right if syllable not superheavy

In order to account for the oscillation of stress between the penultimate and the antepenultimate syllables, Halle and Vergnaud (1987) take the step of declaring all Cairene rime elements (NB not just syllable heads or vowels) stress bearers. The desired result follows automatically, given the parameter settings in (87):

(88)   *   *   *   *   *   *
       **   * * *   *   (**)(* *)(*   *)⟨ *⟩
       ?ad.wi.ya.tu.ma: →   ?ad.wi.ya.tu.hu.ma:

       *   *   *
       ** * *   (**)(*)⟨*⟩
       mar.ta.ba   →   mar.ta.ba

           *   *   *   *   *
       * ** * *   (*)(**)(*)⟨*⟩
       mu.dar.ri.sit   →   mu.dar.ri .sit

The obvious function of the extension of stress-bearer status to all rimal elements is the resetting of the syllable count on the heavy syllables. This result is however achieved in a more direct way in Hayes's framework, given a setting for Cairene feet as leftheaded quantity sensitive (NB word-final heavy syllables become light by last consonant extrametricality; the use of extrametricality to alleviate weight is discussed in Roca 1992a):

(89)   x   x   x
       (X) (x x)(x   x)(x)
       ?a d.wi.ya.tu.hu.ma⟨:⟩

          x   x
       (X) (x   x)
       ma r.ta.ba

             x   x
       (x)(X) (x x)
       mu.da r.ri.s i⟨t⟩

Note importantly that, in addition to laxing the requirements for stress-bearer status, Halle and Vergnaud's analysis requires the accenting of all heavy syllables (cf. (87e)), an obvious duplication of formal resources.

This price is not paid under Hayes's account.

Halle (1990: 167–8) also points out that such accenting must affect the leftmost of the two tautorimal line 0 asterisks, to prevent the generation of incorrect stress contours:

(90)

```
                                    *
     *  ** *  *  *   *  →    *  ** *  *  *   *  →
   mu.qaa.ti .la.tu.hu      mu.qaa.ti .la.tu.hu

            *
   ( *    *   *)
   ( * *)(* *)(* *)⟨*⟩
   muqa  ati  latu hu
```

(*muqaatilátuhu; cf. muqaatilatúhu 'his fighter')

Halle suggests that any such a restriction is arbitrary, and he accordingly reformalises 'accent' as a constituent boundary overlapping by convention with a syllable boundary (i.e. the 'accentual' constituent boundary may not be placed syllable-internally):[12]

(91)

```
     *  ** *  *  *   *  →    * (** *  *  *   *  →
   mu.qaa.ti.la.tu.hu       mu.qaa.ti.la.tu.hu

            *
   ( *   *   *    *)
   ( *)( **)(* *)(*)⟨*⟩
   mu qaa ti la tu hu
```

As can be seen, this approach leads to the correct result, namely *muqaatilatúhu*.

While the stipulation that metrical structure must respect syllable boundaries brings metrical structure into line with the Strict Layer Hypothesis (8), and must thus be welcome from this perspective, it is somewhat at odds with the assumption in Halle and Vergnaud (1987) that metrical structure is autosegmentalised from prosodic structure. This assumption is seemingly maintained in such subsequent works as Halle (1990) and Halle and Kenstowicz (1991).

5.4 WORD STRESS AND ALLIED PROCESSES

5.4.1 Word stress

The discussion so far has been focused on foot-level constituency. As already pointed out, however, besides foot-bound stress, words characteristically exhibit one most prominent syllable, and perhaps also others of intermediate prominence, as illustrated again by the grid of *Apalachicola*:

(92)   *
         *   *
         *   *   *
         *   * *   * * *
         Apalachicola

We shall now direct our attention to the word level, abstracting away the intermediate levels, for simplicity.[13]

As expected, word-level metrical structure is anchored on the next lower metrical level available. In principle, all the parameter settings mentioned are available for the construction of word structure, since in Halle and Vergnaud's parametric theory no discrimination is made between levels with regard to the method of constituent construction. Such uniformity may however be deemed undesirable, since, on the assumption that words carry a prominence peak,[14] the word-level constituent will automatically be set negatively for the Adjacency parameter. If so, the number of elements in such a constituent will potentially be unlimited, as shown in (93):

(93) *
      (* * * * . . .)

Constituent unboundedness clearly renders the Directionality parameter void, since direction of construction only yields a different outcome with bounded constituents. On the other hand, the Flank parameter is still operative, since, besides languages with initial word-stress, as schematically represented in (93), there are many others where the final foot achieves maximal prominence:

                       *
(94) (. . . * * * *)

More controversial is the fate of the Edge parameter. Were such a parameter to be available to unbounded feet, the following structures would be sanctioned:

               *   *
(95) a. (. . . * * * * . . .)   b. (. . . * * * * . . .)

In (95), the head of the constituent is not adjacent to all its dependents. Such a configuration is however ruled out by Halle and Vergnaud (1987) on the basis of the distribution of the ternary feet of Cayuvava. Thus, consider the data in (96), which complement those given in (61) above:

(96)   ikitáparerépeha   'the water is clean'
       Bariékimi   'seed of squash'

Following the procedure so far, we would expect the derivation of *Bariékimi* to proceed as in (97):

(97)   *   *
       (*)(** *)⟨ *⟩
       Bar i eki mi

In particular, the output ought to have been *Báriékimi*, with initial stress. This form, however, is supposedly unattested. The reason for this gap, according to Halle and Vergnaud, lies in the form's constituency ambiguity, the structure in (98) being an obvious alternative to that in (97):

(98)   *   *
       (* *)(* *)⟨ *⟩
       Bari eki mi

The two structures, however, presuppose incompatible settings of the Edge parameter, namely negative for (97) but positive for (98). A situation such as this is at odds with the following 'Recoverability Condition':

(99) Recoverability Condition

Given the direction of government of the constituent heads in the grammar, the location of the metrical constituent boundaries must be unambiguously recoverable from the location of the heads, and conversely the location of the heads must be recoverable from that of the boundaries.

(Halle and Vergnaud 1987: 10)

Thus, in Halle and Vergnaud's terms, the representation of the boundaries and the representation of the heads are 'conjugate', i.e. stand in a relation of mutual implication, for a given setting of the Flank parameter. Now, clearly, in *Bariékimi*, the location of the boundaries is not recoverable from the location of the heads, made explicit in (100):

(100)   *   *
       * ** *⟨*⟩
       Bariekimi

Specifically, we have seen this configuration to be compatible with the two parsings in (97) and (98) above. Consequently, compliance with the Recoverability Condition requires that the word-initial syllable be left unparsed, as apparently corresponds to fact:

(101)
```
              *
  * ( * *   * ) ⟨ * ⟩
  B a r i e k i   m i
```

This success notwithstanding, the Recoverability Condition has been called into question (see e.g. Dresher 1990), as indeed has Halle and Vergnaud's overall approach to trisyllabic stress. For instance, Hayes (1988, 1991) derives such a pattern out of 'weak local parsing', a parametric procedure enabling the skipping of precisely one stress bearer as each ordinary binary foot is constructed. 'Weak local parsing' is obviously incompatible with Halle and Vergnaud's Exhaustivity Condition, stated in (69) above.

5.4.2 Line conflation

Not all languages manifest secondary stress. The simplest formalisation of such data will involve the direct construction of the word constituent on the stress-bearer line, without the intervention of feet.[15]

One example of this type of language is provided by Bengali:

(102) Bengali stress[16]

páromanobik	'atomic, molecular'
ápʃoʃ	'regret'
bánij:o	'trade'
bátʃorik	'annual'
báddohta	'obedience'
próthom	'first'
próʃno	'question'
ápot:i	'dissent'
ápon	'personal'
ápnar	'your own' (honorific)
ɔ́nabɒʃ:ok	'unnecessary'
ónuʃɒron	'pursuit'
bhímrul	'hornet'
bhálobaʃa	'love'
dhã̄ dha	'puzzle'
dhópa	'washerman'
ʈhánɖa	'cold'

According to sources (Lahiri p.c., Hayes and Lahiri 1991), no secondary stresses are discernible in this language, word-initial primary stress being accordingly formalisable as a leftheaded unbounded word constituent built directly on the string of syllable heads, as follows:

(103) Bengali metrical structure

```
     *
(*  *  *  *  *)
paromanobik
```

More complex is the case of (literary) Macedonian, also with no discernible secondary stresses, but where regular word stress is antepenultimate (Comrie 1976, Franks 1985, 1987), as illustrated by the following paradigm:

(104) Macedonian stress

Sg.	Sg. definite	Pl.	Pl. definite	
vodéničar	vodeníčarot	vodeníčari	vodeničárite	'miller'
pólkovnik	polkóvnikot	polkóvnici	polkovnícite	'colonel'
rábota	rabótata	ráboti	rabótite	'work'
véčer	véčerta	véčeri	večérite	'evening'
zbór	zbórot	zbórovi	zboróvite	'word'
gláva	glávata	glávi	glávite	'head'

The rightward shifts of stress in some of the derivatives attest that Macedonian stress cannot be lexical, but must be assigned by the action of our familiar parameters.

In order to derive the target antepenultimate stress, we adopt the algorithm in (105):

(105) Macedonian foot parameter settings
    Head
        a. Adjacency: yes
        b. Edge: yes
        c. Flank: left

    Construction
        d. Directionality: right to left
        e. Extrametricality: right

In particular, Macedonian feet will be binary leftheaded, built from right to left, with the last element extrametrical. In addition, the word-level constituent must be set as unbounded rightheaded. This procedure will in all cases assign primary stress to the penultimate metrical syllable, as sought:

(106) a.
```
                                              *
                     *  *              (*   *)
  *  *  **       *  *  *⟨*⟩     (*)(* *)⟨*⟩     (*)(* *)⟨*⟩
  vodeničar  →  vodeni čar  →  vo deni čar  →  vo deni čar
```

b.
```
                                                      *
                        *   *   *          (*   *   *)
  *  *  **  **      *  *  *  *  *⟨*⟩   (*)(* *)(* *)⟨*⟩   (*)(* *)(* *)⟨*⟩
  vodeničarite  →  vodeni čari te  →  vo deni čari te  →  vo deni čari te
```

The failure of Macedonian secondary stresses to surface lends *prima facie* support to an iterativeness parameter (see e.g. Archangeli 1984, 1984–5, Levin 1989, Hammond 1984, and Hayes 1991 for discussion of this parameter). Specifically, according to this account, foot construction would proceed iteratively in, e.g. Maranungku, but non-iteratively in Macedonian. Non-iterative parsing is of course directly at odds with the Exhaustivity Condition in (69) above. Moreover, as shown in Halle (1990), such an approach runs into difficulties.

Thus, besides regular antepenultimate stress, a handful of Macedonian forms (typically loans), exhibit penultimate stress:

(107) konzumátor   'consumer'
       romántik   'romantic'
       literatúra   'literature'
       nacionálen   'national'

These forms are usually analysed as carriers of a lexical accent on the penult. Now, here too, stress reverts to its regular antepenultimate location when additional syllables are made available, e.g. as a consequence of inflectional suffixation (the two forms in parentheses therefore experience no change):

(108) Sg. definite   Pl.   Pl. definite
       konzumátorot   konzumátori   konzumatórite
       romántikot   romántici   romantícite
       literatúrata   (literatúri)   literatúrite
       nacionálniot   (nacionálni)   nacionálnite

Suppose now that we were indeed to account for this irregular pattern by means of an iterativeness parameter. The derivation of *konzumatórite* would then be as follows:

(109)
```
          *                 *              * *
  *  *  *  *  **      *  *  *  *  *⟨*⟩   *  *  *(* *)⟨*⟩
  konzumatorite  →  konzumatori te  → konzumatori te
```

At this point, the form contains two stresses. In order to obtain the correct surface contour, we would be forced to introduce the rule in (110):

(110) $* \rightarrow \emptyset /$____ $*$ line 1

As it stands, the procedure has been incremented with both the iterativeness parameter and the deletion rule in (110). The alternative offered in Halle and Vergnaud (1987) and Halle (1990) is the postulation of a 'Conflation' parameter. In particular, languages marked positively for this parameter will undergo deletion of the line of foot heads (and, concomitantly, given the Faithfulness Condition (78), of the corresponding constituency brackets):

(111) a.
```
          *
     (*   *)                  *
     (*)(* *)⟨*⟩      *(* *)⟨*⟩
     vo deni  čar  →  vodeni  čar
```

b.
```
                                    *
           *           (*     * *)                        *
   * *  * * * *        (* *)( *)(* *)⟨*⟩     *  *  *(* *)⟨*⟩
   konzumatorite  →  konzu ma tori te  →  konzumatori te
```

This procedure is obviously simpler than its iterativeness-based alternative, and therefore preferred.

5.4.3 Stress Shift

5.4.3.1 Rhythm-inspired

We commented above on the existence of stress shifts in English (see *Jápanese ráilways* and others in (18)), which we used to substantiate the prosodic constituent 'P Phrase'. We are now in a position to investigate the mechanics of such shifts in the context of metrical theory.

The formalisation of these shifts on the metrical grid is in fact straightforward. Thus, consider the metrical structure of *Japanese* in isolation:

(112)
```
                   *
       ( *       * )
       ( *   ) ( * )
       J a p a   n e s e
```

Here the word stress falls on the final syllable *nese*, the initial syllable *Ja(p)* being the head of the subordinate metrical foot *Japa*.

Consider now the metrical structures which are input to the collocation *Japanese railways*:

```
(113)                *             *
          ( *        * )    ( *         * )
          ( *   * ) ( * )    ( * )    ( * )
          J a p a   n e s e   r a i l w a y s
```

It can be readily observed that the two asterisks in line 2 occupy adjacent grid positions, in as much as all the asterisks they dominate down to line 0 are also adjacent. English strongly disfavours such line 2 clashes, and consequently the mark on *nese* slides leftwards to the next landing site in line 1, *Ja(p)*, as shown in (114):

```
(114)     *                   *
          ( *        * )    ( *         * )
          ( *   * ) ( * )    ( * )    ( * )
          J a p a   n e s e   r a i l w a y s
```

Some comments on the procedure are in order. First, the offending configuration must be located in line 2, since similar clashes are readily tolerated in line 1 (for instance, *Américan railwáys* does not become **Américán railwáys*). Second, as shown in Hayes (1984b), the clash configuration does not in fact require strict adjacency (cf. e.g. *Mississípi river* → *Míssissipi ríver*), although the pressure for shift indeed becomes stronger as closeness increases. Third, as explained in section 5.2.1 above, the clash must be encompassed within a P Phrase (cf. [*Japanése* [*ráilways and mótorways*]], with no shift). Fourth, the shift invariably takes place to the left in English (cf. **Japanése ráilwáys*), but not necessarily so in other languages (e.g. in German, as discussed in Kiparsky 1966), a fact that points to parametrisation of shift direction.

The phenomenon of stress shift nicely illustrates the formal superiority of the grid over its numerological and arboreal alternatives. Thus, consider the representation of the phrase at hand in *SPE* notation:

```
(115)   2    1    1    2
        Japanese  railways
```

Prominence reversal will yield the contour in (116):

```
(116)   1    2    1    2
        Japanese  railways
```

While it would be a straightforward matter to delete or alter the clashing number 1 (e.g. 1 → 2 /___ 1), the chain reaction that this change provokes is formally very awkward and unrevealing.

Liberman and Prince's (1977) and Hayes's (1980) arboreal counterpart appears to fare better. Consider the input in (117):

(117) Japanese railways

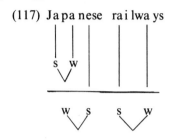

As can be seen, the definition of clash as involving two adjacent *s*s is now straightforward, as also is its correction:

(118) Japanese railways

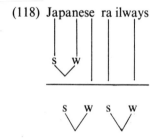

Simply, the sister nodes in the first word have undergone labelling reversal, a process dubbed 'Iambic Reversal' in Liberman and Prince (1977).

Matters are however less straightforward when more complex structures are involved. Consider for instance the derivation of *Apalachicola Falls*. The input is given in (119):

(119) Apalachicola Falls

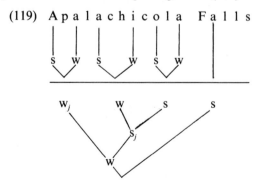

What is now needed is a reversal of the sister nodes we have coindexed '*j*':

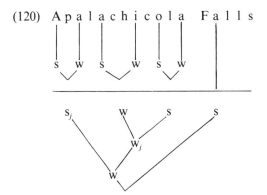

(120)

The motivation for this operation and its interpretation are however far from clear. Thus, consider the clashing structure, which we highlight in (121):

(121)

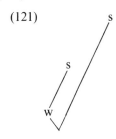

It is not obvious why this structure should be thus definitory of clash, given the different levels of embedding at which the two *s*s occur. As regards the interpretation of the reversal, it is again unclear how the clash has been amended, since both *co* and *Falls* remain dominated by strong nodes.

5.4.3.2 Deletion-triggered

Another class of stress shifts accommodated for in Halle and Vergnaud's (1987) metrical theory follows the deletion of level 0 structure.

Consider the following data from Bedouin Hijazi Arabic (Al-Mozainy *et al.* 1985):

(122) a. Ɂínkisar̩ 'he got broken'   b. Ɂinksár̩at 'she . . . '
        íntiðar̩   'he waited'   intðár̩an   'they-f. . . . '
        íftikar̩   'he remembered'   iftkár̩aw   'they-m. . . . '
        íxtibar̩   'he took an exam'   ixtbár̩aw   'they-m. . . . '

In the context of the stress rules of this language, essentially similar to those of Macedonian in (105) above but with quantity sensitivity (moderated by extrametricality of the final consonant), the stress shift attested by the forms in b. is truly strange (we would instead expect antepenultimate stress: *Ɂínksar̩at*, etc.).

In the b. forms the second stem vowel has been deleted by a syllabically-conditioned rule. Consider in this light the metrical representation which we must assume is input to *Ɂinksár̩at*:

(123)   *
       *   (*   *) ⟨ * ⟩
       Ɂ i n k i s a   r a t

Note in particular that stress does fall on the antepenultimate syllable, *ki*, as predicted by the algorithm.

Consider now the effect of vowel deletion on metrical structure:

(124)   *
       *   (*) ⟨ * ⟩
       Ɂ i n k   s a   r a t

In particular, the deletion of the vowel automatically causes the deletion of its corresponding stress bearer, thus depriving the higher level metrical mark of its level 0 underpinning. Clearly, such metrical mark must immediately look for a substitute anchoring site. The minimal assumption is that such a site will be adjacent to the old one, indeed the case with the stress bearers corresponding to *Ɂink* and *sa*. The choice between these two alternatives is straightforward: simply, the movement of metrical marks is constrained by metrical constituency, and therefore only the *sa* stress bearer can host the orphaned asterisk.

Besides its intrinsic interest, the situation just described constitutes evidence of the strongest kind for the reality of metrical constituency. This counters the proposals by, e.g. Prince (1983) and Selkirk (1984b) (correcting the approach in Selkirk 1980) that the prosodic constituent 'foot' be dispensed with, and stress simply interpreted as constituentless syllable prominence (notationally, as a grid deprived of parentheses).

5.5 UNBOUNDED FEET

All the systems considered up to this point are grounded on rhythmic alternations, whether overt, as in systems exhibiting alternating surface stresses, or covert, as in languages which undergo deletion of bounded feet by conflation (see Roca 1992b for further discussion of this dichotomy). In this section we shall review cases where the source of stress (and a fortiori its manifestation) is patently independent of rhythm.

5.5.1 Quantity-based

In some languages, stress falls on the last heavy syllable or on the last plain syllable, while in others it is carried by the first heavy syllable or by the first plain syllable. These two mirror alternatives are represented by Aguacatec Mayan and Khalkha Mongolian, respectively. We exemplify the latter language in (125):

(125)　Khalkha Mongolian
　　　　bosgú:l　　　　'fugitive'
　　　　bariá:d　　　　'after holding'
　　　　xoyərdugá:r　　'second'
　　　　gará:sa:　　　　'from one's own hand'
　　　　áli　　　　　　'which'
　　　　xő təbərə　　　'leadership'

The pattern of words with no heavy syllables is obviously identical to that of Bengali, discussed above (cf. (102), (103)). Moreover, the contour of their congeners with heavy syllables can readily be assimilated, given the presence of the corresponding quantity-based accents on line 1. We illustrate both possibilities in (126) (we assume that the line 1 gap in a. will be eventually filled in by convention):

(126)　a.　　*　　　　b.　　　　　　*　　　line 2
　　　　　　　　　　　　　　* *　　* *　　line 1
　　　　　　* * * *　　　* * *　* * *　　line 0
　　　　　　xotəbərə　　　gara:sa:→gara:sa:

On the face of it, therefore, such patterns simply do not include metrical constituency.

Consider now the following data from Eastern Cheremis:

(127)　šla:pá:zəm　　'his hat (acc.)'
　　　　ši:nčá:m　　　'I sit'
　　　　tə́ləzəm　　　 'moon's'

As can be seen, the word stress is now carried by the rightmost syllable containing a long vowel, while in the absence of long vowels stress falls on the word-initial syllable. Clearly, therefore, the procedure adopted for Khalkha will not work here. A number of languages behave like Eastern Cheremis, among them Hindi and Classical Arabic. The mirror-image situation is found in Komi, with the first heavy syllable receiving word stress, and, in the absence of heavy syllables, the last syllable.

The solution to the problem is straightforward on the assumption that the Eastern Cheremis system involves the construction of leftheaded feet, crucially on a negative setting of the Adjacency parameter (as in Khalkha, long vowels are obviously accented). In addition, the word constituent will be rightheaded (and, naturally, also unbounded). Unwanted secondary stresses will be disposed of by conflation. We exemplify in (128):

(128) a.
```
                    *
         (*)          *
 * * *   (* * *)   (* * *)
tələzəm → tələzəm → tələzəm
```

b.
```
                                *
            * *        (*  *)           *
 * * *     * * *      (*)(* *)     * (* *)
šla:pa:zəm → šla:pa:zəm → šla:pa:zəm → šla:pa:zəm
```

Note that in *tələzəm* there is only one foot, since this word contains no long vowels. Its counterpart *šla:pa:zəm*, by contrast, originally has two feet, as correspond to the two long vowels.

In Halle and Vergnaud's model, metrical constituency is a universal property of language, as reflected in the Faithfulness and Recoverability Conditions discussed above. Consequently, on their analysis, languages on the Khalkha Mongolian pattern will include unbounded feet, as we have just seen do those on the Eastern Cheremis mould. Clearly, however, the parameter settings of Khalkha cannot all be identical to those of Cheremis, as specified in (129):

(129)　Eastern Cheremis and Khalkha Mongolian settings

		Eastern Cheremis		Khalkha Mongolian	
		Line 0	Line 1	Line 0	Line 1
a.	Adjacency:	no	no	no	no
b.	Edge:	yes	yes	yes	yes
c.	Flank:	left	right	left	left

Let us in this light explore the derivation of the Khalkha forms in (126b) above. Consider first *xötəbərə*:

(130)
```
                          *
              *          (*)              *
        * * * *    (* * * *)  (* * * *)  (* * * *)
```
xötəbərə→xötəbərə→xötəbərə →xötəbərə

Here the same results are obtained with or without foot building. Let us proceed to *gara:sa:*:

(131)
```
                                      *
                * *    * * *   (* * *)     *
        * * *   * * *  (*)(*)(*) (*)(*)(*) (*)* *
```
gara:sa:→gara:sa:→ga ra:sa:→ga ra:sa:→ga ra:sa:

As can be seen, the implementation of foot construction in such words will invariably yield a stress on the initial syllable, in conflict with the facts.

In order to prevent this result, Halle and Vergnaud *de facto* introduce a Construction parameter. This parameter will only be relevant to unbounded constituents, since bounded constituents are by definition created through metrical construction (cf. the template in (51) above):

(132) Construction parameter
      Construct constituents on line *n* (yes/no).

Thus assuming a negative setting for this parameter in Khalkha, the following derivations result:

(133) a.
```
                                      *
                * *    * *    (* *)       *
        * * *   * * *  *(*)(*)  *(*)(*)   *(*) *
```
gara:sa:→gara:sa:→gara:sa:→gara:sa:→gara:sa:

   b.
```
                   *          *
                  (*)              *
        * * * *  (* * * *)  (* * * *)  (* * * *)
```
xötəbərə→xötəbərə →xötəbərə →xötəbərə

The crucial aspect of the new derivations concerns the absence of foot constituency in syllables not headed by a long vowel. In particular, the negative setting of the Construction parameter (132) at Khalkha foot level makes it impossible for an initial weak syllable to head a constituent in the presence of heavy syllables. Conversely, in such cases, all Khalkha feet will be directly derived from the Faithfulness Condition (78), which establishes a mutual implication between heads and constituents. In the absence of accents, therefore, no foot construction will take place, and the word constituent will be built directly on line 0, with the gap in line 1 subsequently filled in by convention (cf. (133b)).

As follows from the discussion, unbounded feet will only be interrupted by the intervention of an extraneous head, or by the limits of the stress domain itself. By contrast, the size of the bounded foot is restricted by the constraints built into the corresponding parameters, as represented in the template in (51) above for the binary foot.

5.5.2 Lexically-induced

The stress system of Sanskrit parallels that of Khalkha Mongolian. Importantly, however, the accents responsible for foot headship are all lexical in Sanskrit.

Consider the following data (gaps indicate morphological boundaries):

(134)   Sanskrit stress
     ásv a nam   'horses'
     dev á nam   'gods'

     ásv a vat i nam 'having horses'
     pad vat i nám   'having feet'

These apparently strange contours are amenable to rule by means of essentially the same parameter settings as in Khalkha Mongolian, provided we hypothesise the underlined vowels as lexically accented. Crucially, as in Khalkha, foot construction must be disallowed, as brought out by the following contrastive derivations of *padvatinam*:

(135) a.

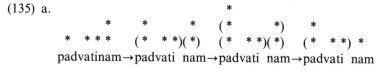

   b.

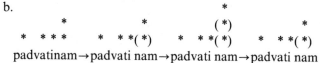

In (135a), with foot construction, the output is, incorrectly, **pádvatinam*. In (135b), by contrast, with no foot construction, the correct *padvatinám* results.

5.6 THE INTERACTION OF MORPHOLOGY AND PHONOLOGY

5.6.1 The cycle

5.6.1.1 Stress

The procedure just proposed for Sanskrit seems to break down in such words as in (136):

(136) rath ín e   'charioteer (dat. sg.)'
       cí kar ay iṣa ti   'wants to cause to make'

In the first form, the accented word-initial syllable is stressless. By contrast, in the second form, the word stress is carried by a word-initial unaccented syllable, notwithstanding the fact that an accented syllable follows. Our discussion above would have led us to expect the contours *ráthiṇe* and *cikaráyiṣati*, respectively, in conflict with the facts.

In order to understand the noted deviations, we must consider the interaction of phonology with morphology throughout the derivation. In particular, Sanskrit affixes have traditionally been classified into two categories, dominant and recessive, on the basis of both their stacking order (dominant suffixes being closer to the stem than recessive ones) and their respective effects on the stress contour of the word, as schematically represented in (137a) and (137b), respectively (S = stem, D = dominant suffix, R = recessive suffix):

(137) a. S D D D → S D D D́   b. S R R R → Ś R R R
         S D D D → Ś D D D   S R R R → S Ŕ R R
         S D D D → S D D D́   S R R R → S R Ŕ R
         S D D D → Ś D D D   S R R R → S Ŕ R R
         S D D D → Ś D D D   S R R R → Ś R R R

As can be seen, identical lexical accentual patterns yield strikingly different surface stress contours, depending on the status of the suffix.

In Halle and Vergnaud (1987), this situation is accounted for by postulating that dominant affixes trigger the application of the stress rules in a cyclic mode, while recessive affixes trigger non-cyclic application. We shall informally represent this difference by enclosing cyclic constituents only within square brackets:

(138) [[rath] ín] e   'charioteer (dat. sg.)'
      [[mitr] ín] e   'befriended (dat. sg.)'
      [[sár] as] vat + i + vant   'accompanied by Sarasvati'
      [práti [cyav] iyas] i   'more compressed'
      [cí [kar] ay] isa] ti   'wants to cause to make'

In forms composed exclusively of recessive (i.e. non-cyclic) affixes stress is distributed in accordance with the procedure we discussed above (cf. *áśv a nam* 'horse' vs *dev á nam*, and *áśv a vat i nam* 'having horses' vs *pad vat i nám* 'having feet'). The problem, as noted, is posed by their dominant (i.e. cyclic) counterparts, which obviously break our expectation.

Halle and Vergnaud (1987) hypothesise that cyclic application of stress rules is automatically preceded by the erasure of all previously erected metrical structure. As we will see below, they attempt to derive this behaviour from the geometrical configuration of the representation. At this point, however, we shall simply stipulate a 'Stress Erasure Convention', as follows:

(139) Stress Erasure Convention
      All existing metrical structure is erased at the start of each cycle

Taking the convention in (139) on trust for the moment,[17] we can provide a solution to the Sanskrit puzzle. Thus, consider in this light the derivations of *rathine* and *cíkarayisati*, which we have mentioned as problematic:

(140) a. [[rath] ín] e

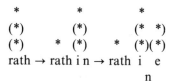

    b. [ci[kar] ay] isa] ti

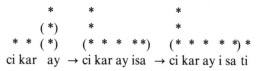

The crucial difference between the two forms concerns the accentual status of their last cyclic suffixes, accented and unaccented, respectively. In (140a), the rightmost dominant suffix, *-in*, is accented, thus eventually qualifying for word stress. In (140b), by contrast, the rightmost dominant suffix, *-iṣa*, is unaccented. Consequently, in the last cycle (associated with *-iṣa*), the word-initial syllable *ci* will be stressed. Naturally, in both cases, the stresses in question are preserved throughout the rest of the (non-cyclic) derivation.

To summarise, the essential ingredients of the Sanskrit stress system are: (i) the Stress Erasure Convention (139); (ii) the status of suffixes as regards cyclicity; (iii) the application of the Sanskrit stress procedure (referred to in the literature as the 'Basic Accentuation Principle' (BAP)) to the domains defined by both the cyclic and the non-cyclic affixes. Notice that the BAP needs to be non-cyclic because not all words contain cyclic suffixes, and in those words the leftmost recessive suffix carries the stress if the stem is unaccented. It also, crucially, needs to be cyclic because, as we have seen, in the presence of cyclic (i.e. dominant) suffixes the location of stress is determined by the accentual status of the last such suffix.

5.6.1.2 Syllables

Besides influencing stress assignment, the cycle typically plays a central role in syllabification. These two domains, therefore, provide direct evidence of cyclic rule application, beyond the effects of the Strict Cycle Condition commented on in Chapter 2.

In Chapter 4 we mentioned in passing the devoicing of German obstruents in the syllable coda. Further illustration of this phenomenon is now given in (141):

(141) a. Ta[k]   'day'   b. Ta.[g]e   'days'
        Ra[t]   'wheel'   Ra.[d]e   'wheels'
        Kin[t]   'child'   Kin.[d]er   'children'
        Kin[t].heit 'childhood'   kin.[d]isch 'childish'
        Ja[k].den 'huntings'   ja.[g]en   'to hunt'
        Ja[kt]   'hunting'   Ja.[g]erei   'hunting'

In each of the pairs in (141), the same underlying consonant appears voiceless in the coda (141a), but voiced in the onset (141b). As we shall now show, the simple rule in (142) is responsible for this alternation:

(142) German Obstruent Devoicing

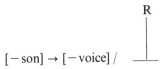

$[-son] \rightarrow [-voice] /$

The proposal in Rubach (1990) is that the German syllabification procedure applies cyclically, whereas the rule of Obstruent Devoicing is non-cyclic. Thus, the Obstruent Devoicing rule (142) cannot be cyclic, since otherwise all the forms in (141b) would also undergo Obstruent Devoicing in the first cycle, and the wrong surface forms would be derived (cf. *Ta[k]e*, etc.). If Obstruent Devoicing is non-cyclic, however, the (universally obligatory) Minimal Onset Satisfaction (MOS) Principle ((37) of Chapter 4) will in the second cycle assign the obstruent in question to the onset of the following syllable, thus preventing the postcyclic application of Obstruent Devoicing (142). We illustrate in (143):

(143)   [[Tag]e]

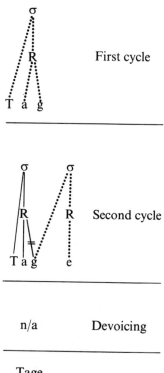

Tage

Notice that in the second cycle the MOS Principle has destroyed the previous coda affiliation of /g/, thus bleeding the non-cyclic Obstruent Devoicing rule (142).

The data in (144) pose an apparent challenge to this analysis:

(144) a. glau[p]lich 'believable'   b. glauben 'to believe'
          fra[k]lich 'questionable'   fragen   'to ask'
          tä[k]lich 'daily'   Tage   'days'
          sor[k]los 'carefree'   Sorge   'care'
          lie[p]lich 'lovely'   Liebe   'love'
          far[p]los 'colourless'   Farbe   'colour'

The forms in (144b) show that each of the obstruents at issue is lexically voiced. In (144a), however, devoicing has seemingly taken place outside the coda, since all the clusters in question constitute well-formed onsets in German, as illustrated in (145):

(145)   Blitz   'lightning'
          glich   'he/she/it resembled'
          blau   'blue'
          Glass   'glass'
          Glocke   'bell'
          blond   'blond'

Moreover, other word-internal instantiations of the same clusters fail to exhibit devoicing:

(146) a. neblig   'foggy'   b. Nebel   'fog'
          hüglig   'hilly'   Hügel   'hill'
          Schmuggler 'smuggler'   Schmuggel 'smuggling'
          Segler   'yachtsman'   Segel   'sail'
          gablig   'forked'   Gabel   'fork'
          wirblig   'giddy'   wirbeln   'to whirl'

The expectation would therefore be that the relevant obstruents in (144) would keep their lexical voicing, the Devoicing rule in (142) being explicitly circumscribed to the rime.

As we shall now show, however, Rubach's (1990) noted assumptions with regard to the cyclicity of the rules in question yield precisely the desired result. Consider first the following (abridged) derivation of *glau*[p]*lich*:

(147)   [[glaub]lich]

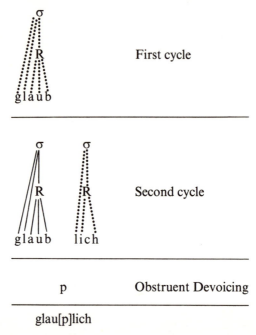

First cycle

Second cycle

p   Obstruent Devoicing

glau[p]lich

The reason for the devoicing of /b/ in *glaublich* is now apparent. Simply, this segment outputs the cyclic phonology in the coda of the first syllable, which structure feeds Obstruent Devoicing. Of interest is the failure of /b/ to resyllabify in the second cycle, contrary to what we saw was the case with /g/ in *Tage* (cf. (143) above). Such a failure must be attributed to the inability of the Maximal Onset Realisation Parameter to affect existing structure. The Minimal Onset Satisfaction Principle, by contrast, is endowed with such power.

An alternative, particularly elegant way of formalising this difference consists in universally assigning extraprosodicity to the final consonant on each cycle (Borowsky 1986, Itô 1986). If so, the allotment of this consonant to the onset in the next cycle will fall out of its unsyllabified status, with no need for resyllabification. Notwithstanding its obvious appeal, we shall show below that this solution runs into serious empirical difficulties.

As already noted, a revealing contrast with *glau*[p]*lich*, etc. in (144) is provided by the forms in (146), in which the obstruent preserves its lexical voicing (*ne*[b]*lig*, etc.). The derivation in (148) is proposed for these forms in Rubach (1990):

(148) [[nebl] ig]

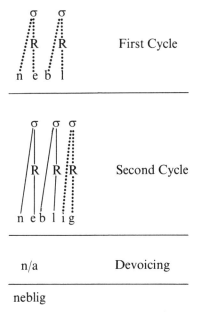

First Cycle	
Second Cycle	
n/a	Devoicing

neblig

The key difference between the devoicing and non-devoicing classes concerns the syllabification of the obstruent. In particular, /b/ in *neblig* functions as the onset of the syllabic consonant *l* (cf. *ne.bl.ig*), while in *glaublich* it is parsed in the coda of the previous syllable, as we saw. The assignment of /b/ to the onset in *neblig* is the direct consequence of the stray status of /l/ that follows the incorporation of /b/ as the coda of *ne* in the first instance, as we now show (the derivation of the first cycle in (148) was accordingly simplified for expository convenience):

(149)

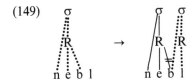

The /l/ originally remains out of syllable structure because of its sonority relationship with /b/ (a syllable *nebl* would contravene the Sonority Sequencing Principle (41) of Chapter 4). Under these circumstances, German, like English, enforces sonorant syllabicity, which gives rise to the configuration *ne.bl*. This automatically accounts for the failure of /b/ to devoice in *neblig*, in contrast with its counterpart in *glaublich*, which is parsed in the coda and thus subsequently undergoes Obstruent Devoicing (142).

The problematic nature of the proposal that the rightmost consonant is universally extraprosodic within each cycle now comes to light. Specifically, *l* extrametricality in *nebl* would sanction precisely the first structure in (149), from which *b* devoicing ought to follow. Similarly, if the /b/ of *glaub* were indeed extraprosodic, it would qualify for incorporation into the onset of the following syllable in the *glaublich* cycle, given the positive setting of the Maximal Onset Realisation Parameter in German. If so, Obstruent Devoicing would be bled, in the obvious way. The consequence of all this is that, rather than declaring the final consonant extraprosodic in each cycle, we must endow the Minimal Onset Satisfaction Principle with the power to destroy structure, thus countenancing a modicum of resyllabification, a strategy already made use of in Levin (1985).

5.6.2 Lexical Phonology

The previous discussion highlights the relevance of morphological structure to phonology. In particular, the seemingly paradoxical facts of German obstruent Devoicing are brought to rule when the syllabi-fication algorithm is applied cyclically (syllable formation thus taking place in step with the morphological derivation), and the rule responsible for obstruent devoicing non-cyclically (i.e. in one fell swoop, after the whole form has been constructed). Similarly, we have accounted for the complex surface stress patterns of Sanskrit on the assumption that the application of stress rules may be cyclic or non-cyclic. As transpires from the discussion, the mode of application of a rule is an idiosyncratic property of the rule, while responsibility for the cyclic or non-cyclic status of any given morphological domain lies (also idiosyncratically) with the affix heading the domain.

5.6.2.1 The Ordering Hypothesis

Consider now the English data in (150) (all in Walker 1924):

(150)	a.	b.	c.
	exclúsive	exclúsiveness	exclusívity
	pássive	pássiveness	passívity
	lógic	lógicalness	logícity
	trágic	trágicalness	tragícity
	incóngruous	incóngruousness	incongrúity
	impétuous	impétuousness	impetuósity

ingénuous	ingénuousness	ingenúity
cúrious	cúriousness	curiósity
précious	préciousness	preciósity
precócious	precóciousness	precócity

The forms in (150b) and (150c) are derivationally related to those in (150a), in the obvious way. The suffixes *-ness* and *-ity* are syntactically parallel, and as close semantically as any two morphemes can be (they are both roughly paraphrasable as 'quality of X'). As can readily be seen, however, their effects on stress are diverse. In particular, the addition of *-ness* is of no consequence, whereas *-ity* suffixation often results in a rightward stress shift.

Stress is not the only process in English with regard to which a different result is associated with different affixes. Thus, for instance, sonorants become syllabic word-finally, and, crucially for our purposes here, also before certain suffixes (cf. *burgled*, *assembling*, and, in rhotic varieties, *hindering*, *remembered*), but not before others (cf. *burglar*, *assembly*, *hindrance*, *remembrance*). An interesting minimal pair mentioned in *SPE* (p. 85) is *twinkling* (= 'instant') vs *twinkling* (present participle), where *l* is syllabic in the latter, but not in the former (ultimately derived from /twinkl + ling/). Similarly, *g* drops after *n* in many dialects both word-finally and before some (but, crucially, not all) suffixes (cf. *lo*[ŋ]*er* 'one who longs' vs *lo*[ŋg]*er* 'of greater length', which involve two different, if homonymous, suffixes). Likewise, the noun-forming suffix *-y* triggers spirantisation in the preceding *t* (*democracy*, *presidency*), but not so its adjective-forming homonym (*chocolaty*, *bratty*). Finally, long vowels (or diphthongs) undergo shortening only before certain suffixes (see *ser*[iː]*ne* → *ser*[ɛ]*nity* vs *d*[iː]*con* → *d*[iː]*coness*).

Thus, some (but, crucially, not all) English suffixes behave as if they were attached to fully-fledged words, since they trigger (or fail to trigger) the same phonological processes as take place (or fail to take place) in word-final position. Importantly, the behaviour of each suffix in this respect is pretty consistent across the range of phonological rules.

Suffixes also differ from each other with regard to their order of concatenation. In particular, it was observed by Siegel (1974) that some suffixes invariably stack closer to the root than others, as we now show in (151) (useful discussion can be found in Strauss 1982):

(151) a. tox-ic
       tox-ic-ity
       tox-ic-ity-less
       tox-ic-ity-less-ness

b. *tox-ic-less-ity
   *tox-ic-ness-ity
   *tox-ic-less-ness-ity

Particularly interesting in this connection is Kiparsky's (1982a) observation that irregular plurals can occur inside compounds in English (cf. *teeth marks, lice-infested*), but usually not so their regular suffixal counterparts (**claws marks, *rats infested*). The reason for this distributional bias obviously cannot be semantic. The suggestion contained in Kiparksy's analysis is instead that both processes (i.e. plural ablaut and plural suffixation) take place at different levels of morphological derivation (basically, pre- and post-compounding, respectively).

Similar ordering constraints apply to prefixes (see Allen 1978 for specific discussion):

(152) a. in-active
     un-in-active
     non-un-in-active

    b. *in-un-active
     *un-non-in-active
     *in-non-un-active

Siegel's original observation is often referred to as the 'Ordering Hypothesis'.

What we now have is a bipartite classification of English affixes based on two independent criteria, namely phonological behaviour and morphological linearisation. If we bring these two strands together, we achieve a particularly close integration of morphology and phonology. Specifically, morphological and phonological processes will now be interleaved, thus potentially interacting with each other throughout the derivation. In particular, the output of a specific set of affixation processes ('class 1 affixation') will be subject to a specific set of phonological rules ('class 1 phonological rules'), the output of which can then be fed through a second set of affixation processes ('class 2 affixation'), to be acted upon by a second set of phonological rules ('class 2 phonological rules'), as we represent in the following diagram (outputs are given in parentheses):

(153) Morphology–phonology interaction (see Siegel 1974: 153):

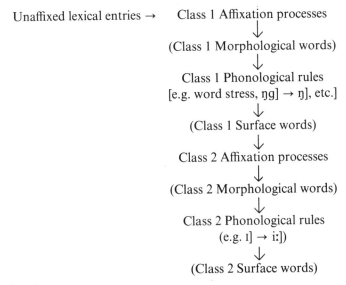

Unaffixed lexical entries → Class 1 Affixation processes
↓
(Class 1 Morphological words)
↓
Class 1 Phonological rules
[e.g. word stress, ŋg] → ŋ], etc.]
↓
(Class 1 Surface words)
↓
Class 2 Affixation processes
↓
(Class 2 Morphological words)
↓
Class 2 Phonological rules
(e.g. ɪ] → iː])
↓
(Class 2 Surface words)

Affixation is assumed to be optional in principle, and in any event subject to the satisfaction of the appropriate subcategorisation and selectional restrictions. Once an affix has been concatenated, the corresponding phonological rules will however apply automatically, allowances being made for the differences between the cyclic and non-cyclic modalities.

The model sketched in (153) differs critically from the conception that underpins *SPE*, where all morphological processing (in fact, syntactic processing within the context in which *SPE* was written) was assumed to precede all the phonological rules. This strict ordering of grammatical modules was of course no obstacle for the cyclic application of phonological rules. Crucially, however, the interaction was uni-directional, i.e. exclusively from morphology to phonology. By contrast, in Siegel's conception, it is possible for a class 1 phonological rule to affect a class 2 morphological process, as indeed corresponds to fact. For instance, -*al* deverbal noun formation in English is limited to stress-final verbs: *recíte* → *recítal*, *propóse* → *propósal* are legitimate, but **vísital*, **prómisal* are not possible formations from *vísit*, *prómise*, respectively.

5.6.2.2 Stratal phonology

The insights in Siegel (1974) and Allen (1978) spurred the birth in the early 1980s of a model known as 'Lexical Phonology' (LP). In this model, the stratal conception of the interaction between morphology and phonology is further elaborated, and extended to the phrasal level (see e.g. Kiparsky 1982a,b, 1983, 1984, 1985, Mohanan 1982, 1986, Strauss 1982, Mohanan and Mohanan 1984, Halle and Mohanan 1985; for a useful summary, see Kaisse and Shaw 1985). Thus, while the scope of the original formulation was restricted to (morphological and phonological) word formation, as embodied in the diagram in (153) above, Lexical Phonology also accommodates the phonological changes that follow syntactic phrasing, as made explicit in (154), which must be understood to follow (153) directly:

(154)

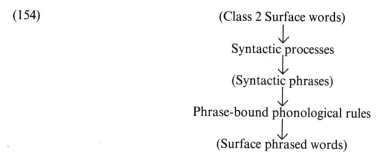

In the new model, the levels originally proposed by Siegel are grouped in a 'lexical' module, while a novel phrasal stratum is introduced 'postlexically'. Moreover, the number of lexical levels is no longer limited to two (in fact a remnant of *SPE*'s essentially dichotomous taxonomy of boundaries), but is increased *ad libitum* to keep pace with descriptive needs (for instance, Halle and Mohanan 1985 propose four lexical levels for English). The postlexical module is however commonly approached as monostratal. The diagram in (155) summarises the fabric of this model (some aspects of the diagram will become clearer as the discussion proceeds):[18]

(155) Classical Lexical Phonology[19]
  unaffixed lexical entries

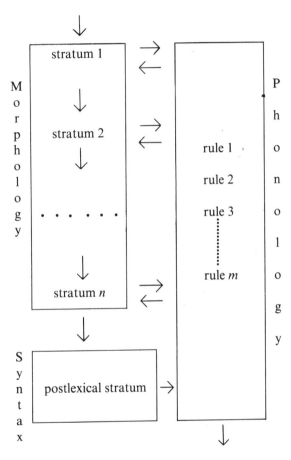

fully formed representations

In the purest incarnation of the model, each of the two modules is associated with a set of differential properties of rule application, as is now summarised in (156) (see Pulleyblank 1986: 7):

(156)   Modular rule-application properties

	Lexical	Postlexical
Accessibility to word-internal structure	yes	no
Cross-word applicability	no	yes
Cyclicity	yes	no
Structure preservation	yes	no
Possible exceptions	yes	no

In addition, of course, cyclic rules will obey the Strict Cycle Condition, and all lexically bound rule applications will precede their postlexical analogues.

For reasons of space, we can only offer a few clarificatory notes on each of these properties. Cyclicity has already been given generous attention. Structure preservation was briefly referred to in Chapter 4, where it was interpreted as involving respect for the basic properties associated with lexical representation (e.g. basic syllabic structures, or the number and identity of the lexical segments). Accessibility to internal structure implies availability of morphological bracketing in the structural description of rules. The general convention is that internal brackets are erased on exit from each of the strata (the 'Bracket Erasure Convention'), a procedure that effectively limits constituency accessibility to the stratum being processed (an obvious corollary of this is that postlexical rules may not make use of any structural information internal to the word). Applicability across words has the obvious meaning, and is by definition restricted to the postlexical stratum. Finally, in the strictest interpretation of the model, only lexical rules are allowed to have exceptions.

Problems with the LP model as described were quick to emerge. Thus, in Halle and Mohanan's (1985) study of English lexical phonology some of the lexical strata are shown to be non-cyclic. Indeed, in Booij and Rubach (1987) the non-cyclicity of the last lexical stratum is given parametric universal status. Conversely, it is not clear that all postlexical rules are non-cyclic (cf. e.g. the Mandarin Chinese tone sandhi rule of Liu 1980 or the English rules of phrasal stress discussed in Halle and Vergnaud 1987). Similarly, several violations of structure preservation have been uncovered. For instance, Mohanan and Mohanan (1984) show that the five underlying places of articulation in Malayalam are expanded to seven in the course of the lexical phonology. Also attested is the possibility of exceptional behaviour with respect to postlexical rules. Thus, postlexical regressive voice assimilation in Dutch is optionally progressive for a number of *d*-initial function words (*op die manier* 'in that way' = *o*[b d]*ie manier* or *o*[p t]*ie manier*).

Problems with the morphology side of the model are also not in short supply. First, there are instances where structures are affected by previous strata. Thus, for instance, in Malayalam (Mohanan 1982), the sub- and co-compounding classes are derived in two separate strata, in this order. Phonologically, both stem-final and stem-initial gemination apply in the subcompounding stratum only (cf. [[*kaaṭ*] [*maṟam*]] → *kaaṭṭəmaṟam* 'forest tree' vs [[[*aaṭ*] [*maaṭ*]] *kaḷ*] → *aaṭəmaaṭəkaḷə* 'cattle', and [[*aana*] [*kutīṟa*]] → *aanakkutīṟa* 'horse that is like an elephant' vs [[[*aana*] [*kutīṟa*]] *kaḷ*] → *aanakutīṟakaḷə* 'elephants and horses', respectively). In addition, subcompounds turn up with a single primary stress irrespective of the number of stems they contain, whereas in co-compounds each stem constitutes a separate stress domain (cf. [[[*ṭáaṟa*] [*kaaṇtan*]] [*maaṟə*] 'Tara's husbands' vs [[[*ácchan*] [*ámma*]] *maaṟə*] 'parents'). Now, paradoxically given the noted stratal ordering, subcompounds may contain co-compounds, e.g. [[[*yakṣan*][*kinnaṟan*]] *kuuṭṭam*] → *yákṣakinnaṟakkuuṭṭam* (cf. the double stress in the embedded co-compound, and the initial gemination of the last stem, the second member of the subcompound). Faced with this situation, Mohanan introduces the formal device of the 'loop', which allows the output of a stratum to be fed back into a previous stratum. Clearly, however, such a strategy amounts to a surrender of the claim that morphological derivation is strictly layered, one of the fundamental tenets of Lexical Phonology (see Christdas 1987 for further discussion).

In addition, languages abound in what is referred to in the literature as 'bracketing paradoxes', i.e. cases where level ordering finds itself at odds with grammatical restrictions or with semantic considerations. Consider, for instance, the English derivative *ungrammaticality*. It has been shown in the literature that *un-* subcategorises for adjectives (see e.g. Sproat 1985: 27ff.), hence the structure [[un grammatical] ity], where a class 2 affix (*un-*) is placed at a deeper level of embedding than a class 1 affix, namely -*ity* (we have already independently shown that -*ity* is stress-affecting, and therefore class 1; cf. (150) above). A perhaps more striking example is provided by the comparative *unhappier*. As is well known, only (underlying) monosyllables select the comparative suffix -*er*. If so, the morphological structure of this word must be [un [happy er]], at odds with the semantics (*unhappier* does not mean 'not happier', but 'more unhappy').

Another morphological assumption of Lexical Phonology subsequently found faltering concerns the stratum-internal freedom of affixation. In particular, affixation is not freely recursive and unordered within each level (see Fabb 1985, 1988), as proposed in the original versions of the model. Thus, Fabb (1988) scrutinises the combinatory possibilities of the 43 most productive derivational suffixes of English, and finds that, out of the 1,849 logically possible combinations, only 40 to 50 actually occur. There exist of course independent selectional restrictions between such suffixes, but these would still allow for 663 combinations, less than 10 per cent of which materialise, as mentioned.

Inevitably, the model is considerably weakened as a result of all these difficulties. Indeed, all that remains uncontroversially unaffected is the choice of a cyclic or non-cyclic mode of application for phonological rules by different groups of affixes. On these grounds, Halle and Vergnaud (1987) do away with stratum ordering in the lexical module, reverting instead to the *SPE* position that all morphological operations take place prior to the phonology, words thus entering the phonology fully formed (*pace* the noted possibility of word formation being sensitive to the output of phonological processes). The distinction between 'lexical' and 'postlexical' phonological rules is however preserved, as is the choice of cyclic or non-cyclic application. Mode of application is however no longer modularly restricted, and, instead, morphemes are allowed to idiosyncratically specify the (cyclic or non-cyclic) mode of application they trigger in their domain. The resulting model is made up of three modules, as represented in (157):

(157) Morphology/phonology interaction in Halle and Vergnaud (1987)

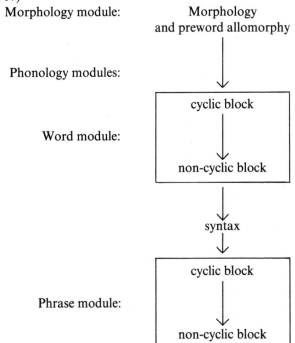

The first module deals with allomorphy, and precedes the phonology proper.[20] Halle and Vergnaud do not say much about this component, but we can assume that it includes all rules with a heavy morphological conditioning. Then comes the word-internal phonology, which basically corresponds to the lexical level(s) of LP. Finally, there is the word-sequence, or phrase, phonology, equivalent to LP's postlexical phonology. Each of these two components includes blocks of cyclic and non-cyclic rules, to be applied in this order, the cyclic block after concatenation of each cyclic affix (or after each process of syntactic phrasing), in the familiar manner, and the non-cyclic block to the fully affixed word (or after the completion of all syntactic phrasing), each affix being consequently marked as to whether or not it triggers the cyclic rules in its domain.

This simple model overcomes the bracketing paradoxes which we have seen marred LP.[21] Thus, consider *ungrammaticality* in this new light:

(158) [[un [grammat + ic + al]] ity]

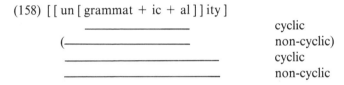

	cyclic
	non-cyclic)
	cyclic
	non-cyclic

The parsing in (158) is consistent with the subcategorisation restrictions noted above. The innermost string *grammatical* will first be subject to the set of cyclic phonological rules. The next constituent, *un-*, is however a non-cyclic constituent, and therefore no phonological rules can apply to it until the word level is reached. Consequently, we proceed to the next (and last) constituent, defined by *-ity*, in which the cyclic rules will apply again. Having thus reached the word level, the non-cyclic rules can come into play. This procedure thus gives a principled account of the fact that, phonologically speaking, *un-* is further removed from the stem than *-ity*, although grammatically the converse is true.

5.6.3 Planar structure

The integration of this approach into the open-book model of phonology introduced in Chapter 1 (see especially 1.7) is not obvious, and a few words must now be said on the subject. This will allow us to close the book in essentially the same area where it was started, a happy occurrence in view of the central position of the issue in current generative phonology.

The core question concerns the interaction between planar phonology and planar morphology, the former having been the object of attention throughout this book. In his studies of Arabic word structure, McCarthy (1979, 1981) proposed the extension of the autosegmental model to morphology by autosegmentalising each (non-concatenative) morpheme. According to this hypothesis, therefore, the spatial structure of the Arabic word $k + t + atab$ 'he copied' will be as in (159) (as usual, misalignment of lines indicates plane distinctness):

(159)

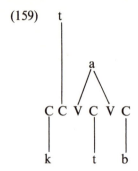

The obvious effect of this move on the phonology is the dislocation of each phonological autosegmental plane into morpheme-bound (sub)planes, as we now illustrate for [coronal] for the form given above (the rest of the features are omitted for simplicity):

(160) [co ron a l]

      |

    C C V C V C

          |

      [c o r o n a l]

Such a situation must be contrasted with the case of tautomorphemic feature realisation, as exemplified by [labial] in the form *samam* 'he poisoned':

(161)

Here, a single instantiation of [labial] is doubly attached to the appropriate template slots, in compliance with the Obligatory Contour Principle.

Halle and Vergnaud (1987) partially extend morpheme autosegmentality to concatenative phonology. In particular, they suggest that cyclic affixes (but, crucially, not non-cyclic affixes) are endowed with their own autosegmental plane, as illustrated in (162):

(162)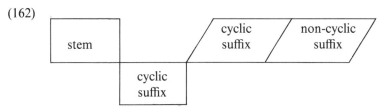

They further point out that the operation of phonological rules requires uniplanarity, and consequently they rule that plane copying must take place prior to the activation of phonological processes (potentially) affecting two planes, as illustrated in (163):

(163)

stem	
copied stem	cyclic suffix

Notice that the contents of the plane containing the stem have been copied onto the plane containing the (cyclic) suffix. Phonological rules can now operate on the resulting merged plane.

A further suggestion made by these authors concerns the fate of metrical structure upon plane copying. In particular, they contend that metrical structure cannot be copied, and is consequently missing from the copied plane (although it remains on the original plane, from which it is therefore conveniently recoverable). Clearly, this procedure subsumes the Stress Erasure Convention in (139) above, which can therefore be dispensed with as an independent principle of grammar.

Halle and Vergnaud's plane copy is reminiscent of McCarthy's (1986) plane conflation, a device he attributes to Younes (1983). Unlike plane copy, however, plane conflation takes place at a particular morpholexical level determined on a language-specific basis. In terms of Lexical Phonology, conflation can therefore occur on exit from each lexical level, or perhaps only at the end of the lexical module. Not surprisingly, thus, plane conflation is usually considered to subsume the bracket erasure of standard LP.

Strong evidence for the proposal of morphology-inspired plane segregation in the early phonology and of plane uniformity in the late stages is presented in McCarthy (1986), essentially relating to the existence of transparency effects at the former, but not at the latter, level (such segregation of planes therefore provides yet another alternative to the projection mechanism provisionally introduced in Chapter 1). One simple example from Modern Hebrew (McCarthy 1986: 238ff.) will suffice for our purposes here.

Of relevance are two (antagonistic) processes of Modern Hebrew: (i) schwa insertion, by which tautomorphemic geminates are broken up; (ii) schwa deletion (related to, but not identical with, its Tiberian Hebrew homologue, which McCarthy (1986: 234) analyses as taking place in a two-sided open syllable, VC____CV). Schwa insertion is illustrated in (164) (e = schwa):

(164)   zalelan   'glutton'
        xatetan   'meddler'
        noxexut   'presence'

These forms can profitably be contrasted with those in (165), with no geminates and therefore no schwa, and with those in (166), which contain fake, rather than true, geminates (see note 12 in Chapter 3):

(165)   dabran   'talkative'
        zaxlan   'very slow'
        malxut   'kingdom'

(166)   dan + nu   'we discussed'
        šavat + ti   'I was on strike'
        it + tamen   'he pretended naivety'

Schwa epenthesis in (164) must therefore be taken to be activated by the multiple attachment of a consonantal melody to the skeleton, as represented in (167):

(167)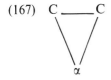

Neither (165) nor (166) possesses this configuration. Note that the epenthesis of schwa in (167) is compatible with the behaviour of geminates attested universally (see again note 12 in Chapter 3), on the backdrop of the lexical planar segregation of vowels and consonants in Modern Hebrew, along the lines of Arabic.

Let us now turn to schwa deletion. The point is that Modern Hebrew exhibits an 'antigemination' effect, whereby such deletion is blocked whenever it would give rise to a genuine geminate, a result that McCarthy (1986) successfully derives from the preventive tutoring action of the Obligatory Contour Principle (in this paper McCarthy presents an impressive survey of such 'antigemination' effects drawing on a wide range of languages). The question that arises for us here concerns the interaction of this rule with planar structure. Notice that, if vowel–consonant plane segregation were maintained throughout the derivation, there would be no possibility of violating the OCP upon schwa deletion in the forms in (164), since the resulting structure would parallel (167) above, and would thus be compatible with the OCP (the motivation for the rule of schwa insertion must therefore be sought elsewhere). Revealingly, however, all the forms in (164) fail to undergo schwa deletion, as do also their congeners in (168), where schwa is lexical or originates from reduction, rather than from epenthesis:

(168) titpaleli   'I will pray'   (cf. titpalel   'thou-f. . . . ')
      kuceca   'she was cut'   (cf. kucec   'he . . . ')
      nadedu   'they wandered'   (cf. nadad   'he . . . ')

By contrast, schwa deletion takes place when there is no liability of OCP contravention:

(169) kašru   'they tied'   (cf. kašar   'he . . . ')
      kušra   'she was tied'   (cf. kušar   'he . . . ')
      hitkašru   'they contacted'   (cf. hitkašer   'he . . . ')

All these facts fall into place on the assumption that the vowel and consonant planes conflate prior to schwa deletion. In particular, at the time of application of schwa deletion, vowels and consonants occupy one and the same plane, and therefore deletion of the schwa in (167) and (168) would indeed give rise to an OCP violation:

(170)

As can be seen, there are now two adjacent occurrences of *d* in the melody tier.

An important recent development in planar phonology concerns directly the issue of plane motivation, clearly an essential matter if circularity and arbitrariness are to be avoided. Because of space pressures, we shall simply present the kernel of McCarthy's (1989a) proposal.

McCarthy's (1989a) key observation is that there are clear and well-motivated cases of planar independence over and above those strictly imposed by the morphology. Thus, in e.g. Yawelmani or Sierra Miwok vowels and consonants do not constitute separate morphemes, in the style of their congeners in Arabic and other Semitic languages, but must none the less be segregated, according to standard analyses (see Archangeli 1983, and Smith 1985, respectively), because of the templatic nature of (part of) the morphology of these languages. This disposes of the strong interpretation of the morphemic plane hypothesis, according to which all and only separate morphemes constitute separate planes. The weaker possibility is that separate morphemes indeed give rise to separate planes, although some planes may not be motivated by morphemes. McCarthy's (1989a) proposal is however that the determinant factor in plane autonomy is not morphemic independence, but rather absence of ordering restrictions. In particular, he shows that in a language like Mayan, with no templatic morphology, segregation of vowel and consonant planes must none the less still be postulated, in order to give a principled account of constraints affecting superficially non-adjacent consonants (in particular, in C_1VC_2 roots, the two consonants must be identical if they are glottalised; see McCarthy 1989a: 81). The solution to the apparent paradox rests on the strict syllabic structure of the Mayan root, basically CVC. This obviously allows the dispensation of ordering for the vowel in lexical representation (the configurations *VCC and *CCV would simply be ill-formed), absence of ordering in turn determining plane autonomy. Clearly, there is a similar absence of linear order between the respective melodies of distinct morphemes in any language, since by definition each of these morphemes occupies its own place in the lexicon. As before, such ordering laxity induces plane autosegmentality, the situation in Arabic or any other such language thus being automatically accounted for.

5.7 CONCLUSION

In this chapter we have reviewed the various domains relevant to the operation of rules, in particular prosodic domains above the syllable, and morphological domains. The specific relevance of the latter concerns the operation of the cycle, the layering of rules, and the arrangement of planes. The higher prosodic domains examined have been found to be grounded on, but not to be isomorphic with, morphological or syntactic structure, although semantic, and even pragmatic considerations are also of relevance for the larger domains. An important, additional area we have lent attention to concerns the metrical organisation of prosodies. The question has been left open as to whether such metrical domains are autosegmentally independent, or whether they must be related to the appropriate constituents in the prosodic hierarchy. Finally, the mode of operation of rules and its interaction with morphosyntactic constituency has also been examined.

Notes

1 PHONOLOGICAL REPRESENTATIONS

1 Among the useful manuals of classical *SPE* phonology are Schane (1973a), Hyman (1975), Sloan *et al.* (1978), and Dell (1980). Particularly thorough is Kenstowicz and Kisseberth (1979), arguably the best generative phonology textbook to date.

2 This new type of phonology is frequently referred to as 'non-linear phonology'. As will become abundantly clear throughout this chapter and the rest of the book, however, far from being non-linear, the new phonology is in fact multilinear, since the representations it licenses are composed of a (large) number of parallel lines. The label 'non-linear' is therefore a terminological red herring, and is best avoided.

3 The term 'obstruent' is used to designate non-sonorant sounds. In *SPE*, sonorancy is contingent on vocal tract configuration: a sound is sonorant if the vocal tract configuration is such as to permit spontaneous voicing, i.e. spontaneous vibration of the vocal folds (see note 11 below for voice and the vocal folds).

4 Sibilants are fricative sounds acoustically characterised by a concentration of energy at a higher pitch, which results in a hissing or hushing effect. Articulatorily, this is achieved by means of a groove-like stricture between the tongue blade and the alveolar ridge.

5 Coronals are made by raising the blade of the tongue, i.e. the front-most area, just behind the tip.

6 The reader familiar with the rise of generative phonology might be surprised at the presence of the term 'phoneme', this construct having been officially banned following several well-known debates in the 1960s (see however Schane 1973b for some arguments in favour of the construct). In our present use, 'phoneme' is not intended to refer to the classical structuralist object, set up on the basis of minimal pair tests, but rather to what is called a 'segment' in *SPE*. As we are seeing, in autosegmental phonology there are no 'segments' as such, but rather parallel lines of 'autosegments'. One of these lines, however, often contains the bulk of the former segments, and the elements in it are nowadays referred to at times as 'phonemes', an instance of terminological liberalisation.

7 Like many of the proposals to be discussed in subsequent chapters, autosegmental phonology does not therefore constitute a theory rival to

generative phonology. Rather, *pace* the grandiosity of the label, it represents a development within this theory. The unity of the field of phonology is in fact quite remarkable, at least when seen from the perspective of syntax. There are indeed a small number of alternative proposals, aspects of which will be discussed as we go along. It is however far from self-evident that such proposals enjoy the status of full-fledged splinter theories, and they are more usefully construed as simple hypotheses on specific points raised by the general theory.

8 The Turkish vowel system is totally symmetric, with two degrees of height, two degrees of backness, and a rounded–unrounded opposition. Thus, Turkish has eight vowels, four [+high] [i, y, ɨ, u] and four [−high] [e, ø, a, o], four [−back] [i, y, ø, e] and four [+back] [ɨ, u, o, a], and four [−round] [i, e, ɨ, a] and four [+round] [y, ø, u, o], as visually displayed in (i):

(i)

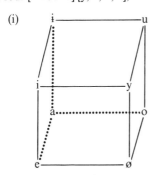

The features [high], [back] and [round] are readily interpreted as in *SPE* to signal deviations from the neutral position of the tongue ([+high] and [+back]), or lip rounding [+round].

9 As transpires from our discussion above, this condition is inapplicable to reduplication, since, for instance, in (29) the segments *ki* remain unassociated. We will be examining the Well-formedness Condition further as we go along.

10 Strictly speaking, this is inexact, since some Turkish consonants in fact influence the harmony process (see Clements and Sezer 1982). We sidestep this complexity, however, since it is not germane to our present purposes.

11 A summary explanation of the mechanism of voice production will help readers unfamiliar with phonetics. The vocal folds are two lip-like structures lodged across the voice box, or larynx (which often protrudes in males as the so-called Adam's apple). The folds can be set in motion by the flow of outgoing air, as follows. If they are closed and the air pressure in the lungs is increased (by raising the diaphragm, and thus decreasing the thoracic volume), the folds will naturally burst open. The rapid flow of pulmonary air going out through the glottis (the name given to the opening between the folds) will cause a drop in intraglottal air pressure (this is the well-known Bernouilli effect), which will allow the folds to close up again by automatic mechanisms of inertia, thus restarting the process. The successive puffs of air thus created give the humming effect characteristic of 'voice'.

12 The feature responsible for the existence of mid tones is [±raised]. The resulting taxonomy of tones is as follows:

	[upper]	[raised]
high	+	+
high mid	+	−
mid	−	+
low	−	−

Of these, low or mid are default, the latter in systems with more than one contrast (see Chapter 2 for formalisation and a full discussion of the significance of default status generally). There are some reports of languages with more than four tones, but the interpretation of the additional tones is far from straightforward. (In Cantonese Chinese, for instance, commonly analysed as possessing six tones, extra tonal aspects come into the formation of tone contrasts.)

13 Exceptions to this generalisation mainly, but not exclusively, affect sonorants, especially nasals. There are also some cases of consonants interfering with the spread of tone. All these phenomena can be sidestepped for our present purposes.

14 A word of clarification about the phenomenon of downstep will be appropriate at this point. As already hinted at above, the pitch height associated with each tone is relative, not absolute. This means that the same pitch level may realise a high tone in one context, and a low tone in another. There are three phenomena involving a lowering of the pitch register. First, 'declination', a gradual fall in the tone baseline. Second, 'downdrift', a lowering of all H(s) after L. Third, 'downstep', a lowering of some H(s) not overtly preceded by Ls, usually attributed to the presence of a floating L. For greater clarity we graphically illustrate the phonetic manifestation of downdrift and downstep (the examples are hypothetical, and abstract away declination):

(i) Downdrift   Downstep

```
   HH                  HH
      HH                  HH
                           H
         H                  H
   L   LL
```

15 In an interesting, if conceptually rather complex, development, Sagey (1988a) contends that the effects of the No Crossing Constraint are derivable from extralinguistic knowledge, and consequently that the constraint must not be included in the formal machinery of phonology. Hammond (1988) takes however exception to Sagey's argumentation, and defends the linguistic validity of a reformulated No Crossing Constraint. For an additional (negative) view on the constraint see Coleman and Local (1991).

16 Note that the interpretation of Maximisation of Association (87) is somewhat unclear. Thus, if taken literally, it would seemingly bring about accumulation of melodic association. This result is possibly prevented by the language-specific licensing conditions on association (e.g. one-to-one association), but the condition remains ambiguous as formulated.

17 Alternative approaches to reduplication are proposed in Clements (1985b) and Mester (1986), involving a parafix and a single melody, respectively, as represented in (i) and (ii) for *taktakki*:

(i) Parafix reduplication

(ii) Single-melody reduplication

The need for melody copy is also obviated by these analyses (but only partially in Clements's parafix formalisation, as can be seen). Note that, under both approaches, reduplication must be followed by linearisation. This remaining complexity is eschewed in Steriade (1988) by maintaining the traditional melody copy procedure and then submitting the copied melody to the filtering action of a set of prosodic conditions (see Chapters 4 and 5 for discussion of prosodic structure).

2 LEXICAL REDUNDANCIES

1 It would of course in principle be possible to differentiate lexical items by means of diacritic tags, such that, e.g. *pin*, *pen*, *pan* and *pun* would be lexically encoded as 1, 2, 3 and 4, respectively. However, one of the most basic tenets of generative phonology is that phonological representations at all levels (including, therefore, the lexical level) are encoded in terms of distinctive features, as expressed in the by now classical 'Naturalness Condition' of Postal (1968), according to which 'the relation between phonological and phonetic structures must be a natural one' (Postal 1968: 55ff.). Requiring that distinct lexical items have distinct phonological representations has the interesting consequence that homophones such as *die* and *dye*, or homonyms, such as *bank* 'financial institution' and *bank* 'slope', cannot constitute independent lexical entries, at least phonologically. On the other hand, while, as we already know, non-suppletive alternants are typically reduced to a unique lexical entry, suppletive variants must be kept apart

lexically, at least within all standard approaches to phonology, which do not countenance extreme lexical abstractness (for a defence of the abstract view, see e.g. Lightner 1975).

2 This use of the term 'segment' may appear to contradict the finding reported on in the previous chapter that the traditional *SPE* feature matrices must be abandoned. Without prejudice to this theoretical advance, we are keeping the term 'segment' as an informal shorthand to refer to a bundle of distinctive features associated to any one skeletal slot (there is in fact no standard label for this configuration in autosegmental phonology).

3 The notion 'distinctness' has been given rigorous content in both *SPE* and autosegmental phonology. In *SPE*, two segments are distinct if they bear opposed specifications for one or more features, and two strings are distinct if they are of different lengths, or if they contain distinct segments in any one position (Chomsky and Halle 1965: 336). According to Pulleyblank (1986: 231), distinctness is defined in autosegmental phonology on the basis of number of skeletal slots, number of phonemes, or identity of autosegmental linkings between the slots and the phonemes. For Archangeli and Pulleyblank (1991: 40), representations can be distinct as to content or structure. The content of two representations is distinct if they differ in the identity or the number of valued features, or in their ordering, while the structure of two representations is distinct if they differ in either the path composition of their valued features (where 'path' can be basically understood in its obvious sense of 'arboreal connectedness') or in the organisation of such features into constituents.

4 Note that, as discussed in Chapter 1, this constraint is relaxed in autosegmental phonology, where in both contour segments and complex segments (in the sense of Sagey 1986) opposite specifications for one feature are allowed to be attached to the same skeletal slot (the difference between contour and complex segments resides in the fact that the two opposing specifications obey phonological linear ordering in the former, but not in the latter).

5 The soundness of this argument is less obvious than may appear at first blush. Thus, while it is undoubtedly true that the tongue cannot be in a raised and a lowered *state* simultaneously, there is no obvious reason for the raising and lowering gestures not to be *attempted* at once. This situation would result in mutual cancellation, and thus, according to this interpretation, the representation in (4a) would be equivalent to [−high, −low]. We shall not explore this interesting question any further here.

6 The contingency of (4b) is proven by the fact that velar laterals have been reported to exist (see Ladefoged 1971). A cogent argument is however made in Levin (1988a) to the effect that the velarity of such segments is only phonetic, their phonological make-up being therefore compatible with the proposed universality of (4b).

7 The Lightner/Stanley objection specifically concerns the ternary use of binary features. There is of course nothing sacrosanct about binarism, which must only be regarded as the working hypothesis on the internal composition of features adopted by classical generative phonology (indeed, as we shall see in Chapter 3, there have also been proposals for the adoption of multivalued and monovalent features at various stages in the development of the discipline). What these authors rightly object to, however, is the effective use of features as ternary in a system overtly proclaimed binary. Thus, consider a

language with the lexical representations in (i), where S_i and S_k are minimally distinct, but S_j is non-distinct with respect to either ('distinctness' has been defined in note 3 above):

(i)
	S_i	S_j	S_k
F_1	+		−
F_2	−	−	−
F_3	−	−	−

Suppose now that this language has the two rules in (ii):

(ii) a. $[+F_1] \rightarrow [+F_3]$
      b. $[-F_1] \rightarrow [+F_2]$

Application of these rules will yield three distinct segments, irrespective of the value assigned to F_1 in S_j:

(iii)
	S_i	S_j	S_k
F_1	+		−
F_2	−	−	+
F_3	+	−	−

The emergence of S_j as a third distinct matrix after the application of the rules in (ii) reveals that the blank for F_1 in S_j has effectively functioned as a third value for this feature, given the fact that both binary values + and − are already exploited for F_1 in the lexical matrices of (i). Such use of blanks is obviously spurious, since blanks should have no influence on the lexical individuation of segments.

8 Most obstruent clusters in English are in fact voiceless. In a few cases, the first consonant is voiced, and the second voiceless. There seem to be no sequences of voiceless + voiced obstruent, and only a handful of obstruent clusters with voice throughout.

9 The applicability of (12b) to *ban* would naturally presuppose that lack of specification in the input of rules be interpreted in a maximally general way, i.e. as application to *any* input (cf. the definition of distinctness in note 3 above).

10 It will be interesting to note that in Kiparsky (1982a,b) the SCC is analysed as a special instantiation of the Elsewhere Condition (13). The key element in this intriguing move is the construal of lexical entries as identity rules. Specifically, the lexical entry for *ban* would in effect be equivalent to (i):

(i) ban → ban

Clearly, if both (12b) and (i) are rules, the latter is more specific than the former, the application of which will thus be blocked by the EC, as desired. The interpretation of lexical entries as identity rules was however subsequently abandoned (Kiparsky 1983, 1985), and the SCC thus reinstated as a primitive.

11 The justification of this assumption would take us too far afield. In fact, it is not always possible to show that rules that obey the SCC must indeed apply cyclically. On the other hand, rules which can independently be shown to be cyclic obey the SCC, and compliance with the SCC appears always to be compatible with cyclic application.

12 The standard label for Constrast-based Underspecification is in fact 'Contrastive Underspecification'. This label is however misleading to the extent that, in this theory, what remains underspecified are the non-contrastive values, while contrastive values are specified. Here as elsewhere, we are endeavouring to adopt a policy of (minimal) terminological rationalisation in the interest of expository transparency.

13 The distinction between stricture and content features is due to Christdas (1988). Briefly, in Christdas's theory, stricture features relate to major class, and are assumed always to be fully specified, regardless of contrastiveness, while content features define secondary traits within these classes.

14 Obviously, the lack of lexical specification of Yoruba /i/ also explains the asymmetric behaviour of this segment with respect to the various processes referred to in (40) above. Simply, an empty matrix is not available as a rule trigger, while naturally being more vulnerable to deletion.

15 The RROC must of course be interpreted in the context of RU theory. Consequently, it is orthogonal to the CU-based analysis of the repercussions of Japanese Rendaku and Lyman's Law presented above (see (61) and (62), respectively). For reasons of space, we shall not explore an RU alternative here.

16 Archangeli (p.c.) informs me however of some problems of data coverage affecting Mohanan's analysis.

3 BASIC ELEMENTS

1 As is well known, it is, for instance, highly natural for nasals to agree in place of articulation with a following obstruent, so that such strings as *pu*[m]*p*, *pu*[n]*t*, and *pu*[ŋ]*k* are favoured over, e.g. *pu*[ŋ]*p*, *pu*[m]*t*, and *pu*[n]*k*. The class subject to such a constraint is readily defined by means of the (phonetically based) distinctive feature [+ nasal], whereas a class made up of, e.g. [m], [s] and [h] would be formally cumbersome, indeed undefinable without the use of the disjunctive operator, a dubious formal device. The claim embodied in the theory of distinctive features is thus that the naturalness of a class is formally translatable into the simplicity of its definition. From this perspective, therefore, the postulation of a feature amounts to the hypothesis that it defines a natural class, i.e. that the segments possessing this feature will exhibit uniform behaviour with regard to such processes as assimilation, dissimilation, strengthening, weakening, and so on.

2 In their phonetic function, feature values are admitted to be scalar, to match phonetic reality. Such fine detail is however relegated to the realm of phonetic realisation and effectively ignored in *SPE* (interestingly, the exception is stress, which, as we will see in Chapter 5, was subsequently found not to be a distinctive feature at all).

3 A currently fashionable interpretation of binarism as involving an 'equipollent' use of features in the Trubetzkoyan sense is debatable. Thus, Trubetzkoy spoke of segments standing in an equipollent opposition as being 'logically equivalent', by which he appears to have meant that the opposition is established by means of *distinct* features, rather than by differences of degree in the substance of the feature (as in 'gradual' oppositions) or simply by the absence of the feature (as in 'privative' oppositions). Thus, for instance, the opposition between English /k/ and /l/ would be equipollent, since there is no one feature that keeps these two

segments apart, gradually or privatively. Rather, they are differentiated by a bundle of features, such as voice, laterality, and so on. In the case of *SPE*'s (and Jakobson's) binarism, however, the opposition between, e.g. /p/ and /b/ is established by precisely one feature, namely [±voice]. In Trubetzkoy's terms, therefore, such an opposition would not be equipollent, but gradual (if we construe it as resting on the assignment of two different degrees of [voice], namely all or nothing), or perhaps privative (if we interpret Trubetzkoy's privativeness as involving a negative marking, rather than the simple formal absence of the feature). From the viewpoint of binarism, therefore, equipollence corresponds to multiple feature differentiation, as indeed it seems to have done in Trubetzkoy's original conception.

4 The OCP was originally proposed by Leben (1973) as a constraint on the distribution of (identical) tones, as follows:

  (i) OCP (Leben 1973)

     At the melodic level of the grammar, any two adjacent tonemes must be distinct. Thus HHL is not a possible melodic pattern; it automatically simplifies to HL.

Essentially abandoned by Goldsmith (1976), the OCP was infused with new life in McCarthy's (1979, 1981) work on Arabic, in order to account for the pattern of distribution of repeated root consonants (*samam*, but **sasam*), thus taking its remit beyond the domain of tone:

  (ii) OCP (McCarthy 1981)

     A grammar is less highly valued to the extent that it contains representations in which there are adjacent identical elements on any autosegmental tier.

                                          (McCarthy 1981:384)

The history of the OCP has been a truly chequered one. Thus, McCarthy (1986) explores the applicability of a strengthened OCP ('At the melodic tier, adjacent identical elements are prohibited' (McCarthy 1986: 208)) in morphological derivation, where he shows it to have blocking effects (for instance, the Afar form *sababá* 'reason' does not become **sabbá*, by syncope, whereas *ʕagára* 'scabies' indeed yields *ʕagrí*), over and above the control it exerts on morpheme-internal structures (cf. again **sasam*). Odden (1986) produces a wealth of tonal evidence against the OCP, which he therefore dismisses as a principle of grammar, interpreting instead its effects as a direct consequence of the general simplicity metric. In a subsequent paper, Odden (1988) purports to complete the demolition work by directly countering McCarthy's (1986) claims from non-tonal phonology. Such claims are, by contrast, regarded as essentially sound by Yip (1988b), who presents further evidence for the role of the OCP as a trigger of rules correcting segmental violations of the principle. Clearly, thus, the inclusion of the OCP in the repertoire of universal grammar allows the simplification of a range of language-specific rules, in addition to shedding explanatory light on the respective processes. On the other hand, the attested cases of OCP failure undoubtedly constitute a motive for moderation in the handling of the issue.

5 A positive specification for [coronal] involves raising of the blade of the tongue, while [+anterior] corresponds to a location of the constriction to the

front of the palato-alveolar area, identified as the place of articulation of English [ʃ]

6 The *SPE* definition of [distributed] is based on the relative length of the constriction, [+ distributed] segments having relatively long constrictions, while their [− distributed] congeners do not.

7 The reported existence of bilabial laterals (see e.g. Catford 1977: 251 on dialects of Irish Gaelic) further stands in the way of the interpretation of [± lateral] as a dependent of [coronal]. According to Levin (1988a), however, the lateral articulation is non-distinctive in such sounds. From an *SPE* perspective, this fact would of course not relieve us from supplying bilabial laterals with the corresponding distinctive feature, but more recent trends in phonological theory do tend to lean heavier on distinctiveness (see e.g. Contrast-based Underspecification theory, examined in Chapter 2), another point of departure from the *SPE* tradition. All this notwithstanding, it will come as no surprise that the incorporation of [± lateral] to the [coronal] class has not met with universal acceptance. For instance, Rice and Avery (1991) argue for the assignment of all sonorants to a separate group, a step that would automatically exclude the dependency of [± lateral] on [coronal]. For lack of space, we must decline to spell out the exact details of this or any other such proposals.

8 The geometry of feature dependencies represented in (17) must be kept well distinct from the geometry of contour (and complex) segments discussed in Chapter 1. In particular, such F-elements as [− continuant] and [+ continuant], which we saw then are necessary to define affricates, occupy one and the same plane, since they correspond to different specifications of one and the same feature. By contrast, the configuration in (17) corresponds to different features, each of which is therefore endowed with its own plane.

9 Note that [labial], [coronal] and [dorsal] all refer to articulator activity. An explicit defence of the construal of place features as relating to articulator activity rather than to stricture locus, as in IPA theory, can be found in Halle (1983, 1988). Problems with this approach arising from the class of gutturals are pointed out in McCarthy (1989b).

10 This feature is not in the *SPE* inventory, and was introduced in the late 1970s following research by Ladefoged (1964, 1971), Steward (1967), and Halle and Stevens (1969), among others. The main argument concerns the harmony systems of some (mainly West African) languages, where vowels are [+ ATR] or [− ATR] throughout a particular domain, in a manner paralleling the [back] harmony of Turkish examined in Chapter 1 (the impoverished [ATR] harmony system of Yoruba has been discussed in Chapter 2). An interesting question concerns the relationship between [± ATR] and the *SPE*–Jakobson feature [± tense]. As is well known, tenseness has proved remarkably elusive phonetically. On the other hand, the feature [ATR] is well substantiated instrumentally, and this includes X-ray evidence. Consequently, it would be desirable to subsume the old feature [tense] under [ATR], but [tense] still appears alongside [ATR] in some recent inventories (e.g. Halle and Clements 1983). More commonly, however, [tense] is nowadays omitted from the list of distinctive features, and we will accordingly say no more about it here.

11 We are adopting these informal features in the interest of expository simplicity. The 'official' features defining laryngeal activity are [± stiff vocal folds], [± slack vocal folds], both of which relate to vocal fold tenseness, and

[$\pm$ spread glottis], [$\pm$ constricted glottis], relating to glottal opening (see Halle and Stevens 1971). The contrasts in the appropriate Thai segments are thus expressed as follows:

(i) /b/ (voiced):

$$\begin{bmatrix} + \text{slack} \\ - \text{spread} \end{bmatrix}$$

(ii) /p/ (voiceless unaspirated):

$$\begin{bmatrix} - \text{slack} \\ - \text{spread} \end{bmatrix}$$

(iii) /pʰ/ (voiceless aspirated):

$$\begin{bmatrix} - \text{slack} \\ + \text{spread} \end{bmatrix}$$

In addition, /b/ will be [$-$ stiff, $-$ constricted], and /p/ and /pʰ/ [$+$ stiff, $-$ constricted].

12 True geminates, as represented in (i), may not be split by epenthesis or undergo change in only one of their component elements:

By contrast, fake geminates (typically, straddling two morphemes) can be subject to such processes:

(ii)
```
x x → x x x  or  x x
| |   | | |       | |
A A   A B A      A C
```

The standard approach, as expounded in the sources mentioned in the text, derives such restrictions from the structure of the representations themselves, in particular from the No Crossing Constraint discussed in Chapter 1.

13 Cf. e.g. the common substitution of [ʔ] for plosives in English under certain conditions, as discussed in Lass (1976) (the use of [ʔ] for [t] is of course one of the salient traits of, e.g. Cockney and Glasgow English), and the historical replacement of three of the Spanish fricative sounds by [h], also under various conditions: [f] (cf. Latin *farina* 'flour' vs Old Spanish [h]*arina*), [x] (cf. Castilian *ca*[x]*a* 'box' vs Andalusian *ca*[h]*a*), [s] (cf. Castilian *más* 'more' vs Andalusian *má*[h]).

14 In what follows, we have slightly reformalised Hayes's (1990) proposal in the interest of simplicity and expository expedience. The substance of the proposal is however not affected by the notational changes.

15 The best known potential counterexample to this claim would be a {root} node empty of dependents, as indeed made use of in some analyses (see e.g.

Borowsky 1985). According to this line of thinking, the two configurations in (i) and (ii) would be distinct (NB 'X' stands for an element in the CV tier):

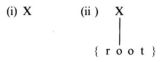

(i) X   (ii)   X
                       |
                       |
                { r o o t }

Clearly, the availability of empty class nodes multiplies possible structural differences, and is therefore best avoided, unless imposed by the facts. To the best of our knowledge, such facts are in short supply, this type of analysis being, in any event, controversial.

16 We are maintaining the autosegmental formalisation of class nodes in faithfulness to the original. A reinterpretation in terms of subindices, in line with our discussion above, is however also possible.

17 Khalkha Mongolian was traditionally thought to possess the front rounded vowels /y/ and /œ/, both partaking in front–back harmony alternations, hence the notation. More rigorous phonetic investigation has however revealed that the relevant trait in this harmony is ATR-ness, as displayed in (51) below (see Rialland and Djamouri 1984 for discussion).

18 The oldest of the three approaches is Dependency phonology, the starting point of which can be ascribed to Anderson and Jones (1974). The body of this theory, which purports to account for the general organisational principles of phonology, is assembled in Anderson and Ewen (1987). Particle phonology stems from the work of Schane, in particular Schane (1984a,b). Its scope is less ambitious, effectively confined to the internal structure of vowels ('I have not investigated whether the principles of particle phonology are applicable to consonants' (Schane 1984b: 154 n. 30)). Finally, Government phonology (fully titled Government and Charm phonology, for reasons which will become apparent below) has its origins in the work of Kaye, Lowenstamm, and Vergnaud in the early 1980s (see e.g. Vergnaud 1982, Kaye and Lowenstamm 1984, and, in particular, Kaye, Lowenstamm and Vergnaud 1985). Like Dependency phonology, it aspires to model all aspects of phonological structure, although its major contributions to date have been in the areas of segment and syllable structure. Unfortunately for the non-initiated, a different terminology and set of notational conventions are in use in each of these theories. In the interest of communication, we shall endeavour to reduce such divergences to a common vocabulary in our presentation.

19 Dependency relations between features have also been postulated in mainstream feature theory, as we have seen above. This practice must be carefully distinguished from the holistic Dependency approach examined in the present subsection. This approach belongs to an altogether distinct tradition (see note 18 above) and is programmatically characterised by the use of the quantal vowels as primes and the complexity of its dependency calculus, as we will see.

20 Unlike the Particle approach, which is basically a theory of vowel structure (see note 18 above), the Dependency framework aims at accounting for the composition of all segments, along the same lines as standard feature geometry. Consequently, also like feature geometry, it contains elements related to phonation and airstream mechanisms, as well as to place and manner of articulation for consonants. Such elements (which are referred to

as 'components' in the Dependency literature) are also grouped into class nodes or 'gestures'. For simplicity, we are limiting our present discussion to vowels, which in fact contribute the most robust data in all the approaches that build on the quantal vowel triangle, as we have already mentioned.

21 For simplicity and consistency across theories we are representing the basic elements in upper case. This is at variance with the Dependency literature, where they appear as lower case letters enclosed in vertical bars: |i|, |a|, |u|. More complex expressions are also enclosed in bars, with the dependency relations formalised as double arrows, as here, or as colons and semicolons (for bidirectional and unidirectional government, respectively). For completeness, we now illustrate these two alternative notations with the front vowels:

(i) /i/: |i| (ii) /i:/ |i|
    /e/: |i⇒a| /e/: |i;a|
    /ɛ/: |a⇔i| /ɛ/: |i:a|
    /æ/: |a⇒i| /æ/: |a;i|

22 Strictly speaking, simple combination, represented by means of a comma, since, in addition to engaging in unidirectional and mutual government, two elements can simply be juxtaposed:

/y/:   I,U
/ø/:   (I,U)⇒A
/œ/:   I,U,A
/Œ/:   A⇒(I,U)

The reason we can dispense with mutual government here is that, as will be seen below, no unidirectional government is allowed between these two elements in the system, juxtaposition being therefore a sufficient relation. For expository and notational simplicity, however, we shall continue operating on the assumption of mutual government. No adverse consequences for the argument follow from the adoption of this presentational strategy.

23 Anderson and Ewen (1987: 32) attempt to justify this inconsistency by appealing to the relational asymmetry of the two instances of the component in such cases: 'it is appropriate to allow up to two instances of each component per segment, provided the two instances are asymmetrically related'.

24 The figures given are derivable from the following series (I owe this information to my colleague Martin Atkinson):

$$n + 3_nP_2 + 7_nP_3 + 25_nP_4 + 121_nP_5 + 721_nP_6 \ldots$$

25 The same problem afflicts the Particle model, as explicitly recognised by Schane (1984a: 41): 'Each complex particle functions within its own network of contrasts so that the interpretation of particles is sensitive to the system as a whole.' He does not appear to be troubled by this situation, however, and further comments that 'the fact that Spanish [e] and English [ɪ] share the same particle configuration is not without interest', since 'these two vowel qualities are surprisingly similar'. It is far from clear what phonological consequences are being predicted to arise from this similarity, or whether other representational identities are also to be welcome.

26 Ironically, Kaye *et al.* (1985: 307) trace the choice of I, U, A as primitive elements back to markedness theory, as represented in *SPE* and in Kean

(1975, 1979). Kaye (1990a) claims that part of the reason [ɪ] may appear to be rare cross-linguistically is that it has often been mistranscribed as a schwa, and he cites Moroccan Arabic as a case in point. He also mentions the merger of short vowels into [ɪ] in this language and in Northern Algonquian as further evidence for the neutrality of this segment. As for [ɯ], he concedes to its rarity and idiosyncratic behaviour within the system.

27 An alternative, pointed out to me by John Harris, consists in stipulating that reduction involves fusion with whatever element(s) may be necessary to account for the specific phonetic implementation. While this strategy will undoubtedly yield the desired variety of output, it obviously subtracts force from the claim implicit in the Government machinery that default vowels are structurally *simpler* than their counterparts.

28 Clause 6 in the *OED* entry for *charm* reads as follows: '*Particle Physics.* One of the quantum properties or flavours that distinguish the different quarks, being possessed only by the *c* quark.'

29 Kaye *et al.* (1985) only allow for positive and negative charm. In our exposition, however, we are taking account of subsequent developments in the theory (see e.g. Kaye 1990a). The three charm categories are at present standard. Coleman (1990b) points out that there are serious theory-internal difficulties with the notion of neutral charm. Thus, an interpretation as a third value will prevent charmless elements from combining with each other, as will be seen in the text directly below. If, instead, we take neutral charm to denote underspecification, we will be in conflict with the principle of Government theory that elements are 'autonomous pronounceable elements defined as fully specified feature matrices' (Kaye *et al.* 1985: 311).

30 A possible exception to this is the ATR feature ɯ, which, according to Kaye *et al.* (1985: 312), 'does not appear to reside on any line'. In more standard terms, this would imply the dependency of [ATR] on the other features. Note that the ATR element exhibits all-round peculiar behaviour in the Government system: 'In normal circumstances it is not the head of a compound segment, and it does not appear as the sole element of a position except in very special circumstances' (Kaye *et al.* 1985: 312). This leads Kaye (1990a: 180) to 'express displeasure at this state of affairs [i.e. that ATR behaves suspiciously, IMR]', and to confess that 'this is a problem that concerns us', to which 'hopefully some insightful solution will be found'.

4 THE SONORITY FABRIC

1 Notice the risk of circularity implicit in this definition, where a subset of the definiendum ([i], [u]) is included in the definiens ('vocalic').

2 Kahn (1976: 97) describes the American 'flap' as a 'one-tap trill', and suggests that the term 'flap' is best kept 'for the ballistic movement of the tongue described for many languages of India (see Abercrombie, 1967: 49–50)'. In Kahn's description, the American sound involves adjustment of the tenseness of the tongue tip so as to allow the Bernouilli effect to take place, the tongue dropping away after the first tap in a manner similar to the Spanish 'simple *r*' of, e.g. *caro* 'dear' (cf. *carro* 'cart', with a fully trilled *r*, [r]).

3 Our current position is that, while the feature [syllabic] does not exist, [consonantal] will be part of the feature geometry, either as an integral element of the root (as in McCarthy 1988) or as one of its daughters (as

proposed by Sagey 1986 and others). Note that, either way, the feature [±consonantal] must be removed from the skeleton (consonantal sounds are defined in *SPE* as 'produced with a radical obstruction in the midsaggital region of the vocal tract' (*SPE*: 302)).

4 A survey of English syllable phonotactics, somewhat unconventionally couched, can be found in Fudge (1969, 1987).

5 Among the languages usually cited as evidence for a marked vc.v parsing are Scots Gaelic (see Clements 1986b) and several Australian languages (see e.g. Sommer 1970). The evaluation of this claim and its repercussions for syllable theory clearly falls outside the scope of the present study.

6 The key argument hinges on the syllabification of Latin *via* /uia/ 'road' as [ui.a], rather than [u.ia], on the assumption that the high vocoids /i/, /u/ are unspecified for [±consonantal], the value of which feature constrains onset formation (in particular, [−consonantal] segments may not be onsets).

7 This principle is the natural successor to the Stray Erasure Convention, stated in (i) in Steriade's (1982: 89) version:

    (i)   Erase segments and skeleton slots unless attached to higher levels of structure.

Steriade attributes the origin of this convention to McCarthy (1979).

8 It is in fact a moot point whether degree of sonority formally corresponds to a special multivalued feature or is a by-product of the values assigned to the standard features. Representative statements of these two positions can be found in Selkirk (1984a) and Clements (1990), respectively.

9 This configuration is referred to in Clements (1990) as the 'sonority cycle' (not to be confused with the standard 'cycle', which will be further discussed in Chapter 5), on the grounds of its (quasi-)periodicity. Clements further suggests that the sonority rise in the onset is optimally maximised, and the fall in the rime optimally minimised. Following on from this, he elaborates a 'Dispersion Principle' to account for degrees of syllable markedness as related to sonority.

10 We could attempt to account for these and other similar facts by means of negative syllable-structure conditions in the style of Clements and Keyser (1983) or Itô (1986). It is far from clear, however, that in the final analysis any such conditions would do other than simply reproduce the facts. Another strategy would be to regard the absence of the sequences in question as an accidental gap.

11 Binary constituents are defended in Kiparsky (1979) (necessarily), and in the Government and Charm framework (maximally), the latter to be examined in section 6 below.

12 Selkirk (1982: 346–7) proposes to analyse *s*C sequences as effectively contour segments (see Davis 1984 for criticism). While such an approach would indeed resolve (most of) the problems related to the distribution of *s* in English, no independent justification for it is apparent.

13 The reader must be warned that the connection between the distinctive feature and syllable components of this framework is less clear than the shared terminology suggests. In Chapter 3 we attempted to show that GC feature theory can plausibly be interpreted as a strong version of Radical Underspecification. The GC contribution to syllables is more original, as will be seen directly.

14 Kaye, Lowenstamm and Vergnaud (1990) refer to Aoun (1979) in support of their claim. They also point to the supposed absence of distributional constraints between the onset and the rime, and offer some additional, theory-internal arguments against the syllable (for a similar stand arrived at from a different perspective, see Hyman 1985: 26ff.).

15 The essential identity of the two modes of representation can be made explicit by means of the graphic transformations in (i):

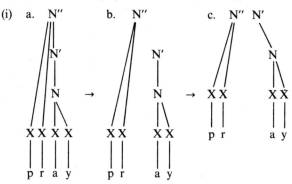

All we have done is in fact dislocate and delink the N' node from its mother, first maintaining it at a lower level, in keeping with the X-bar hierarchy, and then implementing equalisation of levels, to take account of the symmetrical nature of the implication in GC theory, graphically suggested by the leaning towards each other of the two nodes, as if in a gesture of mutual need (NB in GC, N'' is of course relabelled O, and N', R).

16 The obvious question arises at this point of what prevents the R and N nodes from being *both* branching, as represented in (i):

A principled answer to this question will be provided below.

17 This is obviously not true of languages with root-and-pattern morphology, which must necessarily have resort to lexical syllabic templates, as we have shown. The question is whether such templates are necessary in all cases, or whether they can be dispensed with in languages with concatenative morphology.

18 This principle is often referred to as 'locality' in the GC literature, a term which in the present context may lead to confusion with Itô's use. In Itô's sense, locality restricts the scope of syllable-defining conditions to the syllable-internal domain, whereas GC locality alludes to adjacency, as the label in (62) makes transparent.

19 This condition is restated in Kaye (1991–2: 305) as a prohibition against the head itself being licensed. This wording obviously implies the restriction of the scope of the condition to the skeletal level, since, as we know, all heads

but one will necessarily be licensed on the nuclear projection, and therefore at the level of nuclear projection only one head per domain will be unlicensed.

20 This principle obviously subsumes the more conventional CV principle (or rule), since, given a string VCV, the parsing V.CV will result (VC.V would directly contravene the principle).

21 Note that this reasoning only applies in the case of right-to-left directionality. The prediction implicit in the principle in (75) below is however that proper government of nuclei in cases of left-to-right directionality, although formally possible, is empirically irrelevant.

22 As it happens, however, of the neutrally charmed vowels only high vowels can in actual fact partake in onsets, while charmless consonants (sibilants, nasals and liquids) are not assigned to nuclei in the GC analyses available in the literature (hence our previous statement that the domain licensor must be a vowel). The reasons for this mismatch between the predictions of the theory and the apparent facts are at present unclear.

23 Nucleus-to-nucleus government is manifestly exempt from the restrictions in (80), the scope of which must consequently be assumed to be limited to the immediate projection of the heads of the basic constituents, namely O and R/N. This limitation does not appear to follow independently from any of the principles of the theory, and thus further undermines the interpretation of the relation between (non-strictly adjacent) nuclei as G-licensing.

24 The function of charm constraints (both on constituent membership, as in (79), and on government, as in (80)) is clearly the formalisation of sonority distance requirements. In contrast with mainstream approaches, such GC constraints are given strict universal status. Moreover, they are defined on the (charm) categories in (78), rather than on the standard sonority hierarchy.

25 The reason for the interpretation of these consonants as charmless has now become apparent. Unfortunately, however, this interpretation leads to negative results elsewhere, since it awards these sounds the same nucleus status as high vowels (cf. (79)), apparently in conflict with the facts (see note 22 above).

26 The transconstituent analysis of s + C raises the question of the licensing of the empty nucleus corresponding to s, since such a nucleus cannot be properly governed by the following nucleus when a complex onset intervenes, as it does in, e.g. *sprout*. Kaye (1991–2) thus introduces the (as yet mysterious) notion of 'Magic Licensing' to account for the across-the-board legitimacy of sequences involving s + C.

5 DOMAINS AND MODES OF APPLICATION

1 The process of r-Insertion as just described is formalisable by means of a 'domain span' rule, since it applies regardless of the position of the focus elements in the span of the prosodic domain PU, thus (D = a prosodic domain; A, B = segments; X, Y, Z = (strings of) segments, possibly null):

(i) Domain Span Rules
$$A \rightarrow B /\ (_D \dots X\_\_\_Y \dots)_D$$

There are also 'domain juncture' and 'domain limit' rules, as in (ii) and (iii), respectively (see Selkirk 1980: 111–12):

(ii) Domain Juncture Rules

$$A \rightarrow B \ / \ (_{Di} \ldots (_{Dj} \ldots X\underline{\quad}Y)_{Dj} \ (_{Dj} \ Z \ldots)_{Dj} \ldots)_{Di}$$
$$A \rightarrow B \ / \ (_{Di} \ldots (_{Dj} \ldots Z)_{Dj} \ (_{Dj} \ X\underline{\quad}Y \ldots .)_{Dj} \ldots)_{Di}$$

(iii) Domain Limit Rules

$$A \rightarrow B \ / \ (_{D} \ldots X\underline{\quad}Y)_{D}$$
$$A \rightarrow B \ / \ (_{D} \ X\underline{\quad}Y \ldots)_{D}$$

2 Landmarks in the development of the autosegmental approach to (English) intonation are Liberman (1975) and Pierrehumbert (1980). The latter is still a key source on the matter, if superceded in parts. A recent useful summary of the basic principles of autosegmental intonation can be found in Hayes and Lahiri (1991).

3 There are however problems with this position (see Beckman and Pierrehumbert 1986, Ladd 1986, Gussenhoven 1990, and Gussenhoven and Rietveld 1992). It is possible to get a flavour of the issue by comparing the two utterances *But we're **not** telling John* and *But we're **not** going John*, the latter with an IP boundary, but not necessarily a pause, between *going* and *John* (typically represented by a comma in the orthography). What is crucial is that, according to Gussenhoven and Rietveld (1992: 285), both the intonational melody and its distribution over the whole utterance are identical in both cases.

4 This condition is however suspended in the special class of 'directional clitics', where incorporation takes place instead in a given direction (see Klavans 1982, 1985 for further details).

5 Chomsky and Halle's psychological stance must of course be interpreted in the context of the distinction between competence and performance. Specifically, the psychological nature of stress implies its apportioning to the domain of competence, its reflection in performance being indirect. Thus, as pointed out in Hayes (1991: 16ff.), stress can become manifest as the locus of one of the tones in the intonational melody (in particular, the main tone, or 'nucleus'), or as a trigger of segmental rules.

6 Strictly speaking, all non-primary word-internal stresses in (44) must be reduced by one degree, according to Chomsky and Halle's procedure. We deliberately sidestep this detail, which is not germane to our present concerns.

7 Other, related ones can be added to the list: culminativity, rhythmic distribution, hierarchisation, failure to assimilate (see Hayes 1991: 29–30).

8 Liberman and Prince (1977) adopted an essentially equivalent tree formalism:

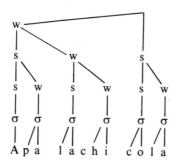

The label 's' stands for strong, and 'w' for weak. The connections between the tree and grid formalisations are obvious. The advantages of the grid over the tree notation will be clarified as we go along (see in particular section 5.4.3.1).

9 In line with our declared policy of seeking terminological unity and perspicacity throughout, we have taken the liberty of adopting novel labels for these parameters. The terminology in Halle and Vergnaud (1987) is as follows: Adjacency = Boundedness; Edge = Head Terminal; Flank = Headedness.

10 A situation suggesting precisely the procedure in (66a) is described in Levin (1988b) for Cahuilla. As Levin shows, however, this stress pattern can be accounted for without surrendering the Directionality parameter, simply by reversing its setting at a certain affixational level. Specifically, in this language Directionality is set as left-to-right in the domain formed by the suffixed root, and as right-to-left in the whole word domain, after prefixation (Levin frames her analysis in the context of the Lexical Phonology model of rule application, which will be examined in 5.6.2). Such a reversal of setting is of course incompatible with the hypothesis of uniformity of setting mentioned above.

11 Hayes also seems to accept this condition under the label 'Bijectivity', which he paraphrases by saying that *'every bracketed domain has a unique grid mark that serves as its "head"* . . . , and every grid mark is the head of some unique domain' (Hayes 1991: 44; my emphasis, IMR).

12 It can also be argued that the success of Halle and Vergnaud's (1987) analysis is an artifact of the fact that Cairene syllables cannot be superheavy word-internally, since the presence of an additional rimal element would also lead to an incorrect result, as exemplified in (i) with the hypothetical form *ʔard.wi.ya.tu.hu.ma*:

(i)
```
     *                        *   *    *    *
   ***  **   *   *   *    (**)(*   *)( *  *)( *)(*)( *)
 ʔard.wi.ya.tu.hu.ma →  ʔar  d.wi . ya.tu. hu.ma
```

The output would thus be mistakenly stressed on the penult.

13 The level intervening between the foot and word levels is often referred to as the 'cola' (strictly speaking, the singular 'colon' ought to be used). Not much research has gone into this level, undoubtedly more elusive than its foot and word analogues. A reasonably robust example is provided by Hungarian. According to Hammond (1987), this language exhibits three degrees of stress, as illustrated by the long form *lɛgmɛgvêstɛgèthɛtêtlɛnèbbɛknêk* 'to those least bribable'. Primary stress is located on the first syllable, and subsidiary stresses on every other syllable thereafter. Among the latter, however, there is a further alternation between tertiary (ˆ) and secondary (`). This pattern is readily obtainable if a cola line is built into the metrical representation, as follows:

(i)
```
   *                                    line 3
  (*           *)         (*)           line 2
  (*      *) (*     *) (*       *)       line 1
  (*    *)(*   *)(*   *)(*   *)(*)       line 0
  lɛgmɛgvɛstɛ gɛthɛ tɛtlɛ nɛbbɛknɛk
```

As can be seen, the word line is now numbered '3', the intermediate line 2 corresponding to the cola. As already mentioned, higher lines have also been postulated to take account of phrasal contours.

14 A few exceptions to this generalisation are reported in the literature, among them Yidinʸ, (Central Alaskan) Yupik, and Tübatulabal. The interpretation of such data is however unclear, and opposing claims are in existence (see Hayes 1991: 29).

15 This situation is of course problematic for the Strict Layer Hypothesis, at least if metrical structure is considered an integral part of the prosodic hierarchy. As already mentioned, an alternative interpretation favoured in Halle and Vergnaud (1987) involves the construal of metrical structure as planarly independent of prosodic structure (see section 5.6.3 below for specific discussion of planar structure).

16 I am indebted to Aditi Lahiri for these data and for discussion of Bengali stress.

17 The reader familiar with *SPE* will be aware that the Stress Erasure Convention (139) directly contradicts the analysis of English stress proposed there. In particular, it was precisely the observation that English stress is preserved irrespective of depth of embedding that prompted Chomsky and Halle (in the footsteps of Chomsky, Halle and Lukoff 1956) to postulate the cycle. The obvious answer to this conundrum is that the *SPE* account fell short of complete adequacy, since the stress pattern of English derivatives does not necessarily stand in a one-to-one correlation with that of their respective bases, as attested by such pairs as *invóke – invocátion, reveál – révelátion, infláme – inflamátion, órigin – oríginal, Páris – Parísian*, etc. (see Halle and Kenstowicz 1991 for some discussion).

18 The reader must be warned against the ambiguity of many of the labels associated with Lexical Phonology. First, the model, as expounded, does not bear exclusively on phonology, and would therefore be better named 'Lexical Morphology and Phonology'. Second, Lexical Phonology, as a model, must be carefully distinguished from the lexical phonology, i.e. from the phonological processes that take place in the lexical module. From this perspective, therefore, 'Interactive Stratal Morphology and Phonology' would perhaps more adequately reflect the substance of the model. Third, the adjective 'lexical' must now be interpreted as referring to the processes (again, morphological and phonological) which contribute to the makeup of words in isolation. It must therefore be kept apart from the 'lexicon', a word which traditionally designates the listing of idiosyncratic properties of morphemes.

19 This diagram corresponds to the conception of LP prevalent in the mid 1980s. Originally (early 1980s), each morphological stratum was assigned its own, specific subset of phonological rules. A mid course can be steered by maintaining a unique list of rules, but allotting each of them idiosyncratically to the various morphological strata (say, by subscripting each rule as to strata), subject to the restriction that strata cannot be skipped (the '[Continuity of] Stratum Domain Hypothesis' of Mohanan 1982). In the model represented by the diagram, all rules are applicable at all morphological (and syntactic) levels, provided they comply with the general principles of grammar (the EC, SSC, the OCP, etc.) operative at each level.

20 Note that this ordering embodies the prediction that morphological processes may not be sensitive to derived phonological information. To the

extent that such sensitivity has been empirically validated, the approach in Halle and Vergnaud (1987) would be in need of further refinement.

21 An alternative solution, involving prosodic analysis, is offered in Booij and Rubach (1984), Cohn (1989), and Inkelas (1989), among others.

REFERENCES

Abercrombie, D. (1967) *Elements of General Phonetics*, Edinburgh: Edinburgh University Press.

Allen, M. (1978) 'Morphological Investigations', Ph.D dissertation, University of Connecticut.

Al-Mozainy, H.Q., Bley-Vroman, R. and McCarthy, J. (1985) 'Stress Shift and Metrical Structure', *Linguistic Inquiry* 16: 135–44.

Anderson, J. and Ewen, C. (1987) *Principles of Dependency Phonology*, Cambridge: Cambridge University Press.

Anderson, J. and Jones, C. (1974) 'Three Theses concerning Phonological Representations', *Journal of Linguistics* 10: 1–26.

Anderson, S.R. (1984) 'A Metrical Interpretation of Some Traditional Claims about Quantity and Stress', in M. Aronoff and R.T. Oehrle (eds), *Language Sound Structure*, Cambridge, MA: MIT Press, 83–106.

Aoun, J. (1979) 'Is the Syllable or the Supersyllable a Constituent?', *MIT Working Papers in Linguistics* 1: 140–8.

Archangeli, D. (1983) 'The Root CV-Template as a Property of the Affix: Evidence from Yawelmani', *Natural Language and Linguistic Theory* 1: 348–84.

—— (1984) 'Underspecification in Yawelmani Phonology and Morphology', Ph.D dissertation, MIT.

—— (1984–5) 'Extrametricality in Yawelmani', *The Linguistic Review* 4: 101–20.

—— (1985) 'Yokuts Harmony: Evidence for Coplanar Representation in Nonlinear Phonology', *Linguistic Inquiry* 16: 335–72.

—— (1988) 'Aspects of Underspecification Theory', *Phonology* 5: 183–207.

Archangeli, D. and Pulleyblank, D. (1989) 'Yoruba Vowel Harmony', *Linguistic Inquiry* 20: 173–217.

—— (1991) 'The Content and Structure of Phonological Representations', MS, University of Arizona and University of Southern California.

—— (forthcoming) *Grounded Phonology*, MIT Press.

Bagemihl, B. (1989) 'The Crossing Constraint and "Backward Languages" ', *Natural Language and Linguistic Theory* 7: 481–549.

Beckman, M.E. and Pierrehumbert, J. (1986) 'Intonational Structure in Japanese and English', *Phonology Yearbook* 3: 255–309.

Bell, A. (1977) 'Accent Placement and Perception of Prominence in Rhythmic Structures', in L. Hyman (ed.), *Studies in Stress and Accent*, Southern

California Occasional Papers in Linguistics 4, Los Angeles: University of Southern California, 1–13.

Bloch, B. (1948) 'A Set of Postulates for Phonemic Analysis', *Language* 24: 3–46.

Bloomfield, L. (1933) *Language*, London: Allen and Unwin.

Booij, G. and Rubach, R. (1984) 'Morphological and Prosodic Domains in Lexical Phonology', *Phonology Yearbook* 1: 1–27.

—— (1987) 'Postcyclic versus Postlexical Rules in Lexical Phonology', *Linguistic Inquiry* 18: 1–44.

Borowsky, T. (1985) 'Empty and Unspecified segments', in J. Goldberg, S. MacKaye and M. Westcoat (eds), *Proceedings of the West Coast Conference in Formal Linguistics* 4, Stanford, CA: Stanford Linguistics Association, 46–57.

—— (1986) 'Topics in the Lexical Phonology of English', Ph.D dissertation, University of Massachusetts at Amherst (distributed by Graduate Linguistics Student Association).

Bromberger, S. and Halle, M. (1989) 'Why Phonology is Different', *Linguistic Inquiry* 20: 51–70.

Brooks, M.Z. (1965) 'On Polish Affricates', *Word* 20: 207–10.

Catford, J.C. (1977) *Fundamental Problems in Phonetics*, Edinburgh: Edinburgh University Press.

Chafe, W. (1968) 'The Ordering of Phonological Rules', *International Journal of American Linguistics* 24: 115–36.

Chomsky, N. (1964) *Current Issues in Linguistic Theory*, The Hague: Mouton.

Chomsky, N. and Halle, M. (1965) 'Some Controversial Questions in Phonological Theory', *Journal of Linguistics* 1: 97–138.

—— (1968) *The Sound Pattern of English*, New York: Harper and Row.

Chomsky, N., Halle, M. and Lukoff, F. (1956) 'On Accent and Juncture in English', in M. Halle, H.G. Lunt, H. MacLean and C.H. van Schoonveld (eds), *For Roman Jakobson*, The Hague: Mouton, 65–80.

Christdas, P. (1987) 'On Constraining the Power of Lexical Phonology: Evidence from Tamil', *Proceedings of the Seventeenth Meeting of the North-Eastern Linguistic Society*: 122–46.

—— (1988) The Phonology and Morphology of Tamil, Ph.D dissertation, Cornell University.

Clements, G.N. (1985a) 'The Geometry of Phonological Features', *Phonology Yearbook* 2: 223–52.

—— (1985b) 'The Problem of Transfer in Non-linear Phonology', *Cornell Working Papers in Linguistics* 7: 38–73.

—— (1986a) 'Compensatory Lengthening and Consonant Gemination in LuGanda', in L. Wetzels and E. Sezer (eds), *Studies in Compensatory Lengthening*, Dordrecht: Foris, 37–77.

—— (1986b) 'Syllabification and Epenthesis in the Barra Dialect of Gaelic', in K. Bogers, H. van der Hulst and M. Mous (eds), *The Phonological Representation of Suprasegmentals*, Dordrecht: Foris, 317–36.

—— (1988) 'Toward a Substantive Theory of Feature Specification', *Proceedings of the Eighteenth Meeting of the North-Eastern Linguistic Society*: 79–93.

—— (1989) 'A Unified Set of Features for Consonants and Vowels', MS, Cornell University.

—— (1990) 'The Role of the Sonority Cycle in Core Syllabification', in J. Kingston and M.E. Beckman (eds), *Papers in Laboratory Phonology I*, Cambridge: Cambridge University Press, 283–333.

—— (1992) 'Place of Articulation in Consonants and Vowels: A Unified Theory', to appear in B. Laks and A. Rialland (eds), *L'Architecture et la géométrie des représentations phonologiques*, Paris: Editions du CNRS.

Clements, G.N. and Keyser, S.J. (1983) *CV-Phonology: A Generative Theory of the Syllable*, Cambridge, MA: MIT Press.

Clements, G.N. and Sezer, E. (1982) 'Vowel and Consonant Disharmony in Turkish', in H. van der Hulst and N. Smith (eds), *The Structure of Phonological Representations*, vol. 2, Dordrecht: Foris, 213–55.

Cohn, A. (1989) 'Stress in Indonesian and Bracketing Paradoxes', *Natural Language and Linguistic Theory* 7: 167–216.

Comrie, B. (1976) 'Irregular Stress in Polish and Macedonian', *International Review of Slavic Linguistics* 1: 227–40.

Cole, J. (1987) 'Planar Phonology and Morphology', Ph.D dissertation, MIT.

Cole, J. and Trigo, L. (1988) 'Parasitic Harmony', in H. van der Hulst and N. Smith (eds), *Features, Segmental Structure and Harmony Processes (Part II)*, Dordrecht: Foris, 19–38.

Coleman, J. (1990a) 'Charm Theory Defines Strange Vowel Sets', *Journal of Linguistics* 26: 165–74.

—— (1990b) 'Vowel Sets: A Reply to Kaye', *Journal of Linguistics* 26: 183–7.

Coleman, J. and Local, J. (1991) 'The "No Crossing Constraint" in Autosegmental Phonology', *Linguistics and Philosophy* 14: 295–338.

Davis, S. (1984) 'Some Implications of Onset-Coda Constraints for Syllable Phonology', in *Proceedings of the Twentieth Meeting of the Chicago Linguistic Society*, Chicago: Chicago Linguistics Society, 46–51.

—— (1985) 'Topics in Syllable Geometry', Ph.D dissertation, University of Arizona.

—— (1988) 'Syllable Onsets and Stress Rules', *Phonology* 5: 1–19.

Dell, F. (1980) *Generative Phonology*, Cambridge: Cambridge University Press.

Dresher, B.E. (1990) 'Review of Morris Halle and Jean-Roger Vergnaud, *An Essay on Stress*', *Phonology* 7: 171–88.

Ewen, C. and van der Hulst, H. (1988) '[high], [low] and [back] or [I], [A] and [U]?', in P. Coopmans and A. Hulk (eds), *Linguistics in the Netherlands 1988*, Dordrecht: Foris, 49–57.

Fabb, N. (1985) 'The Relation between Phonology and Morphology. A New Approach', MS, University of Strathclyde.

—— (1988) 'English Suffixation is Constrained only by Selectional Restrictions', *Natural Language and Linguistic Theory* 6: 527–39.

Firth, J.R. (1957) *Papers in Linguistics 1934–51*, Oxford: Oxford University Press.

Foley, J. (1977) *Foundations of Theoretical Phonology*, Cambridge: Cambridge University Press.

Franks, S. (1985) 'Extrametricality and Stress in Polish', *Linguistic Inquiry* 15: 144–51.

—— (1987) 'Regular and Irregular Stress in Macedonian', *International Journal of Slavic Linguistics and Poetics* 35–6: 93–142.

Fudge, E. (1967) 'The Nature of Phonological Primes', *Journal of Linguistics* 3: 1–36.

—— (1969) 'Syllables', *Journal of Linguistics* 5: 253–86.

—— (1987) 'Branching Structure within the Syllable', *Journal of Linguistics* 23: 359–77.

Goldsmith, J. (1976) 'Autosegmental Phonology', Ph.D dissertation, MIT; published by Garland, New York and London, n.d.

—— (1985) 'Vowel Harmony in Khalkha Mongolian, Yaka, Finnish and Hungarian', *Phonology Yearbook* 2: 251–75.

Grammont, M. (1933) *Traité de Phonétique*, Paris: Librairie Delagrave.

Gussenhoven, C. (1990) 'Tonal Association Domains and the Prosodic Hierarchy in English', in S. Ramsaran (ed.), *Studies in the Pronunciation of English*, London: Routledge, 27–37.

Gussenhoven, C. and Rietveld, A.C.M. (1992) 'Intonation Contours, Prosodic Structure and Preboundary Lengthening', *Journal of Phonetics* 20: 283–303.

Halle, M. (1959) *The Sound Pattern of Russian*, The Hague: Mouton.

—— (1964) 'On the Bases of Phonology', in J. Fodor and J. Katz (eds), *The Structure of Language*, Englewood Cliffs, NJ: Prentice-Hall, 324–33.

—— (1983) 'On Distinctive Features and their Articulatory Implementation', *Natural Language and Linguistic Theory* 1: 91–105.

—— (1985) 'Speculations about the Representation of Words in Memory', in V. Fromkin (ed.), *Phonetic Linguistics*, Orlando, FL: Academic Press, 101–14.

—— (1988) 'Features', MS, MIT; published as 'Phonological Features', in W. Bright (ed.), *International Encyclopedia of Linguistics*, vol. 3, Oxford: Oxford University Press, 1992, 207–12.

—— (1990) 'Respecting Metrical Structure', *Natural Language and Linguistic Theory* 8: 149–76.

Halle, M. and Clements, G.N. (1983) *Problem Book in Phonology*, Cambridge, MA: MIT Press.

Halle, M. and Kenstowicz, M. (1991) 'The Free Element Condition and Cyclic versus Noncyclic Stress', *Linguistic Inquiry* 22: 457–501.

Halle, M. and Mohanan, K.P. (1985) 'Segmental Phonology of Modern English', *Linguistic Inquiry* 16: 57–116.

Halle, M. and Stevens, K. (1969) 'On the Feature "Advanced Tongue Root" ', *Quarterly Progress Report* 94, Research Laboratory of Electronics, MIT, 209–15.

—— (1971) 'A Note on Laryngeal Features', *Quarterly Progress Report* 101, Research Laboratory of Electronics, MIT, 198–213.

Halle, M. and Vergnaud, J.-R. (1987) *An Essay on Stress*, Cambridge, MA: MIT Press.

Hammond, M. (1984) 'Constraining Metrical Theory', Ph.D dissertation, University of California, Los Angeles.

—— (1987) 'Hungarian Cola', *Phonology Yearbook* 4: 267–9.

—— (1988) 'On Deriving the Well-Formedness Condition', *Linguistic Inquiry* 19: 319–25.

Harris, J.W. (1969) *Spanish Phonology*, Cambridge, MA: MIT Press.

Harris, Z. (1944) 'Simultaneous Components in Phonology', *Language* 20: 181–205.

Haugen, E. (1949) 'Phoneme or Prosodeme', *Language* 25.

—— (1956) 'The Syllable in Linguistic Description', in M. Halle, H.G. Lunt, H. MacLean and C.H. van Schoonveld (eds), *For Roman Jakobson*, The Hague: Mouton, 213–21.

Hayes, B. (1980) 'A Metrical Theory of Stress Rules', Ph.D dissertation, MIT (distributed by Indiana University Linguistics Club).

286   References

—— (1984a) 'The Phonetics and Phonology of Russian Voicing Assimilation', in M. Aronoff and R.T. Oehrle (eds), *Language Sound Structure*, Cambridge, MA: MIT Press, 318–28.

—— (1984b) 'The Phonology of Rhythm in English', *Linguistic Inquiry* 15: 33–74.

—— (1985) 'Iambic and Trochaic Rhythm in Stress Rules', *Proceedings of the Second Annual Meeting of the Berkeley Linguistics Society*: 429–46.

—— (1986) 'Inalterability in CV Phonology', *Language* 62: 321–51.

—— (1987) 'A Revised Parametric Metrical Theory', *Proceedings of the Meeting of the North-Eastern Linguistic Society* 17: 274–89.

—— (1988) 'Metrics and Phonological Theory', in F. Newmeyer (ed.), *Linguistics: The Cambridge Survey*, vol. II, *Linguistic Theory: Foundations*, Cambridge: Cambridge University Press, 220–49.

—— (1989a) 'Compensatory Lengthening in Moraic Phonology', *Linguistic Inquiry* 20: 253–306.

—— (1989b) 'The Prosodic Hierarchy in Meter', in P. Kiparsky and G. Youmans (eds), *Rhythm and Meter*, Orlando, FL: Academic Press, 201–60.

—— (1990) 'Diphthongisation and Coindexing', *Phonology* 7: 31–71.

—— (1991) 'Metrical Stress Theory: Principles and Case Studies', MS, University of California, Los Angeles.

Hayes, B. and Lahiri, A. (1991) 'Bengali Intonational Phonology', *Natural Language and Linguistic Theory* 9: 47–96.

Hockett, C. (1955) *A Manual of Phonology*, Baltimore: Waverly Press.

Hooper, J.B. (1972) 'The Syllable in Phonological Theory', *Language* 48: 525–40.

—— (1976) *An Introduction to Natural Generative Phonology*, New York: Academic Press.

Hyman, L. (1975) *Phonology: Theory and Analysis*, New York: Holt, Rinehart, Winston.

—— (1985) *A Theory of Phonological Weight*, Dordrecht: Foris.

Hyman, L., Katamba, F. and Walusimbi, L. (1987) 'Luganda and the Strict Layer Hypothesis', *Phonology Yearbook* 4: 87–108.

Inkelas, S. (1989) *Prosodic Constituency in the Lexicon*, New York and London: Garland, 1990.

Itô, J. (1986) 'Syllable Theory in Prosodic Phonology', Ph.D dissertation, University of Massachusetts, Amherst (distributed by Graduate Linguistics Student Association).

Itô, J. and Mester, A. (1986) 'The Phonology of Voicing in Japanese: Theoretical Consequences of Morphological Accessibility', *Linguistic Inquiry* 17: 49–73.

Jakobson, R., Fant, G. and Halle, M. (1952) *Preliminaries to Speech Analysis*, Cambridge, MA: MIT Press.

Jespersen, O. (1904) *Lehrbuch der Phonetik*, Leipzig and Berlin.

Jones, D. (1950) *The Phoneme*, Cambridge: Heffer.

Kaisse, E. (1985) *Connected Speech: The Interaction of Syntax and Phonology*, New York: Academic Press.

Kaisse, E. and Shaw, P. (1985) On the Theory of Lexical Phonology, *Phonology Yearbook* 2: 1–30.

Kahn, D. (1976) 'Syllable-based Generalizations in English Phonology', Ph.D dissertation, MIT (distributed by Indiana University Linguistics Club), published by Garland, New York and London.

Kaye, J. (1982) 'Harmony Processes in Vata', in H. van der Hulst and N. Smith (eds), *The Structure of Phonological Representations (Part II)*, Dordrecht: Foris, 385–452.

—— (1985) 'On the Syllable Structure of Certain West African Languages', in D. Goyvaerts (ed.), *African Linguistics: Essays in Memory of M.W.K. Semikenke*, Amsterdam: John Benjamins, 285–397.

—— (1986–7) 'Government in Phonology', *The Linguistics Review* 6: 131–59.

—— (1990a) 'The Strange Vowel Sets of Charm Theory: The Question from Top to Bottom', *Journal of Linguistics* 26: 175–81.

——(1990b) ' "Coda" Licensing', *Phonology* 7: 301–30.

—— (1991–2) 'Do you Believe in Magic? The Story of $s + C$ Sequences', in A. Görkel and E. Parker (eds), *SOAS Working Papers in Linguistics and Phonetics*, London: School of Oriental and African Studies, 293–313.

Kaye, J. and Lowenstamm, J. (1984) 'De la syllabicité', in F. Dell, D. Hirst and J.R. Vergnaud (eds), *Forme Sonore du Langage*, Paris: Hermann, 123–59.

—— (1986) 'Compensatory Lengthening in Tiberian Hebrew', in L. Wetzels and E. Sezer (eds), *Studies in Compensatory Lengthening*, Dordrecht: Foris, 97–132.

Kaye, J., Lowenstamm, J. and Vergnaud, J.R. (1985) 'The Internal Structure of Phonological Elements: A Theory of Charm and Government', *Phonology Yearbook* 2: 305–28.

—— (1990) 'Constituent Structure and Government in Phonology', *Phonology* 7: 193–231.

Kean, M.-L. (1975) 'The Theory of Markedness in Generative Grammar', Ph.D dissertation, MIT (distributed by Indiana University Linguistics Club).

—— (1979) 'On the Theory of Markedness: Some General Considerations and a Case in Point', *Social Sciences Research Report* 41, UC Irvine.

Kenstowicz, M. and Kisseberth, C. (1979), *Generative Phonology*, New York: Academic Press.

Kenyon, J.S. and Knott, T.A. (1944) *A Pronouncing Dictionary of American English*, Springfield, MA: Merriam.

Kiparsky, P. (1966) 'Über der deutsche Akzent', *Studia Grammatica* 7: 69–98.

—— (1979) 'Metrical Structure Assignment is Cyclic', *Linguistic Inquiry* 10: 421–41.

—— (1982a) 'Lexical Morphology and Phonology', in I.-S. Yang (ed.), *Linguistics in the Morning Calm*, Seoul: Hanshin, 3–91.

—— (1982b) 'From Cyclic Phonology to Lexical Phonology', in H. van der Hulst and N. Smith (eds), *The Structure of Phonological Representations (Part I)*, Dordrecht: Foris, 131–75.

—— (1983) 'Word-formation and the Lexicon', in F. Ingemann (ed.), *Proceedings of the 1982 Mid-America Linguistics Conference*, Laurence: University of Kansas, 3–29.

—— (1984) 'On the Lexical Phonology of Icelandic', in C.-C. Elert, I. Johansson and E. Strangert (eds), *Nordic Prosody III*, Stockholm: Almqvist and Wiksell, 135–64.

—— (1985) 'Some Consequences of Lexical Phonology', *Phonology Yearbook* 2: 83–138.

Klavans, J. (1982) 'Some Problems in a Theory of Clitics', Ph.D thesis, University College, London.

—— (1985) 'The Independence of Syntax and Phonology in Cliticization', *Language* 61: 95–120.

Kuryłowicz, J. (1948) 'Contribution à la théorie de la syllabe', *Biuletyn Polskiego Towarzystwa Jezykoznawczego* 8: 80–114.

Ladd, D.R. (1986) 'Intonational Phrasing', *Phonology Yearbook* 3: 311–40.

Ladefoged, P. (1964) *A Phonetic Study of West African Languages*, Cambridge: Cambridge University Press.

—— (1971) *Preliminaries to Linguistic Phonetics*, Chicago: University of Chicago Press.

—— (1975) *A Course in Phonetics*, New York: Harcourt Brace Jovanovich.

Ladefoged, P., Cochran, A. and Disner, S. (1979) 'Laterals and Trills', *Journal of the International Phonetic Association* 7: 46–54.

Lahiri, A. and Evers, V. (1991) 'Palatalization and Coronality', in C. Paradis and J.-F. Prunet (eds), *The Special Status of Coronals*, New York: Academic Press, 79–100.

Langendoen, D.T. (1968) *The London School of Linguistics*, Cambridge, MA: MIT Press.

Lass, R. (1976) *English Phonology and Phonological Theory*, Cambridge: Cambridge University Press.

—— (1984) *Phonology*, Cambridge: Cambridge University Press.

Leben, W. (1973) 'Suprasegmental Phonology', Ph.D dissertation, MIT.

—— (1978) 'The Representation of Tone', in V. Fromkin (ed.), *Tone: A Linguistic Survey*, New York: Academic Press, 177–219.

Lehiste, I. (1970) *Suprasegmentals*, Cambridge, MA: MIT Press.

Levin, J.(1983) 'Reduplication and Prosodic Structure', MS, MIT.

—— (1985) 'A Metrical Theory of Syllabicity', Ph.D, MIT.

—— (1988a) 'A Place for Lateral in the Feature Geometry', MS, University of Texas at Austin.

—— (1988b) 'Bidirectional Foot Construction as a Window to Level Ordering', in M. Hammond and M. Noonan (eds), *Theoretical Morphology*, New York: Academic Press, 339–52.

—— (1989) 'Evidence for an Iterative Footing Parameter', paper presented at the GLOW meeting at Utrecht.

Liberman, M. (1975) *The Intonational System of English*, Ph.D dissertation, MIT (distributed by Indiana University Linguistics Club), published by Garland, New York and London.

Liberman, M. and Prince, A. (1977) 'On Stress and Linguistic Rhythm', *Linguistic Inquiry* 8: 249–336.

Lightner, T. (1963) 'A Note on the Formation of Phonological Rules', *Quarterly Progress Report* 68, Research Laboratory of Electronics, MIT: 187–9.

—— (1975) 'The Role of Derivational Morphology in Generative Grammar', *Language* 51: 617–38.

Liu, Feng-Hsi (1980) 'Mandarin Tone Sandhi: A Case of Interaction between Syntax and Phonology', paper presented at the Summer meeting of the Linguistic Society of America at Albuquerque, NM.

McCarthy, J. (1979) *Formal Properties of Semitic Phonology and Morphology*, Ph.D dissertation, MIT (distributed by Indiana University Linguistics Club), published by Garland, New York and London.

—— (1981) 'A Prosodic Theory of Nonconcatenative Morphology', *Linguistic Inquiry* 12: 373–418.

—— (1986) 'OCP Effects: Gemination and Antigemination', *Linguistic Inquiry* 17: 207–63.

—— (1988) 'Feature Geometry and Dependency: A Review', *Phonetica* 45: 84–108.

—— (1989a) 'Linear Order in Phonological Representation', *Linguistic Inquiry* 20: 71–99.

—— (1989b) 'Guttural Phonology', MS, University of Massachusetts, Amherst.

McCarthy, J. and Prince, A. (1986) 'Prosodic Phonology', MS, University of Massachusetts, Amherst.

McCawley, J. (1968) *The Phonological Component of a Grammar of Japanese*, The Hague: Mouton.

Maddieson, I. (1984) *Patterns of Sounds*, Cambridge: Cambridge University Press.

Marantz, A. (1982) 'Re Reduplication', *Linguistic Inquiry* 13: 435–82.

Mascaró, J. (1976) 'Catalan Phonology and the Phonological Cycle', Ph.D dissertation, MIT (distributed by Indiana University Linguistics Club).

—— (1983) 'Phonological Levels and Assimilatory Processes', MS, Universitat Autònoma de Barcelona.

Mester, A. (1986) 'Studies in Tier Structure', Ph.D dissertation, University of Massachusetts, Amherst (distributed by Graduate Linguistics Student Association).

—— (1988) 'Dependent Ordering and the OCP', in H. van der Hulst and N. Smith (eds), *Features, Segmental Structure and Harmony Processes (Part II)*, Dordrecht: Foris, 128–44.

Milner, J.C. (1967) 'A French Truncation Rule', *Quarterly Progress Report* 86, Research Laboratory of Electronics, MIT, 273–83.

Mohanan, K.P. (1982) 'Lexical Phonology', Ph.D dissertation, MIT (distributed by Indiana University Linguistics Club).

—— (1983) 'The Structure of the Melody', MS, MIT.

—— (1986) *The Theory of Lexical Phonology*, Dordrecht: Reidel.

—— (1991) 'On the Bases of Radical Underspecification', *Natural Language and Linguistic Theory* 9: 285–325.

Mohanan, K.P. and Mohanan, T. (1984) 'Lexical Phonology of the Consonant System of Malayalam', *Linguistic Inquiry* 15: 575–602.

Murray, R.W. and Vennemann, T. (1983) 'Sound Change and Syllable Structure in Germanic Phonology', *Language* 59: 514–28.

Myers, S. (1987) 'Tone and the Structure of Words in Shona', Ph.D dissertation, University of Massachusetts, Amherst (distributed by Graduate Linguistics Student Association).

—— (1991) 'Persistent Rules', *Linguistic Inquiry* 22: 315–44.

Nanni, D. (1977) 'Stressing Words in *-ative*', *Linguistic Inquiry* 8: 752–63.

Napoli, D.J. and Nespor, M. (1979) 'The Syntax of Word Initial Consonant Gemination in Italian', *Language* 55: 812–41.

Nespor, M. (1990) 'On the Rhythm Parameter in Phonology', in I.M. Roca (ed.), *Logical Issues in Language Acquisition*, Dordrecht: Foris, 157–75.

Nespor, M. and Vogel, I. (1982) 'Prosodic Domains of External Sandhi Rules', in H. van der Hulst and N. Smith (eds), *The Structure of Phonological Representations (Part I)*, Dordrecht: Foris, 225–55.

—— (1986) *Prosodic Phonology*, Dordrecht: Foris.

—— (1989) 'On Clashes and Lapses', *Phonology* 6: 69–116.

Newman, P. (1986) 'Tone and Affixation in Hausa', *Studies in African Linguistics* 17: 249–67.

Odden, D. (1981) 'A Nonlinear Approach to Vowel Length in Kimatuumbi', MS, Ohio State University.
—— (1986) 'On the Role of the Obligatory Contour Principle in Phonological Theory', *Language* 62: 353–83.
—— (1988) 'Antigemination and the OCP', *Linguistic Inquiry* 19: 451–75.
Öhman, S. (1967) 'Numerical Models of Coarticulation', *Journal of the Acoustic Society of America* 41: 310–20.
Paradis, C. (1988–9) 'On Constraints and Repair Strategies', *The Linguistic Review* 6: 71–97.
Paradis, C. and Prunet, J-F. (1991) *The Special Status of Coronals*, New York: Academic Press.
Pierrehumbert, J. (1980) 'The Phonology and Phonetics of English Intonation', Ph.D dissertation, MIT.
Pike, K. (1944) *The Intonation of American English*, Ann Arbor, MI: University of Michigan Press.
Pike, K. and Pike, E. (1947) 'Immediate Constituents of Mazateco syllables', *International Journal of American Linguistics* 13: 78–91.
Postal, P. (1968) *Aspects of Phonological Theory*, New York: Harper and Row.
Prince, A. (1983) 'Relating to the Grid', *Linguistic Inquiry* 14: 19–100.
—— (1984) 'Phonology with Tiers', in M. Aronoff and R.T. Oehrle (eds), *Language Sound Structure*, Cambridge, MA: MIT Press, 234–44.
Pulleyblank, D. (1983) 'Tone in Lexical Phonology', Ph.D dissertation, MIT.
—— (1986) *Tone in Lexical Phonology*, Dordrecht: Reidel.
—— (1988a) 'Vocalic Underspecification in Yoruba', *Linguistic Inquiry* 19: 233–70.
—— (1988b) 'Underspecification, the Feature Hierarchy and Tiv vowels', *Phonology* 5: 299–326.
Rialland, A. and Djamouri, R. (1984), 'Harmonie vocalique, consonantique et structures de dépendance dans le mot en Mongol Khalkha', *Bulletin de la Société Linguistique de Paris* 79, 333–83.
Rice, K. and Avery, P. (1991) 'On the Relationship between Laterality and Coronality', in C. Paradis and J.-F. Prunet (eds), *The Special Status of Coronals*, New York: Academic Press, 101–24.
Roca, I.M. (1988) 'Theoretical Implications of Spanish Word Stress', *Linguistic Inquiry* 19: 393–423.
—— (1992a) 'Constraining Extrametricality', in W. Dressler, H. Lüschutzky, O. Pfeiffer and J. Rennison (eds), *Phonologica 1988*, Cambridge: Cambridge University Press, 239–48.
—— (1992b) 'On the Sources of Word Prosody', *Phonology* 9: 267–87.
Rubach, J. (1990) 'Final Devoicing and Cyclic Syllabification in German', *Linguistic Inquiry* 21: 79–94.
Rubach, J. and Booij, G. (1990) 'Syllable Structure Assignment in Polish', *Phonology* 7: 121–58.
Sagey, E. (1986) 'The Representation of Features and Relations in Non-linear Phonology', Ph.D dissertation, MIT.
—— (1988a) 'On the Ill-formedness of Crossing Association Lines', *Linguistic Inquiry* 19: 109–18.
—— (1988b) 'Degree of Closure in Complex Segments', in H. van der Hulst and N. Smith (eds), *Features, Segmental Structure and Harmony Processes (Part I)*, Dordrecht: Foris, 169–208.

—— (1988c) 'Place Feature Geometry', *Proceedings of the Eighteenth Meeting of the North-Eastern Linguistic Society*: 451–64.

Saussure, F. de (1916) *Cours de linguistique générale*, Lausanne and Paris: Payot.

Schane, S. (1973a) *Generative Phonology*, Englewood-Cliffs, NJ: Prentice-Hall.

—— (1973b) 'The Phoneme Revisited', *Language* 47: 503–21.

—— (1984a) 'Two English Vowel Movements: A Particle Analysis', in M. Aronoff and R.T. Oehrle (eds), *Language Sound Structure*, Cambridge, MA: MIT Press, 32–51.

—— (1984b) 'The Fundamentals of Particle Phonology', *Phonology Yearbook* 1: 129–55.

Schein, B. and Steriade, D. (1986) 'On Geminates', *Linguistic Inquiry* 17: 691–744.

Selkirk, E.O. (1972) *The Phrase Phonology of English and French*, Ph.D dissertation, MIT (distributed by the Indiana University Linguistics Club), published by Garland, New York and London.

—— (1980) 'Prosodic Domains in Phonology: Sanskrit Revisited', in M. Aronoff and M.-L. Kean (eds), *Juncture*, Saratoga, CA: Anma Libri, 107–29.

—— (1981) 'On Prosodic Structure and its Relation to Syntactic Structure', in T. Fretheim (ed.), *Nordic Prosody II*, Tapir, 111–40.

—— (1982) 'The Syllable', in H. van der Hulst and N. Smith (eds), *The Structure of Phonological Representations (Part II)*, Dordrecht: Foris, 337–83.

—— (1984a) 'On the Major Class Features and Syllable Theory', in M. Aronoff and R.T. Oehrle (eds), *Language Sound Structure*, Cambridge, MA: MIT Press, 107–36.

—— (1984b) *Phonology and Syntax: The Relationship between Sound and Structure*, Cambridge, MA: MIT Press.

—— (1990) 'On the Nature of Prosodic Constituency', in J. Kingston and M.E. Beckman (eds), *Papers in Laboratory Phonology, vol. I*, Cambridge: Cambridge University Press, 179–200.

Shaw, P. (1991) 'Consonant Harmony Systems: The Special Status of Coronal Harmony', in C. Paradis and J.-F. Prunet (eds), *The Special Status of Coronals*, New York: Academic Press, 125–57.

Siegel, D. (1974) *Topics in English Morphology*, Ph.D dissertation, MIT, published by Garland, New York and London.

Sievers, E. (1881) *Grunzüge der Phonetik*, Leipzig: Breitkopf and Hartel.

Sloan, C., Taylor, S.H. and Hoard, J.E. (1978) *Introduction to Phonology*, Englewood Cliffs, NJ: Prentice-Hall.

Sloan, K. (1991) 'Syllables and Templates: Evidence from Southern Sierra Miwok', Ph.D dissertation, MIT.

Smith, N. (1985) 'Spreading, Reduplication and the Default Option in Miwok Nonconcatenative Morphology', in H. van der Hulst and N. Smith (eds), *Advances in Nonlinear Phonology*, Dordrecht: Foris, 363–80.

Snider, K. (1990) 'Tonal Upstep in Krachi: Evidence for a Register Tier', *Language* 66: 453–74.

Sommer, B. (1970) 'An Australian Language without CV Syllables', *International Journal of American Linguistics* 36: 57–9.

Stanley, R. (1967) 'Redundancy Rules in Phonology', *Language* 43: 393–436

Steriade, D. (1982) 'Greek Prosodies and the Nature of Syllabification', Ph.D dissertation, MIT.

—— (1984) 'Glides and Vowels in Romanian', *Proceedings of the Tenth Meeting of the Berkeley Linguistic Society*: 47–64.

—— (1985) 'A Note of Coronal', MS, MIT.

—— (1987) 'Redundant Values', in A. Bosch, B. Need and E. Schiller (eds), *Papers from the Parasession on Autosegmental and Metrical Phonology*, Chicago: Chicago Linguistics Society, 339–62.

—— (1988) 'Reduplication and Syllable Transfer in Sanskrit and Elsewhere', *Phonology* 5: 73–155.

Stevens, K. (1972) 'The Quantal Nature of Speech: Evidence from Articulatory-acoustic Data', in E.E. David and P.B. Denes (eds), *Human Communication: A Unified View*, New York: McGraw-Hill, 51–66.

—— (1989) 'On the Quantal Nature of Speech', *Journal of Phonetics* 17: 3–45.

Stevens, K., Keyser, S.J. and Kawasaki, H. (1987) 'Toward a Phonetic and Phonological Theory of Redundant Features', in J. Perkell and D.H. Klatt (eds), *Symposium on Invariance and Variability*, Hillsdale, NJ: Lawrence Erlbaum.

Steward, J.M. (1967) 'Tongue Position in Akan Vowel Harmony', *Phonetica* 16: 185–204.

Strauss, S. (1982) *Lexicalist Phonology of English and German*, Dordrecht: Foris.

Thráinsson, H. (1978) 'On the Phonology of Icelandic Preaspiration', *Nordic Journal of Linguistics* 1: 3–54.

Trubetzkoy, N.S. (1939) *Grunzüge der Phonologie*, Prague: Travaux du Cercle Linguistique de Prague.

Tryon, D.T. (1970) *An Introduction to Maranungku*, Pacific Linguistics, Series B, no. 15, Canberra: Australian National University.

Vennemann, T. (1972) 'On the Theory of Syllabic Phonology', *Linguistische Berichte* 18, 1–18.

Vergnaud, J.R. (1977) 'Formal Properties of Phonological Rules', in R.E. Butts and J. Hintikka (eds), *Basic Problems in Methodology and Linguistics*, Dordrecht: Reidel, 299–318.

—— (1982) 'On the Theoretical Basis of Phonology', paper presented at the GLOW colloquium, Paris.

Walker, J. (1924) *Rhyming Dictionary*, revised and enlarged by L.H. Dawson, London: Routledge and Kegan Paul.

Walli-Sagey, E. (1986) 'On the Representation of Complex Segments and their Formation in Kinyarwanda', in L. Wetzels and E. Sezer (eds), *Studies in Compensatory Lengthening*, Dordrecht: Foris, 251–95.

Welmers, E. (1946) *A Descriptive Grammar of Fanti*, Supplement to *Language* 22, no. 3.

Whitney, W.D. (1865) 'The Relation of Vowel and Consonant', *Journal of the American Oriental Society* 8.

Williams, E. (1976) 'Underlying Tone in Margi and Igbo', *Linguistic Inquiry* 7: 463–84.

Williamson, K. (1977) 'Multivalued Features for Consonants', *Language* 53: 843–71.

Woodrow, H. (1951) 'Time Perception', in S. Stevens (ed.), *Handbook of Experimental Psychology*, New York: Wiley.

Yip, M. (1980) 'The Tonal Phonology of Chinese', Ph.D dissertation, MIT (distributed by Indiana University Linguistics Club).

—— (1988a) 'Template Morphology and the Direction of Association', *Natural Language and Linguistic Theory* 6: 551–77.

—— (1988b) 'The Obligatory Contour Principle and Phonological Rules: A Loss of Identity', *Linguistic Inquiry* 19: 65–100.

Younes, R. (1983) 'The Representation of Geminate Consonants', MS, University of Texas, Austin.

INDEXES

INDEX OF AUTHORS

INDEX OF SUBJECTS

(Number italicisation indicates definition.)

INDEX OF LANGUAGES

(Genealogical affiliation is given in parentheses [and geographical distribution in square brackets].)

Abbreviations